A Circle of Trust

A Circle of Trust
Remembering SNCC

Edited by Cheryl Lynn Greenberg

R *Rutgers University Press*
New Brunswick, New Jersey, and London

Library of Congress Cataloging-in-Publication Data

A circle of trust : remembering SNCC / edited by Cheryl Lynn
Greenberg.
    p. cm.
   Includes index.
   ISBN 0-8135-2476-8 (cloth : alk. paper). — ISBN 0-8135-2477-6
(pbk. : alk. paper)
   1. Student Nonviolent Coordinating Committee (U.S.)   2. Civil
rights movements—United States—History—20th century. 3. Afro-
Americans—Civil rights—History—20th century.   4. Civil rights
workers—United States—Interviews.   5. United States—Race
relations.   I. Greenberg. Cheryl Lynn.
E185.61.C58 1998
323'. 0973—dc21   97-23093
                                                  CIP

British Cataloging-in-Publication data for this book is available from the British
Library

Manufactured in the United States of America

to the spirit of the beloved community

Contents

Jack Chatfield

"Give us the wisdom to understand this world."
—The Reverend Charles Sherrod, speaking in the Mount
Olive Baptist Church, Sasser, Georgia, July 25, 1962

Foreword

In 1987, the year before Cheryl Greenberg and I organized the Trinity SNCC conference, an administrator asked me if I would teach a course on the civil rights era. I told her that I no longer could; I was in fact turning away from recollections that filled me with pain and regret. When I thought of my experience in the early civil rights movement—the excitement, the laughter, the music, the enervating fear—I thought of accounts unsettled, mysteries unresolved, friendships severed, and feelings of serenity, even momentary ecstasy, now lost beyond recovery. I thought of what Willa Cather called the "incommunicable past." What a strong attachment I once felt for the South—and not only for the people, both black and white, whom I met there. Though a sojourner, I felt a native's love for the flat, fertile land, the sweltering heat, the crickets after nightfall, the cotton bolls and the dust rising as the tractors moved across the parched fields. There I found a world so rich that it conveyed at times a kind of enchantment. There I began to feel a new personal identity, a new sense of nationality, a new set of intellectual prospects and challenges. There I became a true student of American history.

Memories of my days in the South returned in force when, in January of 1987, I watched the PBS documentary "Eyes on the Prize." The few minutes I saw on the Albany Movement—together with the riveting documentary footage on events ranging from the Emmett Till murder to the Selma crisis of 1965—set in motion a train of thoughts that finally resulted in the SNCC conference the succeeding year. But to explain the impact of "Eyes on the Prize," I must describe what brought me to southwest Georgia in September of 1962 and some of what I saw when I got there.

I cannot remember clearly how or when the civil rights movement entered my consciousness. Between 1956 and 1960 I attended Randolph-Macon Academy, a segregated Methodist military boarding school in northern Virginia, where I was immersed in sports, music, and intense friendships that survive to the present day. I became an avid reporter and columnist for the student newspaper, but I wrote only about academy affairs. I had never read a daily newspaper or watched a television news broadcast. I was unaware of the momentous events that followed the *Brown* decision of 1954, and I was utterly unmoved when I learned that Warren County, in which Randolph-Macon was located, had closed its public schools rather than obey a desegregation decree. Despite my New England roots and my presence at a junior high in Bethesda, Maryland, which underwent peaceful desegregation the year after the *Brown* decision was handed down, I saw the separation of the races as part of the natural order of things. I have no recollection of the sit-in movement that swept the South in the winter and spring of 1960 when I was a senior. Nor do I recall clearly the Freedom Rides of 1961, which occurred when I was completing my first year as an undergraduate at Trinity College in Connecticut. Yet somehow, by the autumn of that year, the black student movement of the South had become the focal point of much of my youthful passion.

Two of my undergraduate friends were primarily responsible for this: J. Ronald Spencer and George F. Will. Both young men, deeply influenced by thinkers such as Albert Camus and André Malraux, tutored me in the reform liberalism of the Americans for Democratic Action, whose members were among the ardent supporters of the "Negro revolution" spearheaded by the *Brown* petitioners, the Montgomery movement, and now the thousands of student sit-in demonstrators who had carried the desegregation campaign to nearly every major city in Dixie. The Negro students of the South, said Will in the undergraduate paper, were teaching Americans how to be citizens.

The civil rights crusade gave us the elements of a new civic and moral identity. The newspapers were now full of reports from the South: mass marches and prayer vigils had virtually paralyzed the city of Albany, Georgia; high school students and SNCC activists had organized demonstrations in McComb, Mississippi; sit-ins continued in the upper and lower South; and voter registration drives had been launched in some of the most refractory counties of the rural Black Belt. At times we were consumed by the stories we read. It is no exaggeration to say that we had begun to feel powerful fraternal bonds with the men and women—especially the students—whose names we had learned from the columns written by Murray Kempton and James Wechsler in the *New York Post* and the vivid dispatches by Claude Sitton in the *New York Times*. Nearly every day seemed to bring a new story or a new revelation. The civil rights activists and the dedicated journalists covering the South were conducting us along a new frontier of understanding and moral imagination. Within a year of my departure from a military boarding school in the segregated upper South, I had come to know a new America and to embrace a new vision of our national democracy.

Early in my sophomore year, Spencer and I traveled as reporters to Wesleyan University in Middletown to hear a speech by Marian Wright, a former sit-in leader who was then a student at Yale Law School. I was transfixed by the flowing, sonorous words of this impassioned black woman who seemed to embody the humane and gentle spirit of the movement. I felt a kind of exultation. This was an emotion I was to feel again when, at a conference at Sarah Lawrence College, I met Tom Hayden, Bayard Rustin, and—most important—Charles McDew. Slow talking and sardonic, an Ohio native who had enrolled in a black university in South Carolina, McDew had become the chairman of the Student Nonviolent Coordinating Committee (SNCC) and was a veteran of chilling experiences in McComb and Baton Rouge.

Still, neither philosophical commitments nor inspirational encounters with Marian Wright and Charles McDew were sufficient to catapult me into the southern movement. I failed to pass Trinity's mathematics and science requirements by the end of my sophomore year, a circumstance that forced me to repair to summer school in June of 1962. There, despite my academic burdens, I followed events in Albany, Georgia, where street demonstrations and mass jailings had resumed after a lull of several months during the late winter and spring. Devouring the sometimes daily dispatches of Claude Sitton and the columns that Murray Kempton wrote from the region when he visited in early August, I felt a deepening spiritual kinship with Charles Sherrod, Charles Jones, and Cordell Reagon (SNCC field secretaries in Albany); William Anderson and C. B. King (the president and the attorney of the Albany Movement); and Penny Patch and Bill Hansen (northern white students who had arrived in Albany during the summer months). But nothing prepared me for the article by Sitton that appeared on the front page of the *New York Times* on July 27, 1962.

The article was extraordinary by any measure: historian Taylor Branch has rightly called it the "most remarkable news dispatch of the entire civil rights generation." Appearing under the headline "Sheriff Harrasses Negroes at Voting Rally in Georgia" and bearing the dateline of Sasser, a hamlet eighteen miles from Albany, Sitton's long article described the disruption of a voter registration meeting by a menacing band of white men that included Terrell County's sheriff, Z. T. Matthews, two seething deputies, the sheriff of nearby Sumter County, and a body of supporters characterized by Matthews as "disturbed white citizens." Containing vivid descriptive passages anchored in details so exact and evocative as to give the report a pictorial quality, the dispatch is perhaps most notable for its rendering of the plain English words—both spoken and sung—that Sitton transcribed as he sat with two other white journalists, thirty-six black citizens, and four SNCC workers (two white and two black) in Sasser's Mount Olive Church. One of the student workers was my Trinity friend Ralph Allen, who I had supposed was at home in Massachusetts. A quirk of fate had brought him to Atlanta, where he had impulsively enlisted in the small but swelling regiment of SNCC workers. In the days before the Mount Olive meeting, he and Prathia Hall, a black student from Philadelphia, had been threatened by a pistol-waving Sasser policeman, and Allen had been badly beaten in Dawson, the county seat. When I read these details, the newsprint swam before my eyes. In a flash, what had been unimaginable became ineluctable, and I was in southwest Georgia by early September.

Personal details aside, it is clear that Sitton's story is a prism through which much of the early history of SNCC may be viewed. The gathering in the plain wooden church signaled a new and as yet unheralded phase in the struggle for racial equality in America: the inauguration of voter registration campaigns in rural Black Belt counties that had once composed the heart of the Cotton Kingdom. Isolated and impoverished, their populations checked by the steady flow of emigration and their folkways shaped by a white supremacy so potent as to seem a force of nature, these counties stood as a separate nation even within the states of the Old Confederacy. With its heavy black majority, and with 51 of its 8,209 black residents on the voting rolls, Terrell County exemplified these bastions of the ancient ways as Sheriff Matthews embodied the consensual culture of the ruling caste. "We want our colored people to go on living like they have for the last hundred years," the sheriff told the Mount Olive crowd. "I tell you cap'n, we're a little fed up with this registration business." "As the 70-year-old peace officer spoke," reported Sitton, "his nephew and chief deputy, M. E. Matthews, swaggered back and forth fingering a hand-tooled black leather cartridge belt and a 38-caliber revolver. Another deputy . . . slapped a five-cell flashlight against his left palm again and again. The three officers took turns badgering the participants and warning of what 'disturbed white citizens' might do if this and other rallies continued." As SNCC workers and local activists were learning, the inflamed emotions that gripped these local whites were all too common across the Deep South. Indeed, by the time of the Mount Olive gathering, SNCC's southern Mississippi beachhead had resulted in savage beatings, ceaseless threats, jailings, and the death of Herbert Lee, an Amite County farmer who had boldly aligned himself with the movement. Bob Moses and his co-workers decided to evacuate Amite and Pike counties (the latter included McComb) rather than continue to risk their own lives and those of others. By the summer of 1962, however, organizing was proceeding in a handful of Delta counties north of Vicksburg and Jackson.

SNCC's Mississippi and southwest Georgia projects marked the beginnings of a political movement without precedent in the history of modern America: an effort to implement the provisions of the Fifteenth Amendment in the predominantly black counties of the most traditional regions of the agrarian South. "This is where CORE and SCLC stop," said Sherrod one night as we turned onto a dirt path from a lonely highway north of Albany in the fall of 1962. His remark reflected the sense of uniqueness and righteous mission that increasingly defined the young activists in their work in the rural areas. It reflected as well the kind of revolutionary ethos—a prime ingredient of the "SNCC mystique"—that encouraged the staff to see itself as a group apart as it labored to transform a set of social arrangements whose roots rested in plantation slavery.

In southwest Georgia, the presence of white field secretaries—both women and men—was an essential feature of SNCC's ambitious enterprise, and Sherrod was to sever his ties with the organization when it embraced the Black Power philosophy and expelled the remaining white workers from its ranks in 1966 and 1967. The partnership of black and white workers, of course, symbolized the visionary integrationist aims that animated the Albany Movement and SNCC's southwest Georgia project. But the visible presence of whites—as Sherrod said on many occasions—was also calculated to increase media attention, bring much-needed financial support, and gain the sympathy of influential people in the nation's political and cultural capitals. Sherrod's interracial vision, in short, was anchored in strategic as well as spiritual considerations. In this respect it reflected the aims of the movement as a whole: the recasting of social relations between the races, the reduction in the level of black poverty and the opening of paths of higher opportunity, and the growth of black political power.

During the early days of SNCC—from the sit-ins through the Mississippi Summer Project of 1964—none of these aims was deemed separable from the others. It is almost forgotten today that the emblem of the Student Nonviolent Coordinating Committee—adopted during the massive sit-in campaigns of 1960—was that of a black and white hand clasped together in friendship. Many have said—and many continue to say—that this represented a forlorn hope. But it was a hope nonetheless—one ultimately resting in the assurance that democratic America possessed a conscience and a political system to which black citizens could appeal. Indeed, this compound faith—anchored at once in political calculations and the visionary egalitarianism that has been the hallmark of social and religious movements in the American past—led to the boldest and most ambitious experiment of all: SNCC's recruitment of over eight hundred young Americans, nearly all of them white, to work in Mississippi during the summer of 1964.

It is precisely this faith in the moral and political foundations of American life that was so powerfully conveyed in the dispatch that Sitton wrote nearly two years before the Mississippi Summer Project was launched. Standing in Mount Olive Church near a calendar displaying the images of John F. Kennedy and other American Presidents, a Terrell County leader, Lucius Holloway, welcomed the white intruders ("Everybody's welcome. This is a voter registration meeting.") and made a plea for racial reconciliation. Sherrod read Bible verses ("If God be for us, who can be against us?"), raised hymns and prayers, and led the assembly in the singing of "Climbing Jacob's Ladder," a spiritual representing the timeless aspirations of blacks, both slave and free. Most tellingly, he prayed: "Give us the wisdom to understand this world. Oh Lord, we've been abused for so long; we've been down so long; oh, Lord, all we want is for our brothers to understand that in Thy sight we are all equal. . . . We're praying for the courage to withstand the brutality of our brethren." Sitton reported that as Sherrod spoke, loud voices could be heard calling out the numbers of license plates. "[The] faces of the audience," he wrote, "stiffened with fear." The spiritual arsenal of the movement—rooted in the ancestral Protestant faith—might lessen but could not banish the apprehension stirred by the white vigilantes. This emotion was well founded: in early September, Mount Olive and another black church were destroyed by fire, and night riders poured three shotgun blasts into the home of Carolyn Daniels, a Dawson hairdresser who housed the SNCC staff. For the next several months, the Terrell County voter registration movement was moribund.

It is hardly surprising that the ardent—one might say, utopian—hopes of the early movement began to dissipate despite the sea change in federal policy that brought the enactment of the Civil Rights Act of 1964 and the Voting Rights Act of 1965. Within a year of the passage of the latter, many SNCC veterans were expressing grave doubts about the character of the liberal Democratic establishment and reassessing the interracial partnership that had given the movement its broader identity and much of its political clout. The causes of this development were complex: the anger and frustration bred by the unbroken stream of white violence, particularly in the isolated countryside; the inability—or, as some believed, the unwillingness—of federal agencies to protect civil rights workers and stem the terror; the increasingly strong identification that SNCC organizers felt with the most impoverished and dependent segment of the rural black population; and the rising mood of cultural separatism within the ranks of SNCC workers whose intellectual disposition and movement experience had fostered a pronounced and often bitter sense of alienation from the dominant society. Still, it is possible that the forces of the new separatist radicalism might have been deflected but for the momentous events at the national convention of the Democratic party in Atlantic City in August of 1964 at the height of the Mississippi Freedom Summer. There, despite painstaking preparations, tireless lobbying, and the spellbinding testimony of Fannie Lou Hamer before the Credentials Committee, the Mississippi Freedom Democratic Party failed in its effort to unseat the regular delegation and achieve official recognition as the state branch of the national party. Surely Mrs. Hamer spoke for her delegation and for the SNCC staff members who had labored to build the MFDP when she told the Credentials Committee, "[If] the Freedom Democratic Party is not seated now, I question America."[1] And surely Stokely Carmichael (now Kwame Toure) reflected the views of many SNCC comrades when he wrote: "The major moral of [Atlantic City] was not merely that the national conscience was unreliable but that . . . black people in Mississippi and throughout this country could not rely on their so-called allies. . . . These black people knew that they would have to search for and build new forms outside the Democratic party—or any other; forms that would begin to bring about the changes needed in this country."[2]

When Carmichael wrote these words in 1967, I was a graduate student in American history at Columbia University in New York (and George Will, incidentally, had long since completed his conversion to conservatism). The next year I returned to the South as field director of a short-lived organization called the Southern Elections Fund, which a wealthy friend had founded as a vehicle to bring financial assistance to blacks running for office. In 1969 I spent two months exploring the history of the civil rights movement in Claiborne County, Mississippi. But after 1970 I lost touch with nearly all my old civil rights friends. Burdened with family and professional duties, I never returned to the South. When I began teaching at Trinity in 1976, I initially created courses on the civil rights era, and was often invited to reminisce about my time in the movement. But gradually I became more and more reluctant to do so: my SNCC experience had become increasingly remote, part of the "incommunicable past." One day I surprised a group of students; instead of speaking, I sang some movement songs: "Oh, Freedom," "Eyes on the Prize," "We Are Soldiers in the Army," "Get on Board, Chillun, Chillun," and "We Shall Not Be Moved." I knew the songs would do more to recapture the mood of these bygone days than my arid, Yankeefied words. I knew as well how music had been used—as it was used in Mount Olive Church that July evening in 1962—to forge a transcendent sense of communal and spiritual purpose that guided the movement and buoyed it during the storms it faced.

It is easy, then, to understand the impact that "Eyes on the Prize" had on me when I saw it in early 1987. There was Sherrod speaking to a packed mass meeting in Albany in 1962; there were the high school girls, electric with excitement and laughter, belting out the movement songs; there were the mass marches, the prayer vigils, the police bullhorns, the arrests. And there as well were the aging veterans offering reflections and reminiscences about their activist days. Before long, I began to think about organizing a conference on the movement. The result was the April 1988 gathering and the memories that follow. They not only contribute to our knowledge of America's Second Reconstruction but offer us at least a portion of the wisdom necessary to understand this world.

Notes

1. Quoted in Clayborne Carson, *In Struggle: SNCC and the Black Awakening of the 1960s* (Cambridge, Mass., 1981), p. 125.
2. Stokely Carmichael and Charles Hamilton, *Black Power* (New York, 1967), pp. 96–97.

Acknowledgments

I could not have completed this work without the financial and technical support of Trinity College, especially the Office of the Dean of Faculty and the Audio Visual Department. And while many people contributed to the success of this project, a few must be singled out for special thanks. My editor, Marlie Wasserman, believed in me and in the project even after the many delays and crises that almost derailed it, and offered encouragement and sage advice. Joy Wright, one of the best students I have ever had the pleasure of teaching, worked with me all summer to prepare the manuscript; her research and organizational skills are matched by her historical competence and generosity of spirit. My two research assistants at Harvard, Tracey Wollenberg and Eliana Menzin, did a fabulous job of fact checking and glossary building with both alacrity and grace. Finally, this SNCC reunion would never have happened without the vision and energy of Jack Chatfield, who has supported every stage of the process. I thank them all, as well as all the participants in this inspiring conference.

Cheryl Lynn Greenberg
December 1996

A Circle of Trust

Introduction

In 1988 activists from the Student Nonviolent Coordinating Committee (SNCC) and some of their friends and admirers gathered, in what was for many their first reunion in twenty-five years, to reflect on their experiences in the civil rights movement. It was a remarkable moment, a blend of historical reminiscence and ongoing activism, of thoughtful analysis and raw energy, of singing and hugging and sharp and pointed disagreement. Conference participants resisted all attempts at structure. Panelists consistently ran over time. Those not on panels spoke from the floor. At one moment two presenters might be engaged in heated debate; in the next we were all on our feet, arms locked, swaying with the force of "Oh, Freedom" or "This Little Light of Mine." That conference, with its fusion of thought and action, of love and confrontation, epitomized the very nature of SNCC from its vigorous and idealistic inception in 1960 to its no less energetic and contentious decline less than a decade later.

SNCC originated with the decision in February of 1960 of four black college freshmen from North Carolina Agricultural and Technical College in Greensboro to challenge segregation by requesting service at their local Woolworth's counter.[1] When they were not accommodated they insisted that they would stay until served, and remained seated at the counter for the rest of the day. The store closed that evening and the four men left without incident. The next day more students joined them, and tensions escalated. Although the students sat peacefully and politely, they were spat on and harassed by white onlookers. Finally, after several days, with growing numbers sitting inside and demonstrating outside, the students agreed to a brief halt to

1

negotiate with the store owner. By then, aided by wide media coverage, the sit-in idea had spread to cities and towns across the South; fifteen cities in five southern states saw sit-ins during those first two weeks. Within a year, more than 50,000 people had participated in at least one such demonstration, and some 3,600 had gone to jail.[2] Two cities in particular proved crucial training grounds for SNCC: Atlanta, whose student movement was remarkably large and well organized, and Nashville, where sit-in leaders set up training workshops in the theory and practice of nonviolent civil disobedience. Harassment by onlookers and by police often took a violent turn. Demonstrators were beaten, burned with cigarettes, kicked, poked with cattle prods, and hauled off to jail. The home of Z. Alexander Looby, a black lawyer in Nashville who defended the jailed protesters there, was bombed.

Although these sit-ins occurred without coordination, they were the product of a long struggle for civil rights that stretched back to abolition and slave resistance. In this century, the Niagara Movement in 1905 that launched the National Association for the Advancement of Colored People (NAACP), the "Don't Buy Where You Can't Work" campaigns of the Great Depression, and the Montgomery bus boycott of 1955–56 are three examples of the persistent efforts of African Americans to gain full citizenship; there are thousands more that are less well known but no less significant. This tradition of activism reminded African Americans frustrated by the slow gains and unfulfilled promises of the Fourteenth Amendment, the 1954 decision in *Brown v. Board of Education*, and the Civil Rights Act of 1957 that acquiescence was not the only alternative. Particularly for young people, who despite those federal commitments to equality still faced the same constricted set of choices their parents had endured, resistance had great appeal. And they had seen the limits of legal decisions and federal legislation in the lurid images of lynching victim Emmett Till or of black high school students in Little Rock, Arkansas, brutally attacked when they entered all-white Central High School in 1957 in full compliance with the *Brown* decision.

The international scene had an impact on their decision to act as well. Anticolonial efforts in Asia, Africa, and the Middle East resonated with those in this country enduring their own form of domination, and the ability of nonwhites abroad to challenge white supremacy emboldened some people of color in the United States. Then too the strategies of these movements, most particularly those of Mohandas Gandhi in India, seemed to offer an effective means of achieving equality. Like the nineteenth-century American Transcendentalists before them, these practitioners of civil disobedience (publicly confronting and violating unjust laws peacefully but determinedly) demonstrated the moral force of living one's ideals, of refusing to acquiesce in one's own oppression. And although the Cold War ultimately tempered the demands and strategies of much of the civil rights movement with its attack on any effort to subvert the status quo, it also provided an opening for civil rights because of America's struggle to gain the allegiance of the nonaligned nations of Asia and Africa. The United States could not plausibly argue for the virtues of its system while blatantly repressing nonwhite members of its own population. Thus although Jim Crow segregation remained, its most outrageous excesses were opposed, at least rhetorically, by the federal government. Civil rights efforts that publicized contradictions between the American creed and American reality could therefore occasionally mobilize government support. At the same time, only certain forms of civil rights struggles could gain legitimacy in this period. Nationalist or economically radical challenges to the status quo were routinely suppressed, sometimes in blithe disregard for the niceties of civil liberties. But civil rights programs whose means and goals were integrationist fared slightly better because they could appeal to the fundamental principles Americans claimed as the moral basis for their international leadership. As Gerald Horne and others have observed, Cold War America constrained the choices of those who believed in black equality and set the stage for a civil rights movement that was integrationist in vision, and whose demands began with social and political rather than economic equality.[3]

Thus it was both the potential of effective struggle and the frustration of hard-won promises still unfulfilled that ultimately energized thousands of activists in the mobilization that we call the civil rights movement. Although many organizations contributed to that struggle, SNCC was unique. Emerging from the spontaneous actions of the Greensboro college students and the demonstrations they inspired elsewhere, SNCC's underlying tenets included a belief in the importance of every individual, the redemptive nature of love and community, and the potential of local people to mobilize effectively on their own behalf. It formed in April of 1960, when sit-in participants from all over the South and others who hoped to join them gathered at Shaw University in Raleigh, North Carolina. They came for a series of meetings called by longtime activist Ella Baker (1903–1986). A North Carolina native who had spent considerable time in Harlem, Baker was the first full-time executive secretary of the Southern Christian Leadership Conference (SCLC), a former field secretary of the NAACP, and the veteran of numerous civil rights campaigns. She recognized the potential in these students' actions and set up the Shaw conference to help them establish a formal organization. The result was the Student Nonviolent Coordinating Committee. (Actually, a temporary organizing committee was created first, becoming formalized in another conference in Atlanta in October.) Mostly African American, mostly college educated, mostly young, these activists and their organizational style could not have contrasted more strongly with that of the hierarchical SCLC led by Dr. Martin Luther King, Jr., or the NAACP with its focus on the courts, although all shared the same commitment to racial justice and nonviolence. The new group's philosophy was perhaps closest to that of the Congress of Racial Equality (CORE), established in 1942 by a group from the Fellowship of Reconciliation, but that organization was based primarily in the North. The historian and activist Howard Zinn has described participants in SNCC:

> They are prepared to use revolutionary means against the old order. They believe in civil disobedience. They are reluctant to rely completely on the niceties of negotiation and conciliation, distrustful of those who hold political and economic power. They have tremendous respect for the potency of the demonstration, an eagerness to move out of the political maze of normal parliamentary procedure and to confront policy-makers directly with a power beyond orthodox politics—the power of people in the streets. . . .
>
> They believe, without inflicting violence, and while opening themselves to attack, in confronting a community boldly with the sights and sounds of protest.[4]

SNCC members tried to live their politics by avoiding hierarchy and seeking unanimity in decision making. In their commitment to civil disobedience, grassroots organizing, decentralization, and consensus politics, and in their willingness to put their bodies on the line for their beliefs, this "beloved community," as SNCC members called themselves, took a moral philosophy and turned it into a political force. SNCC's founding statement of purpose declared: "We affirm the philosophical or religious ideal of nonviolence as the foundation of our purpose, the pre-supposition of our faith and the manner of our action. Nonviolence as it grows from Judaic-Christian traditions seeks a social order of justice permeated by love." At the same time, although members' vision of the redemptive power of love was clearly, if idealistically, spelled out, they had no real ideology beyond a commitment to nonviolent civil disobedience. This would prove a weakness when SNCC floundered later in the decade, but it was also one of SNCC's greatest strengths. Unlike most other liberal organizations of the period, SNCC did not reject the support of leftists and communists or demand adherence to any particular political credo but instead welcomed all who were willing to work for black people's freedom. This brought them the crucial support of leftist activists such as Carl and Anne Braden of the Southern Conference Educational Fund, Myles Horton of Highlander Folk School, Virginia and Clifford Durr in Alabama, and the National Lawyers Guild.

Virtually all of the SNCC leadership was African American. In 1960 Marion

Barry became SNCC's first chairman, followed almost immediately by Charles (Chuck) McDew, then succeeded by John Lewis in 1963, Stokely Carmichael in 1966, and H. Rap Brown the following year. Ed King served as SNCC's first executive secretary, followed by James Forman in 1961, Ruby Doris Smith Robinson in 1966, and Stanley Wise in 1967. Virtually all of its project directors and most committed activists were African American as well, including Courtland Cox, Victoria Gray (Adams), Lawrence Guyot, Gloria House, John Jackson, Bernard Lafayette, Bob Moses, Diane Nash, Silas Norman, Martha Prescod (Norman), Charles Sherrod, and Hollis Watkins. From the start, however, SNCC was an integrated organization. Jane Stembridge, a white Virginia native then studying at Union Theological Seminary in New York, became the SNCC office's first secretary. Robert (Bob) Zellner, hired in 1961 to recruit other white southern students into the movement, quickly became a full SNCC staff member, involved in SNCC programs and protests from McComb, Mississippi (where he was beaten and jailed), to Talladega, Alabama (where he was beaten and jailed). Other white activists, including Ralph Allen, Sally Belfrage, Jack Chatfield, Bill Hansen, Sandra (Casey) Hayden, Mary King, and Mendy Samstein, played similarly long-term and important roles in SNCC, while hundreds joined the effort more briefly.

SNCC had only 16 staff members in 1961. By early 1964 there were over 150. They certainly did not join for the money—a SNCC "field secretary" (as field staff were called) earned $10 a week, $9.64 after deductions. Indeed, the whole organizational budget was minuscule compared with those of other civil rights groups, and was patched together from individual and organizational donations. In 1963, for example, SNCC operated on only $300,000. Headquartered in Atlanta, SNCC established projects across the South, often consisting of only one or two SNCC members who then recruited local people. Project staffers launched desegregation efforts, marches, demonstrations, and voter registration drives, or tried to aid the spontaneous protests that were erupting all over the region. Central loci of struggle included southwest Georgia, where former divinity student Charles Sherrod became project director in 1961; the Mississippi Delta, under Bob Moses, former Harvard student and mathematics teacher; and the area around Selma, Alabama, where Bernard Lafayette and his wife, Colia, and later Silas Norman, ran the voter registration projects. SNCC also, however, had outposts in Pine Bluffs, Arkansas; Danville, Virginia; Cambridge, Maryland; and anywhere else courageous men and women were willing to brave white violence to help bring social change. Howard Zinn called them the "new abolitionists."

Who were these activists? Zinn, who interviewed forty-one SNCC staff members in Mississippi in 1963, or a third of all SNCC workers in the Deep South, found that thirty-five were African American. Of them, twenty-five came from the Deep South, all from working-class homes. Two of the six whites were southern. Of the northerners, some blacks and all the whites came from middle-class homes. Virtually all were young; three-quarters of the Mississippi staff, for example, were between the ages of fifteen and twenty-two. Two-thirds had had at least some college education. By 1964, although their numbers had grown, their profile remained the same—primarily young, 80 percent black, most of whom were southern, with the majority of whites coming from the North.[5]

Sometimes they lived in houses rented by SNCC, called Freedom Houses, but more often they relied on the local black community to support and house them. Taking in SNCC workers required great courage, as white attacks were frequent and dangerous. The SNCC headquarters in Selma burned; in Greenwood, Mississippi, a mob attacked the office. Nor were these attacks limited to property. Every project met with immediate and violent white resistance. Demonstrators and any of their perceived supporters could be attacked at any time. Hundreds were hurt, many killed. More surprisingly, in SNCC's early years its activists also faced the suspicion of some of the older civil rights and liberal leaders and organizations, who believed they were going too fast or moving too confrontationally. They pointed to SNCC's strategies of publicly confronting white supremacy, packing the jails (called "jail–no bail," intended to dramatize the injustice of the segregated system), and refusing any compromise with the racial apartheid of the Jim Crow system. Meanwhile, the pace of activity was picking up.

CORE launched a series of interracial bus rides through the South in the spring of 1961 to test the recent Supreme Court decision in *Boynton v. Commonwealth of Virginia*[6] desegregating all terminals serving interstate travel. Modeled on CORE's 1947 Journey of Reconciliation, which employed a similar strategy on a smaller scale but was met largely with silence, the Freedom Rides of 1961 were splashed on front pages across the nation as black and white riders were brutally attacked at every stop in the Deep South. Local police either absented themselves from the scene or in some cases actually coordinated their arrival time with the mobs. The U.S. Justice Department refused to intervene. By the time the Riders arrived in Birmingham, Alabama, so much violence had occurred that no bus driver would agree to carry them any further. CORE members decided to fly to New Orleans, their intended destination. But a Nashville student leader and SNCC staffer, Diane Nash, determined not to let white supremacists have the last word, rounded up volunteers to board the buses to keep them rolling. Eventually the violence became so overwhelming, the violations of Riders' civil rights so egregious, that the federal government was compelled to act. Even then, however, its actions were hardly an endorsement of the Riders' efforts. Finally organizing protection for the Riders and drivers, those at the national level also compromised with local officials by permitting them to arrest Riders for violating the same segregation laws the Supreme Court had just declared unconstitutional. Attorney General Robert Kennedy then called for a "cooling off" period, urging the Riders to desist. Not unexpectedly, they refused to do so. Ultimately the Justice Department persuaded the Interstate Commerce Commission to formalize the Court decision against segregation by issuing new regulations. At great cost, the Freedom Rides had succeeded.

In that same year, in Albany, Georgia, the largest series of demonstrations and protests since the Montgomery bus boycott began, organized by Charles Sherrod and Cordell Reagon (later joined by Charlie Jones). The Albany Movement brought together SNCC, the NAACP, black ministers, the Federation of Women's Clubs, and others in a great coalition. Zinn has written that the Albany Movement "became the prototype for demonstrations that later rocked Birmingham and dozens of other cities throughout the nation. It represented a permanent turn from the lunch counter and the bus terminal to the streets, from hit-and-run attacks by students and professional civil rights workers to populist rebellion by lower-class Negroes. And the Albany crisis revealed clearly for the first time the reluctance of the national government to protect constitutional rights in the Deep South."[7] The white violence and mass arrests were unprecedented, as was the police repression under Chief Laurie Pritchett. In what was for many the final blow, in August of 1963 the Justice Department charged civil rights protesters with conspiring to obstruct justice. The Freedom Rides as well as SNCC's early experiences in Albany and elsewhere raised many issues for SNCC workers concerning the potency of direct action (confrontational activities designed to challenge segregation), the efficacy of nonviolence, the importance of media coverage, and the complicity of the federal government in maintaining the racial status quo.

In 1961 SNCC's central Coordinating Committee began another series of meetings to discuss the organization's strategies and priorities in light of members' experiences. The final meeting, held that August in Tennessee at Highlander Folk School, saw a showdown of sorts between the faction who insisted SNCC should focus on direct action and those who believed SNCC should instead concentrate on voting rights. President Kennedy's Justice Department urged the latter, since direct action seemed the more dangerous and created such a fierce white response. This, of course, only strengthened the conviction of the direct action advocates that theirs was the course better calculated to challenge the entrenched racial system. The disagreement was resolved in typical SNCC fashion—the group would do both. In the South, voter registration was so dangerous, so threatening to white supremacy, and so revolutionary that it *was* direct action. Diane Nash headed up the direct action projects, and Charlie Jones the voter registration efforts.

In cities, towns, county seats, and rural hamlets, the struggle against Jim Crow continued. Sometimes SNCC worked in concert with SCLC, CORE, the National Student Association, the YWCA, the Southern Conference Educational Fund, or the Council of Federated Organizations (COFO, an umbrella group designed to coordinate civil rights efforts in Mississippi). Several of the most active SNCC workers in fact came out of these other organizations. Most often, however, SNCC acted alone, organizing in areas other groups deemed too dangerous. By all accounts, such judgments were correct. SNCC activists met with fire hoses, attack dogs, and rock-hurling white mobs. Arrested by angry police, SNCC members were beaten in jail or released into the arms of waiting Klansmen. Increasingly, these images were captured by newspapers and television cameras. Everywhere these direct action struggles went hand in hand with voting drives, union-organizing campaigns, food distribution, and demands for economic justice.

Although SNCC participated in the March on Washington in 1963, the site of Martin Luther King, Jr.'s "I Have a Dream" speech, many considered it inappropriately deferential to the Kennedy administration. John Lewis, who represented SNCC on the podium, initially planned to give a fiery speech deeply critical of government collusion with the forces of white supremacy. Though he was ultimately prevailed upon to temper his remarks, his original draft (and even his revised speech) presaged SNCC's later repudiation of integrationist liberalism. It criticized the proposed civil rights bill put forward by the Kennedy administration as far too weak, and rehearsed the many apparent examples of collaboration between the federal government and the forces of Jim Crow. "I want to know, which side is the federal government on?" he asked. "We will not wait for the President, the Justice Department, nor Congress, but we will take matters into our own hands and create a source of power outside of any national structure that could and would assure us victory."[8] Lewis had good reason to be distrustful of government promises. The federal government had refused to intervene to protect the rights of demonstrators or even of those merely wishing to register to vote. The Justice Department would not send representatives or observers to investigate violations or to enforce existing civil rights laws. But the failures of liberalism emerged most clearly in the area of voting rights.

In Mississippi, voter registration efforts took the form of a Freedom Vote (or Aaron Henry Campaign) in 1963 and Freedom Summer in 1964. As early as 1961 Bob Moses and Amzie Moore had launched unsuccessful voter registration efforts that had generated a level of white violence overwhelming even for the South; it became clear that a different strategy would be needed. The theory for such a strategy, provided by sociologist Ernst Borinski of Tougaloo College, was called "parallel institutionalism." Black people barred from participating in the regular political structure registered instead in a parallel party. The gubernatorial election in 1963 pitted two segregationists against one another; SNCC (through COFO) launched the campaign of Aaron Henry, a black NAACP leader, and asked supporters to vote for him in an unofficial "Freedom Vote." Eighty thousand voted in that parallel election and inspired the creation of an entire parallel party, the Mississippi Freedom Democratic Party (MFDP), in 1964, to serve as the vehicle for voting in the presidential primary. The program to launch and promote the MFDP was called Freedom Summer. At a contentious planning meeting for Freedom Summer held in Greenville, Mississippi, in November 1963, SNCC decided to invite northern college students, white and black, to join in the effort. The bitter debates over the merits of inviting white people to organize local black people, though resolved for the moment, continued until three years later, when the opposing position triumphed and SNCC became an all-black organization.

Freedom Summer was a great success in its mobilization of black southerners, in its turning national attention to the issue of black voting rights, and in the historical, cultural, and political education programs (called Freedom Schools) it launched simultaneously. Hundreds of northern students participated. The MFDP completely failed, however, in its effort to have its delegation, rather than the one elected in the official, all-white Mississippi Democratic Party primary, seated at the Democratic National Convention in 1964. In fact liberal organizations, both black and white, urged the MFDP to back down from its demand to officially represent Mississippi at the convention. Instead of confronting the racism of its own southern wing, the party offered the MFDP what it considered a compromise: the Mississippi Democratic Party would be seated as Mississippi's official delegation, but the MFDP could have two at-large seats, with the promise of later party reform. The MFDP angrily refused the offer and while the Democratic Party did ultimately insist that future delegations be integrated, the change did not come quickly enough for many in SNCC. Already disillusioned by the media and government attention showered on white summer volunteers, as well as the occasionally patronizing attitudes of the white volunteers themselves, many black members of SNCC questioned whether a movement with whites in it could ever truly succeed in a nation as riven by racism as the United States. In the intensive FBI search for missing civil rights workers (white) Andrew Goodman and Michael Schwerner and (black) Jim Chaney during Freedom Summer, agents dredging the river discovered the bodies of black victims of lynchings they had never bothered to investigate. Nor, given the fury and stubbornness of white resistance, was it clear any longer that nonviolence was an appropriate or effective tactic. And with mobilizations like Freedom Summer, the movement was growing too large to effectively educate all the newcomers into the finer points of SNCC's radically egalitarian philosophy. It could be said that the beloved community became another casualty of white racism.

Freedom Summer had a radicalizing effect on its volunteers, though, many of whom went on to participate in other movements. Mario Savio left the South and became a founding member of Berkeley's Free Speech Movement; Kathie Sarachild helped found the feminist Redstockings after realizing the possibility of mobilizing against sexism the way SNCC mobilized against racism. Tom Hayden worked in the South before going to Michigan and writing the Port Huron Statement, the founding document for Students for a Democratic Society. And this broader radicalism in turn came back into SNCC. When in 1964 SNCC called a conference at Waveland, Mississippi, to reassess its direction, Mary King and Casey Hayden submitted an anonymous position paper urging that attention be paid to the unequal status of women in the movement. The memo was taken seriously by only a few at the time (Stokely Carmichael mocked it by insisting that the position of women in the movement should be "prone," a joke he later regretted when some feminists, believing he was serious, used him to exemplify male chauvinism), but their signed piece sent to "other women in the peace and freedom movement" a year later was much more widely read and debated, demonstrating both the staying power of such concerns and the distance SNCC (and the nation) had traveled in that year.

After Freedom Summer SNCC's rhetoric began to shift. Frustration and anger against the liberal establishment, white and black, exploded into the open. Some, like Cleveland Sellers, who became SNCC's program director in 1965, began to argue against SNCC's traditional decentralization, insisting that more internal structure and discipline were necessary to successfully unseat white supremacy. Many urged a greater emphasis on black rather than interracial projects. Alabama proved a central battleground for these debates. An SCLC-sponsored march from Selma to Montgomery in 1965 in which SNCC workers joined was attacked by Sheriff Jim Clark and state troopers at the Edmund Pettus Bridge. Martin Luther King, Jr., agreed to postpone the remainder of the march, and without informing SNCC of his intentions, at the next encounter with the police he instructed the protesters to pray and then turn back. SNCC members were disgusted and continued to demonstrate—and clash violently with police—in Montgomery. Jim Forman preached to one crowd, "If we can't sit at the table of democracy, then we'll knock the fucking legs off."[9]

A 1965 voter registration project led by Stokely Carmichael, Robert Mants, Willie Vaugn, and Judy Richardson in Lowndes County, Alabama, encountered white violence even after the passage of the Voting Rights Act (which ostensibly protected black people's right to vote), including the shooting of two white organizers, Jonathan Daniels and Reverend Richard Morrisroe, by a white deputy who was later acquitted. Revealing how far SNCC had moved from its earlier commitment to complete nonviolence, staffers in Alabama advocated African Americans' right to armed self-defense. As in Mississippi, SNCC created a separate political party, the Lowndes County Freedom Organization, which took for its logo a black panther. Although SNCC workers insisted on "black power for black people," the party was not explicitly separatist. Nevertheless, given the overwhelming racial tensions in the county, only African Americans joined. Again police intimidation, along with escalating attacks in the media and Congress against SNCC's radicalism and alleged communism, reinforced SNCC's disenchantment with liberalism.

Out of these experiences a more militant, more nationalist core of activists emerged, primarily from SNCC's Atlanta headquarters, who supplanted SNCC's traditional battle cry of "Freedom Now!" with "Black Power!" (The two words had been used before, but the phrase was first employed as a mobilizing tool by Willie Ricks at a Mississippi march in 1966 protesting the shooting of black activist James Meredith.) At a 1966 SNCC staff meeting, this separatist group presented a position paper urging the expulsion of whites as a crucial step toward the creation of a politically potent racial consciousness among black people. A majority of the staff opposed the move, but the paper articulated a long-festering set of grievances. Malcolm X's fiery rhetoric, the writings of political theorist Frantz Fanon, an eye-opening trip to Africa by several SNCC leaders in 1964, and SNCC's own history had forced many to rethink the potential of liberalism to deliver on its promise of racial justice. Such voices had been heard earlier, but the events of the past few years seemed to prove them right. And the Civil Rights Act of 1964 and Voting Rights Act of 1965 complicated the question of what to do next. Now that political equality had been won on paper, how could true, structural equality be achieved?

This newer militancy was institutionalized in 1966 when Ruby Doris Smith Robinson replaced James Forman as executive secretary and, in a hotly contested election, Stokely Carmichael replaced John Lewis as chairman. Carmichael became Black Power's chief spokesperson, and although he had not been aligned with the separatists, his position as chairman as well as his heated oratory quickly made him a lightning rod for attacks by both blacks and whites who viewed Black Power and separatism as one and the same. By this time most whites had left SNCC, some for the anti–Vietnam War, feminist, or student movements, some because they distrusted SNCC's emerging nationalism. By the time of the December decision at the estate of the black entertainer "Peg Leg" Bates to make SNCC an all-black organization, there were hardly any white members to exclude. (It was a close and contentious vote; of the one hundred or so attending, the final tally after days of debate was nineteen for expulsion, eighteen against, and twenty-four abstaining.) By that time even many African-American SNCC stalwarts, including Julian Bond, Charlie Sherrod, Marion Barry and John Lewis, had resigned, frustrated by the growing stridency and declining effectiveness of the organization. SNCC had begun few new projects, and those it had organized enjoyed little success in mobilizing either local or national support.

A heightened government and media campaign against SNCC (which escalated after SNCC announced its opposition to the Vietnam War in early 1966), an FBI campaign of disruption and disinformation called COINTELPRO, and the continued criticism of former black and white allies pushed SNCC farther into a militant radicalism aligned with the Third World and with the urban unrest in American ghettos. H. Rap Brown became SNCC's chairman in 1967, and Carmichael, increasingly convinced of the importance of an anticapitalist Pan-Africanism, took a position in the Black Panther Party and in 1968 moved to Guinea and changed his name to Kwame Toure. By that time SNCC had been decimated by infighting, paranoia, and external attacks. A year later Brown convinced the staff to become a paramilitary organization and change SNCC's name to the Black Revolutionary Action Party. Although SNCC sporadically launched projects for several more years, its existence as an effective force for social change had ended.

It is to this history that the SNCC reunion conference turned in 1988. For the first time in twenty-five years, activists from the movement gathered to reminisce, to assess their actions and decisions, and to analyze the movement's contributions and limitations. They were brought together by a former SNCC worker, Jack Chatfield. He and Mary King came up with the idea for a SNCC reunion conference and although I was co-organizer, Jack did the lion's share of the work. Over 150 people gathered at Trinity College in April to hear SNCC activists reflect on their experiences, evaluate SNCC's legacy, and weigh in on the historical controversies that have swirled around the organization. Lambasting the journalists and historians who, many believed, had distorted SNCC's true role, these speakers desperately wanted to set the record straight. The tone of the presenters was striking—laudatory of SNCC, of course, but bordering on the defensive—as they attacked those who had criticized the movement in any particular. Female activists, black and white, including those who had written the original position paper on women, flatly rejected the notion that SNCC was in any way sexist. And though at the time many felt embittered by SNCC's militant nationalism, even this turn in the organization's direction came in for little criticism at the conference. Virtually every speaker stressed instead the revolutionary structure of SNCC's early days—its radical egalitarianism, its transformative and empowering potential, its crucial support system of love and trust. The bitterest of fights seemed to most of them, in retrospect, only another indication of their depth of commitment to the movement and to one another. Clearly the perceived distortions of the historians and media, and a certain romanticization of the past, affected the tone and content of their shared reminiscences.

At the same time, however, each participant grappled with the same questions posed by those writers they criticized: what was SNCC and why did its structure and style change so radically between 1960 and 1967? What lessons does SNCC's history hold for progressive activists today? What is community? Which strategies and goals were effective and appropriate, and which were misguided? What were SNCC's limits, and what were its strengths? What gave SNCC activists the strength to go on organizing in the face of cattle prods, beatings, fire hoses, dogs, jails, and gun-wielding sheriffs and Klansmen? And, just as historians did, the conference participants returned repeatedly to points of conflict within SNCC: the conferences at Highlander and Greenville, at Waveland and Peg Leg Bates's, questions of Black Power, the experience of women, the role of the federal government, and the tensions between voting and direct action. Thus does the "politics of memory" play itself out in contemporary America; our memories may be selective, but what we select is at least in part determined by the contemporary context in which we are doing the remembering.

Speakers also disagreed on particular details—who was at what meeting, when a decision was made—as well as on their analysis of what went right and what went wrong. Their differences remind us that we must not only criticize historians whose conclusions we disagree with, but sympathize with the difficulties facing even the most conscientious scholar. The term "revisionist" has become almost an epithet in recent years, and indeed several conference participants condemned revisionist historians as passionately as the more common critics on the right. But I believe the term, or at least the mission, should be reclaimed. Revisionist history has made substantial contributions to the study of history. First, it challenges conventional presumptions about the past by using previously unexamined sources or asking new questions of traditional sources. For example, it has raised questions about America's culpability in the Cold War, its involvement in various foreign coups, and its support for certain dictatorships abroad. Revisionists have countered widely held myths about the lack of an authentic African-American culture, the classless nature of American society, and the fixity of the "traditional" family stucture. Second, revisionists have broadened the question of history from simply a study of white males in political power to include the lives and the struggles of black people, of other minority groups, of women, of the poor and the disenfranchised. The revisionist commitment is to give voice to the previously voiceless, to integrate their experience into the broader narrative of history. Nevertheless, the perils of attempting to do this kind of history were certainly in evidence at the conference.

If contemporary historical debates over feminism, nationalism, and liberalism affected the participants' perception of the past, so too did the political realities of 1988. The mood of the conference was cautiously upbeat. Ronald Reagan was still President, but in other ways the fruition of civil rights promises seemed imminent. Jesse Jackson, a movement veteran, had launched his second campaign for the Democratic nomination. African-American officials had been elected all over the country, most impressively in southern towns and municipalities that thirty years ago allowed virtually no African-Americans to register to vote. African-American and student protest had challenged South African apartheid through a divestiture movement. The ills of the nation in 1988—failing schools, homelessness, growing poverty, mind-numbing commodification, a corporate-controlled media—did not go unnoticed by the conference participants, but one speaker after another insisted that the legacy of the civil rights movement held out the promise of an effective mobilization against them. What SNCC and the broader civil rights movement had accomplished had transformed the nation and, if properly harnessed, could continue the process of building a more just society. Indeed, the continued activism of these SNCC workers was striking. They were still hard at work organizing in the South, serving in political office, challenging those in political office, teaching, preaching, writing, staffing campaigns of all descriptions. Their energy for political action had not diminished; in some cases it had been channeled in new directions, but in every case the central motivating force appeared to be the same commitment to radical equality that had led them to SNCC so many years earlier.

I edited the transcripts of this SNCC reunion conference eight years later, when the political scene looked rather different. Despite the election of a Democratic President in 1992, the social safety net that had been in place since the Great Depression had been decimated, and previously sacrosanct, if limited, programs of racial redress such as affirmative action were everywhere under attack. Republicans held majorities in both the Senate and the House. Homelessness, poverty, and the deterioration of cities had all increased, but those in need saw aid programs slashed and their right to whatever meager subsistence support they had been receiving replaced by harsh limits and exclusions. The entire political dialogue had moved to the right, with Democrats aping Republicans and Republicans doing them one better. Supreme Court decisions had thrown out voting districts that while limiting African-American input in races across the board by concentrating their votes, at least permitted the election of a number of congressional representatives who reflected the concerns of African-American communities. Other cases had raised questions about the constitutionality of affirmative action programs, minority business set-asides, and voluntary school desegregation plans. Debates over intellectual differences between the races had again become legitimate in academic discourse.

In such a context, what can the musings of SNCC workers offer us? Read today, the optimism about black voting strength seems at first glance naive. The stubborn persistence of poverty suggests that SNCC's goal of economic empowerment was an unrealizable dream. The confidence that one could still mount an effective mass protest appears absurd given the official containment structures that have been carefully created, best embodied by the 1996 National Democratic Convention's strategy: those groups wishing to demonstrate entered a lottery the winners of which could take the microphone for a specified length of time at a prearranged protest site. (This revolution would be televised.)

And yet the reminiscences, observations, and critiques offered by SNCC members remain moving and fresh. They remind us that whatever problems we face today, SNCC and other civil rights organizations dismantled Jim Crow, expanded economic opportunity, and opened the voting booth to millions of the disfranchised while facing guns and dogs and jails and beatings and death to do it. And they did so with a vision of the society they hoped would replace the one they inhabited, one they called the beloved community, a band of brothers and sisters, a circle of trust. SNCC's radical egalitarian vision, its idealism, its faith in grass-roots mobilization and empowerment, its commitment to racial and economic justice, and its unwavering conviction that one cannot achieve a just society in the future without living it in the present make the organization uniquely inspirational for our own time. Even its members' disagreements and lapses in judgment should inspire, because they remind us that fallible human beings, not saints and martyrs, challenged the fundamental institutions of our society and brought about real social change.

A word about the editing. Oral histories are vivid and evocative, offering unexpected insights and delightful nuggets of new information; it is the strength of these oral histories and the powerful and compelling voices of the speakers that make this volume a contribution to the history of SNCC and of the civil rights struggle more broadly. Nevertheless, publishing oral histories poses a real challenge. The conference itself was a free-wheeling affair, so each of the original presentations had to be edited and in some cases reorganized to make the arguments fully comprehensible to readers. Entire sessions were broken up and restructured to highlight more effectively the conference's central themes. Some material, fascinating in itself, had to be excluded as too particular to 1988 or too far off the subject of SNCC. In some cases I have added a first or last name or a date, or clarified or amplified an offhand aside.

Many presenters, speaking to their colleagues and friends, referred only in passing to people or events that may be unfamiliar to many readers. To avoid cluttering the text, these references have been gathered into a Glossary of Names and Terms which provides further information. This is followed by brief biographical sketches of each participant.

Although I tried to retain the flavor of each presenter's speaking style, translating from an oral to a written presentation inevitably required some grammatical adjustments to the original text. I tried to keep those alterations to a minimum. And some material was lost or mistranscribed as it was transferred from audio tapes to typewriter and then to computer. I have sought to correct the transcription errors and speakers' unintentional misstatements, and to bring the participants' comments up to the present wherever possible (I updated figures on black voting, homelessness, and so on). But inevitably mistakes remain—names misheard by the transcribers, or details of which I was in ignorance misremembered by a speaker. Some will disagree with my alterations and deletions, others might have wished for more. I take responsibility for all the editing that I did to create what I hope is a coherent, vibrant, and inspiring record of a remarkable conference by remarkable people living in a remarkable time.

Notes

1. There are hundreds of books on the civil rights movement, and dozens on SNCC alone. The three broadest accounts of SNCC are Howard Zinn, *SNCC: The New Abolitionists* (Boston, 1964); Clayborne Carson, *In Struggle: SNCC and the Black Awakening of the 1960s* (Cambridge, Mass., 1981); Mary King, *Freedom Song: A Personal Story of the 1960s Civil Rights Movement* (New York, 1987).
2. Zinn, *SNCC*, p. 16.
3. See, for example, Gerald Horne, *Black and Red: W.E.B. Du Bois and the Afro-American Response to the Cold War, 1944–1963* (Albany, 1985).
4. Zinn, *SNCC*, pp. 13-14.
5. Ibid., pp. 9–10.
6. *Boynton v. Commonwealth of Virginia* 364 U.S. 454 (1960).

7. Zinn, *SNCC*, p. 123.
8. The original speech can be found in Joanne Grant, *Black Protest* (Greenwich, Conn., 1968), pp. 375–77.
9. Quoted in Carson, *In Struggle*, p. 160.

The Beloved Community: Origins of SNCC

The Student Nonviolent Coordinating Committee emerged out of the spontaneous demonstrations against racial segregation that began in Greensboro, North Carolina, in 1960 and quickly spread across the South. The fledgling organization, dominated by African-American young people, consciously modeled its style and strategies on preceding grass-roots political struggles, especially those of Mohandas Gandhi in India and leftist and civil rights demonstrations in the United States. Rooted in the philosophy of nonviolent civil disobedience, SNCC's approach included faith in the power and wisdom of local people and a commitment to radical egalitarianism. These civil rights workers believed that they should themselves live in the sort of loving and equal community they sought to create in the larger society; they called themselves the "beloved community, a band of brothers and sisters, a circle of trust." SNCC thus represented both a continuity with the past and a challenge to it.

DIANE NASH: I think history's most important function is to help us better cope with the present and the future. So I'd like to talk about the philosophy behind the civil rights movement that drove it in its very early stages. We aspired in the sixties to the redeemed community or, as we frequently called it, the beloved community. A community recovered or fulfilled, a community that could become more of what its potential was. We defined the beloved community as a community that gave to its citizens all that it could give and allowed its members to then give back to the community all that they could. Our goal was to reconcile, to heal and to rehabilitate, to solve problems rather than to simply gain power over the opposition, and it really comes to the question of do you believe that human beings can be healed, can be rehabilitated. It's very interesting to me that so many of the struggles for liberation in the world seek to create a beloved society, a society where human beings get along, where democracy is practiced, but those struggling for liberation try to achieve these ends by killing people. And in spite of the fact that efforts toward liberation had been going on for thousands of years and in each generation, it's surprising to note with all that effort for so long, that there are still relatively few places on earth where the level of social, economic, and political liberation is very high. So it pays, I think, to go back and look at our methods and see if it isn't possible to become more efficient in terms of how we struggle for liberation. I think that the philosophy behind the movement of the sixties was very special, unique in terms of my own life in the late sixties. In the early sixties I had been very much dedicated to what we called nonviolence; in the late sixties I decided that it was an impotent, probably ineffective way to struggle for liberation. And I felt that way for a few years until I noticed that I hadn't killed anybody, I hadn't been to the rifle range, I hadn't blown up anything and truly, I had done very little during that period of time where I had decided that violence was the way to go, and I also noticed that the movement had not attracted large numbers of people in the kind of meaningful social action that it had attracted while we were using the philosophy of nonviolence.

Now, there is a connectedness with other historical periods and also a connectedness worldwide. We really used the philosophy that Mohandas Gandhi developed in India. He called it *satyagraha*, which is the Hindi word for holding onto truth. A young minister by the name of James Lawson had been to India, had spent some time in prison in this country because he was a conscientious objector. He refused to go into the Korean War, but he had studied Gandhi's philosophy in India and brought that philosophy to Nashville. Many of us who were students there at the time attended workshops regularly and became educated in the philosophy and the techniques that Gandhi used toward the independence of India from Great Britain.

I would like to mention a few of the basic tenets underlying the philosophy. First, we took truth and love very seriously. We felt that in order to create a community where there was more love and more humaneness, it was necessary to use humaneness and love to try to get to that point. Ends do not justify means. As Gandhi said, everything is really a series of means. We took truth very seriously; in fact, I'm sure I've lived an entirely different kind of life as a result of having been exposed to the philosophy in those early years. Truth now for me has very little to do with being good or doing what's right. It's more relevant to me in terms of providing oneself and people around one with accurate information upon which to base our behavior and base our decisions.

That principle has been very well understood I think in the natural sciences. It's quite clear that when scientists are calculating their mathematical problems or conducting experiments, they try to be as accurate and as truthful as possible. I think that that might be one reason why the natural sciences are in the space age and the social sciences are in primitive stages. Lying is institutionalized in our social relations. Countries lie to countries. The whole purpose of the CIA is to spy and to lie, and the FBI also. Governments of countries lie to the citizens. Boyfriends lie to girlfriends, girlfriends to boyfriends, husbands and wives to each other. In our personal relationships or governmental, economic, and business relationships we come to expect a great deal of untruth.

I think another fundamental quality of the movement is that we used nonviolence as an expression of love and respect of the opposition while noting that a person is never the enemy. The enemy is always attitudes, such as racism or sexism, political systems that are unjust, economic systems that are unjust, some kind of system or attitude that oppresses. Not the person himself or herself. We had some illustrations of that in that one of the managers in particular of a lunch counter in Nashville who was the opposition the first year that we had sit-ins, 1960, became an ally the second year and he was talking to managers of the restaurants that we were trying to desegregate the second year and saying, "Well, I know how it is, it sounds really difficult but it's not so bad," and was actually encouraging the managers to desegregate.

Another important tenet, I think, of the philosophy was recognizing that oppression always requires the participation of the oppressed. So that rather than doing harm to the oppressor, another way to go is to identify your part in your own oppression and then withdraw your cooperation from the system of oppression. Guaranteed if the oppressed withdraw their cooperation from their own oppression, the system of oppression cannot work. An example of that would be the Montgomery bus boycott in 1955-56. [For more details on the boycott and other events and individuals mentioned in the text, see the Glossary of Names and Terms.] For many years, Montgomery blacks assumed that Alabama whites were segregating them on buses. But in order to have segregated buses, it was necessary for the blacks to get on the bus, pay their fare, and walk to the back of the bus. When Montgomery blacks decided that there weren't going to be segregated buses anymore, there were segregated buses no more. It didn't take any change on the part of whites; when the blacks decided, then there were no longer segregated buses. So then, you have to ask yourself the question, well, who was segregating the buses all this time?

I think there's a thin line between what's known as blaming the victim and identifying appropriate responsibility, and I think that when you do identify your own responsibility in an oppressive situation, it then puts you in a position of power, because then you are able to withdraw your participation and therefore end the system.

There is so much about the philosophy that people as a whole never knew, because what was reported in the newspapers was just the fact that the demonstrators were not hitting back or not creating violence. But there were five steps in the process that we took a community through. The first step was investigation, where we did all the necessary research and analysis to totally understand the problem. The second phase was education, where we educated our own constituency to what we had found out in our research. The third stage was negotiation, where you approach the opposition, let them know your position, and try to come to a solution. The fourth stage was demonstration, where the purpose was to focus the attention of the community on the issue and on the injustice. And the last stage was resistance, where you withdraw your support from the oppressive system, and during this stage would take place things such as boycotts, work stoppages, and nonsupport of the system.

I think that the philosophy that started in Nashville, that was borrowed from India, the philosophy of the Student Nonviolent Coordinating Committee in its early days, has a great deal of merit. Everything considered, there was a considerable amount of social change achieved. There were some deaths, a number of injuries. But in looking at the efficiency of that struggle and comparing the number of casualties, I think that the philosophy that Gandhi developed works, and appears to me to be more efficient than many violent struggles. I would really urge you to do some studying of the history of nonviolence and some reading of how it works. I think it's got great potential for today and I think that we need to really get past the idea that going to the polls and voting is enough. I think we'd better take this country and its economics and politics into our own hands. We, the people. If we don't, we're going to lose more and more control of it. Nonviolence is certainly an approach that we should look into.

Some people think it was the influx of northerners, of whites, that made the redemptive community idea dissipate. I don't agree; I think it's possible for even a large-scale movement to operate as a band of brothers and sisters, a circle of trust. The reason wasn't that new people came in, I think we did not devote enough time and energy into the education of the people coming in. In Nashville, we started the teaching process before the sit-ins began in Greensboro on February 1, 1960. So there was quite a bit of time for them to become well versed. But what happened was that we got involved in going to jail and organizing and what have you and I think did not devote enough time and energy into training new people. When I first got exposed to the philosophy, I really didn't think it would work. And I had had a lot of training in it. But it was the only thing that was going on in Nashville that was trying to do something to combat the problem. And so I said well, I'll go along with it, but I really didn't think it would work. It was only in the process of using it that I finally became convinced. I always had the feeling that many of the people from throughout the South, including a number of people who were in SNCC, probably did not understand it to the level that many of us did in Nashville. And so I think education was the key.

It's true that one of the things that worked for us was that people like Bull Connor played into our hands by attacking us and getting it all onto the news. Now it seems that the system has learned to play the game, and people have wondered if a nonviolent movement can still succeed when those in power understand how to defuse it. Well, I do believe it can. One of the problems that we had was with the term "nonviolence" because it means absence of violence. And that term does not really describe the process. Absence of violence is really just one aspect of it. This is a whole, very active program, a process that a community is taken through. I think that the many demonstrations or efforts that are called "nonviolent" are only in terms of there being an absence of violence. They are not using the whole spectrum of activities in preparation and withdrawal of support. You really have to analyze what supports the system, what's financial, what's political, what's PR, and how the people as a whole are participating. So I think we haven't really been using the entire process of nonviolence. So even if the opposition understands this and we understand it, I think we can prevail.

Another thing. I think it's important to understand that today we are past the point of protests and attempting to show the government or show the powers that be that we don't like X, Y, or Z. I think we have to begin thinking of how we are going to solve it and make the ends of any demonstrations or efforts along that line what it is that we are going to do. For instance, if we object to the way the media is covering something, then we know that the media is controlled by the powers that be. It has very limited use to let the media or the government or whomever know that we don't like it. They know that we don't like it already. The idea is, decide what you need and do it yourself. Take matters into your own hands and do it yourself.

I sometimes think that there is kind of a mass masochism that we're all suffering from right now. Our water is poisoned. Our air is being poisoned. The soil, the toxic waste. We're eating food with cancer-causing chemicals. All kinds of gross things that go on and we read about them in the newspapers and maybe make a comment or two to each other, "Isn't that awful that they are doing this to us?" and then we turn the page of the newspaper and go on off to work the next morning or to school the next morning, tra la. As though our life isn't being threatened. If you were about to eat and I told you that the cook who was about to bring your food was in the next room poisoning your food and you just proceeded to go on and eat it, it would be clear that you were crazy. With all the social problems that we have right now, it's clear to me that we're not acting in a psychologically healthy manner. I think one thing that we need to do is stop lying to ourselves and realize that our life is being threatened.

MARY KING: I think it's very important to ask what exactly was this organization, the Student Nonviolent Coordinating Committee—what made it unique in a unique struggle that flourished in the South between 1955 and, to my mind, 1965. One of the things that made SNCC so distinctive is that it grew out of a phenomenon that was completely unplanned. At the start of the decade of the 1960s, February 1, four students in Greensboro, North Carolina, following a bull session, fed up with the laws of segregation, decided to go downtown to Woolworth's and to sit in. They didn't call it a sit-in, they just decided to order a Coca-Cola and not to leave when they were refused. That sparked other students across the South who similarly went to lunch counters and sat, ordered a Coca-Cola or whatever, and refused to leave. Within three months there were 35,000 students who had sat in. By then it had a name. And by the end of the year, 50,000 students had sat in. Thirty-six hundred had gone to jail.

For most of those students who were sitting in who were the first of their generation to go to college, going to jail was about the worst possible thing that could happen and yet they were willing to put everything on the line; they were willing to sacrifice not only their future but their family's investment in them. What was it that made that happen at that point in time that had launched the brushfire of reaction? Within hours, the students in Nashville who were already preparing themselves in biweekly seminars on nonviolence had moved downtown. Shortly thereafter students in Orangeburg, South Carolina, had moved to sit in. In Texas. It spread all across the South like lightning. What made that happen at that time?

Well, I think that one of the most significant, if not *the* most significant, global phenomenons since World War II was the sweep of anticolonialism throughout the world. And if you remember when television came, black families had begun to see leaders from Africa. They had heard about the Algerian War, which was still raging at the time of the sit-ins—one million Algerians had been killed in a struggle with the French for control of their own country. The British Raj had ended in 1947. At the time of the sit-ins, Fidel Castro was in the news almost every night. It was absolutely inevitable that at some point in time American blacks would launch an anticolonial struggle in the United States.

What happened with the sit-ins I believe is partly attributable to the studying that was going on. I mentioned the Nashville group. This group of students had been studying the works of Mohandas Gandhi and Henry David Thoreau, they had been studying the nonviolent civil disobedience and the nonviolent resistance of the Indian struggle, they had studied the basic philosophy of Christianity, and also there was the influence of the existentialists. There was a belief for many of the people who became involved that you are what you believe. It was a part of the times. And following that sit-in in February 1960 in Chattanooga, Tennessee, a remarkable woman named Ella Baker called a conference in April in Raleigh, and that was the start of this organization. If there is any one person that I think deserves the credit for SNCC's philosophical framework, it's probably Ella Baker. She profoundly influenced many of us with her beliefs, which had been constructed through a lifetime of organizing.

She was born in 1903 and she was organizing all during the 1920s and the 1930s with the YWCA, as a founder of CORE, and as an important leader in the NAACP. She was there when SCLC was born. She was the person who took $800 from SCLC for the first conference on SNCC, and she is the person that you find repeatedly from the twenties right through the sixties as the pivot, as the catalyst for many of the civil rights organizations. And she profoundly believed that there is leadership in everyone, in the most humble hamlet. I was to encounter her two years later. I was twenty-two years old when I went to work for SNCC. There were forty-one staff members at the time, spread across about ten southern states, and it was the most extraordinary group of students, of young people, that I had ever met.

The moment that I met the staff in the SNCC headquarters in Atlanta, I knew that my place was with the movement; there was no turning back. I was part of a campus group that traveled from Ohio Wesleyan to Nashville and Atlanta and Tuskegee in my senior year, and I met Bernard Lafayette and Jim Forman and Julian Bond and others, and that was it. I knew that that's where I belonged. So even in my own response, I had something of that self-sacrifice, that willingness to throw everything to the winds for this force.

It's hard for me to impart to you fully the strength of that commitment but there is no one, no matter how jaded or how worldly, among my peers who would disagree with me when I say that we were willing to die for each other. We believed in something bigger than ourselves and we were willing to sacrifice everything for it. We believed that ideas should come from action, not from ideology. We had a stern insistence that our conceptualization, our thinking, our framework, should grow from engagement with the people that we were working with rather than any doctrine or any ready-made philosophy. We were not ready to accept anyone's -ism. We wanted to do it ourselves.

The sit-ins were profound in their insistence that belief and action are one. What those students were doing was saying that nothing else counts except the willingness to act out your beliefs. SNCC also had the most pure vision of democracy that I have ever encountered. We never doubted the feasibility of democracy; we had no doubts about that at all. We struggled for consensus. It was never easy, it was always a struggle, but we believed that everyone had a right to speak and everyone's opinion was important.

One of the most vital distinctions between this extraordinary organization and the organization headed by Dr. King, the Southern Christian Leadership Conference, was its view of leadership. We believed that leadership was something inherent in every individual—to be biblical about it, even the least of these—and we believed that our role was that of organizers. We talked about ourselves frankly as an organization of organizers and that we had to move on. We saw ourselves as working ourselves out of a job. The first time that I met Julian Bond, he said to me, "I think SNCC's going to be gone in another five years. There isn't going to be a need for us and we're going to be moving on to other things." We never had any sense of institutionalizing ourselves.

We thought of leadership as a matter of development, a process, a matter of becoming, and that our role was to help it emerge and flourish. And we were also an incredibly diverse group of young people. Howard Zinn did a survey in 1962 [reported in *SNCC: The New Abolitionists*] of forty-one SNCC workers, and at that time thirty-five of them were black, twenty-five came from the Deep South. All of the southern blacks were from homes where their mothers worked as domestic servants and their fathers were farmers, truck drivers, factory workers, bricklayers, or carpenters. So the organization had that cadre at its core, but also there were many others from a variety of different homes and ethnic backgrounds that were part of the organization.

For myself I have to say that one of the most important things that was at work for me when I went to work for SNCC was the studying that I had done of a theologian named Dietrich Bonhoeffer. He was involved in a bomb plot to kill Hitler. He was a German theologian who believed that being Christian meant taking sides. He was incarcerated; he was locked up in Buchenwald and was hanged by the Nazis, but he believed two things that profoundly influenced me then and, frankly, influence me now. He believed that freedom is expressed in the willingness to assume responsibility and he believed that freedom without responsible action is not freedom.

I think that one of the other things I would like to highlight about this extraordinary organization is the fact that there is nothing that we were afraid to discuss. We asked astounding questions of each other. There was nothing that was too cosmic, too enormous for us to consider. In fact, the debates in our organization straddled some of the great philosophical questions of the century and I think it contributed to that debate on a global basis.

I mentioned the question of leadership, our position that leadership had to come from the bottom up in contrast to the more conventional perception of leadership in SCLC centered around a singular leader, centered in the historical leadership of the black church. We debated questions of reform versus revolution. We debated the question of nonviolence as opposed to armed struggle. We debated the question as to whether a centralized method of organizing our struggle was better than a decentralized method of organizing. In other words, should we have a strong central organization to serve as the catalyst or should we attempt to decentralize as much as possible to local communities? We also debated the question of whether there weren't some virtues in authoritarianism or should we be manifestly as democratic as we could be. And finally we debated the question of the power and psychology of men and women.

Certainly there was a two-centuries-old, if not longer, tradition of grass-roots resistance right from the earliest days of slavery. There were all sorts of efforts to overturn and end slavery, including petitions and work stoppages and all sorts of devices, buying one's way into freedom, and finally, armed resistance. There was a long tradition of resistance and faith and endurance, but what was remarkable about SNCC is that it came together and despite its almost anti-ideological position, particularly in the early years, it developed a framework for social change that spark-plugged and catalyzed a whole series of other movements. There was no guidebook for how to organize. A lot of the very basic principles of organizing were subsequently used by Saul Alinsky and in the grape strike in California, and any number of other movements and endeavors. We took some from the labor movement, it's true. We took some from study. But, primarily, the tactics that were developed grew out of the experience and the engagement with the people in the Black Belt counties in which we were working. But that movement went on to catalyze the emergence of the modern women's movement. It certainly was the spark plug for the resistance to the Vietnam War. Those two movements profoundly influenced the techniques used by the environmental movement. One of our volunteers [Mario Savio] launched the Free Speech Movement in Berkeley. If you look at where people are now you see the tentacles going out from SNCC throughout the intervening three decades.

J ULIAN BOND: There is an interconnectedness in the movement. Not just from the period of the beginning of SNCC until its end, but from the period shortly after the first slaves came to this country until today. A book called *The Origins of the Civil Rights Movement* by Aldon Morris [1984] details this connectedness, and shows the essential role of the NAACP and NAACP youth chapters in helping to organize essential early sit-ins in several cities in North Carolina before the Greensboro sit-in in February of 1960. There's the Baton Rouge bus boycott of 1953, and the developer and leader of that boycott, Reverend T. J. Jemison, whose father was head of the National Baptist Convention. Jemison was able to go to the Baptist Convention and tell the Reverend C. K. Steele of Tallahassee and another minister from New Orleans about what he had done in Baton Rouge, and later he was able to share his experiences in Baton Rouge with Martin Luther King and Ralph Abernathy. So there is a long string of connected relationships in what the Student Nonviolent Coordinating Committee was able to do from its beginnings until its demise.

J OANNE GRANT: The leadership that functioned in the movement of the sixties came out of movements that had existed in the South for a long time. Amzie Moore, for instance, was somebody with whom Ella Baker had worked very early, and he was key in voter registration work in Mississippi, but there were a lot of local people like that who had been working before the sixties and continued to work during the sixties. One of the great things about the movement was that it spanned the generations; the movement was a continuum.

H OWARD ZINN: It was a little over thirty years ago that I and my wife and our two little kids trundled ourselves into our old Chevy and headed south into Atlanta for me to take a job teaching at Spelman College, a black southern college for young women. This was in 1956. And things looked very quiet. The campus was quiet. The city looked quiet. My students were quiet. And you could easily get the impression—and so many people did—that nothing is ever going to happen here. Yes, there's racial segregation. Yes, people are being humiliated. Yes, terrible things are going on behind the scenes, behind closed doors, out in the streets, but nobody's talking about it and there doesn't seem to be much that's being done about it. My students fit the description that they often give of students today: "Oh, how apathetic students are, look how quiet they are, look they're not doing anything, they're just interested in promoting their careers"—you might have said the same thing about Spelman students in 1956–57. Of course, it's no wonder that young people need to promote their careers given the kind of society that they face, the kind of odds that they face whether they're white or black, but especially if they're black and especially if they're women. And so, yes, they were going about their duties trying to just move up in the ranks of society, and it seemed as if that was all that they were interested in then. And then in a few years this quiet campus exploded and the adjacent campuses exploded. And these students who had just been studying and walking quietly along the campus, suddenly they were outside the walls, outside the barbed wire, outside that little enclave that had been set up for them. They were out in the city, they were demonstrating, they were sitting in, they were marching, they were going to jail, they were sacrificing, and they were beginning to make a tumultuous change in the South and in this country.

And I mention that because I have to remind myself every once in a while, and then I try to remind other people when they say, "Nothing is going to happen, we really don't have a chance, look at all the power that 'they' have"— you know who I mean by "they." There is a "they." There is a "we." And people are always saying, "Look at all the power 'they' have and look at us and what can we do?" Well, what happened there in the South in that period of history showed what ordinary people could do once they woke up, once they got together, once they talked together, once they joined: they created a power that was heard and seen all over the world. And it seems to me that we ought to remember that. We ought to remember that power, the power to change things. That power doesn't depend simply on having the uniforms and having the military power, having the police and army on your side, having the money on your side—as strong and ferocious as that is, that can be overcome by people who struggle together. And that's what happened in the South, and we could see that happening. You could see the young people from all over the South, black college students, a few white friends joining them, getting together, forming SNCC and then going out into the small towns of the South talking to the ministers, talking to the local people, getting a place to live in local homes and then creating the kind of commotion which is necessary to create in order to bring about change.

That kind of remarkable time is not unique. It has happened again and again in American history except that just after it's over, people forget, and "they" want us to forget. And the reason for having discussions like this is so that we won't forget, so that we'll recognize what it is possible for us to do and, I think, so that we'll go out ready to start again.

One thinks very often—maybe especially if one has not been involved in a social movement and is looking at it from afar—"It's too serious, it's too hard, it's too grim, it's too sacrificial, it's no fun." If there's one thing that needs to be said to those people who want to have fun—and this is what I saw again and again in SNCC and what I felt in SNCC—it was the most beautiful, most fascinating, most alive time for the people who were in it. Fun is too trivial a word to describe the kind of feeling that people had when they were doing what they were doing and doing it not just for themselves but doing for others, and it seems to me that sense of coming alive in a movement, feeling more human than you ever had before is what SNCC people felt and what they showed to others and what I think they show to coming generations.

I want to follow up on what Joanne said about historical continuities, because it seems to me such an important point. History tends to be written around great cataclysmic events and so they all say, "The civil rights movement started in 1955 with the Montgomery bus boycott," or "Things started in 1960 with the sit-ins"; it's easier to think of things that way. But it's misleading, because it doesn't explain where it came from. Did it come out of nowhere? And how many people know that before the 1955 Montgomery bus boycott there was a bus boycott in Baton Rouge, Louisiana, in 1953, or that between 1900 and 1906 there were boycotts of streetcars all over the South? You could trace it—and you would have to work at it because the tracks are very faint now—connections going all the way back to the turn of the century and before that. And I think of William Monroe Trotter, a black leader in Boston who is not well known but who organized a demonstration against Booker T. Washington at the turn of the century, and he was arrested. And W.E.B. Du Bois was so filled with indignation at this arrest that he called a gathering at Niagara called the Niagara Conference. This then led to the formation of the NAACP in 1909. The formation of the NAACP led not just to creating a legal organization in New York or a fund-raising organization but it led to little groups throughout the South, NAACP chapters, youth chapters of the NAACP in which people who were not known, who were not heroes, who were not leaders, carried on a remarkable struggle. Some of the kids who participated in the 1960 sit-ins had been involved in the local chapters of the NAACP. Rosa Parks was not just a person who just happened to be sitting in the wrong place on the bus in Montgomery because, as they said, she was just tired. Other people have been tired, but she had been to Highlander Folk School, she had been in the local NAACP. The connections go on and on over the decades and over the generations and people carry it on. And it's important to know this, because otherwise we will not see the importance of the little things we do that carry on the struggle, the things that don't make the history books but have passed the baton on from person to person, from movement to movement.

PAUL LAUTER: Muhammad Kenyatta was very active in starting the movement in Chester, Pennsylvania. He went downtown with a sign one day in 1962 or 1963 and started standing outside one of the stores downtown and the sign said, "Don't buy where you can't work." He got arrested, knocked around. He got out and went back and people began to join him. The Chester movement is a very important seedbed for lots of people, particularly later on in Students for a Democratic Society, SDS. One of the lessons, I think, for people who were involved in that group was the possibility of taking that individual action that really moved people and that gave people the freedom and the sense of possibility to break out of what people call apathy.

One other thing in that respect. When we trace history back we tend to do it in terms of these great figures, Martin Luther King, his ideas of nonviolence that he got from Gandhi who got them from Henry David Thoreau, right? Thoreau got his ideas from where? It was a commonplace of evangelical Christianity in the early nineteenth century to stand against laws that were evil. Ten years before Thoreau the women in the Boston Female Antislavery Society, being attacked by a mob of well-dressed men in Boston, stood up against them in a nonviolent manner. Angelina Grimké, twelve years before Thoreau, wrote about the need to break the law. If we get away from the notion that great ideas are transmitted by great minds and think about the work that goes on at every level and the continuity of that work, that is very liberating.

TOM HAYDEN: I was reading *Man's Hope* [1938], a novel written by André Malraux about the Spanish Civil War. There is an interesting connection with SNCC because the Spanish Civil War of the 1930s, in which a popular social democratic government was toppled by a fascist movement led by Francisco Franco supported by the Nazis and by Mussolini's Italy, was one of the immediate events precipitating World War II and holocaust and devastation for much of the planet. There was a failure on the part of the West, and the Soviet Union for that matter, to defend Spain, and when Spain fell, it was an incentive for the Germans to begin to move their empire. And a number of people from around the world, including the United States, went to Spain and they fought in Spain in the Abraham Lincoln Brigade, and went through an experience which for the 1930s generation was something like Vietnam and civil rights for the 1960s generation. They were divided into many camps—very similar in all movements—there were pure anarchists who believed that all authority resided in the individual and all decisions have to be made in the whole movement by individuals alone, all the way over to members of the Communist Party who were highly structured and believed in top-down discipline and in a structured approach, and everything in between. And they just couldn't agree on structure. They were split, overrun, and finally defeated. But they created a legacy for the next fifty years. They created a standard of courage, a standard of sacrifice, and most of them who lived through the experience in Spain came back and organized in America in teachers' unions, in trade unions in general, in intellectual circles—every significant American intellectual of the 1930s who then dominated the next twenty years had some relationship to Spain. It was the touchstone of their lives when they were young, just as Mississippi was, for many of us, or Vietnam was.

In the course of reading this book I came across a passage that I thought was pretty universal. There are these two people in the Popular Front and they're arguing over whether you need in modern warfare to rely on experts and technology or whether you need just the inspiration and the will of people. They were up against mechanized warfare and an air force and they had people who were building barricades in the streets with mattresses. And as they're arguing about this, out in the streets the people are shouting "Salud" and singing revolutionary songs and marching around and preparing for the enemy to advance on Madrid, and this one fellow who has been convinced that you need experts says out the window, "'As to those sounds coming in through the window . . . —I might define them as an Apocalypse of fraternity.'" In other words, everyone on the street was no longer living the life of business as usual, they were completely engulfed in this historical moment that they'd given their lives to. It was apocalyptic. And he said, "'The apocalyptic mood clamors for everything right away. . . . But that fervor spells certain defeat . . . and for a very simple reason: it's in the very nature of an apocalypse to have no future. . . . Even when it professes to have one.' Putting his pipe back in his pocket, he added, sadly, 'Our humble task, Mr. Magnin, is to *organize* the apocalypse.'" [pp. 116, 118]. That is, I would submit, exactly what happened also in the 1960s and is a universal dilemma. We tried to organize the apocalypse. I don't think it can be done.

The apocalypse happens now and then—a fever comes. I think it has to do with people being left outside the system for long enough and having serious grievances that are not addressed and starting to throw off that hatred of self that usually goes with being oppressed and starting to replace that with pride, then some fearless young people step forward and everybody follows. That happens. That will happen again. So what Malraux is saying in this book is that when you're in that situation, trying to organize that consciousness is virtually impossible.

It was one of those moments I think that only come very rarely in American history, where movements arise that do not have simply in mind a specific demand like the right to vote, but circles of people come together who are possessed with a far more inspired vision that they can change the world and *will*. I don't know where that comes from. That's the way it was. For whatever reason, young people came together and believed for at least a two-year period that we would change the world. That is heady stuff. That is far more than we would achieve civil rights or we would reduce the military budget or something like that—those were givens, and it was going to be something far more than that.

And there was a period of time when all this seemed quite true, a year or two, and people gave their whole lives to it. They put their future out of the way, they cast themselves off from their families, they gave themselves to a movement. From that they got purpose, a new family, a substitute community; they grew up together through that experience. Income—enough to live on, that room for $1.50 at the YMCA—everything was provided as long as you were willing to provide body and soul. And it was necessary. I don't think you could have gotten the catalytic energy together to go into Mississippi and confront the violence of the state without such a community. Nobody who worked in an office as opposed to a community was going to take the office to Mississippi on an afternoon and crash into the wall of segregation, because it was an axiom that you would probably die. So you had to have something around you strong enough to take the fear of death and dissipate it, and that was this community.

And this was how SDS was born as well, much of SDS. I started in the South, not in Ann Arbor; I spent two years in the South. And a purpose was served. We were the catalyst for a great many reforms, some of which we didn't accomplish ourselves, but we started. And that was the function, I think, that we performed, an all-important function. Some of it was aborted because of events that were out of our control: the killing of the two Kennedys, Dr. King, Malcolm X; those killings cast a question mark over the whole enterprise. As a friend of mine said, we all became might-have-beens.

After serving that initial function, I think a number of things set in but, primarily, it's very difficult to sustain a revolutionary commitment without roots for very long, without either becoming unrealistically radical or burning out or starting to realize that you can't perfect the human being before society changes. So we started thinking we could change the whole world and within six years realized we couldn't even hold our own organization together. It was a very humbling and devastating experience for a lot of people.

My friend Howard Zinn was saying that there were organizers who were quietly organizing, holding workshops, and Rosa Parks attended one and that gave her the skills and the consciousness, so she sat down on the bus, and I agree with that. But the mystery remains, why that day, that person? Because a lot of Rosa Parkses went through those workshops and they didn't sit down on buses. I think there is an element of magic and spark and spontaneity to it that's unexplainable.

The other thing that's quite important is that all of us are talking from a context that is utterly and radically and permanently different than today's context. You cannot underestimate how important it was that no black person in the South could vote, and no college student in America could vote. The two active constituencies did not have the option of working in the system open to them. I could not vote until I graduated from the University of Michigan when I was twenty-one years old. So all during those four years I was a student, an editor expressing my opinions, yelling at the administration, picketing—those were the only choices I had: do nothing versus speak out outside the system. There was no inside the system. Civil disobedience and speaking out were the options open. Today, I suppose to most people civil disobedience seems strange if you haven't first voted and tried to work within the system. So it's a hopelessly different context.

Today, too, students are treated relatively as adults whereas we were treated as infants. The student government at UCLA is like a big patronage system; they have hundreds of thousands of dollars and the different ethnic groups on the campus fight over it like it's New York in 1911. It used to be that student government was totally a sandbox, it didn't have a budget. So a lot of energy gets absorbed in the system, the campus system, at least in the California campuses. Then, also, the job pressure is terrible today. It seems that the only way to insure some kind of material success for yourself is to study like crazy and so if you protest, if you get active in something, it puts you at a competitive disadvantage next to the other person who's trying to get a good grade.

Why is that different from the sixties? Partly because we didn't care as much about that because the economy, believe it or not, was relatively good. I mean, in Ann Arbor you could leave school for a year and get arrested in the South twice, come back and use that as a credential for getting into law school. They'd think this was a career step. If you advised that to somebody today, they'd think that you had checked out from the human race.

So I think as a rule that—this is a Hayden law of social change—you should work within the system as far as possible, and where it fails, go outside the system, but not knowing how far you can go, not having a dogma about how far you can take things. Working within the system always has some utility, and I don't think there's any handbook on social change. I no longer believe in the catechism of "what is the right way to effect social change," because it usually happens in surprising ways, unexpected ways.

My life was changed, I would say totally, by my experience in the South. I wanted to be a foreign correspondent or a newspaper editor, and actually I was the editor of the college paper and I was supposed to go to the Washington bureau of the *Detroit News*, which is where my family wanted me to go. At least if I wasn't going to be a doctor or a lawyer, they wanted me to be a journalist. And Georgia and Mississippi changed all of that. My outlook was changed almost overly romantically, I suppose, to the view that the people who were considered to be excluded and at the bottom and the least qualified actually knew more about reality than college students with degrees. And that no movement for justice or political movement could be complete until it included opportunities for the poor, and that the poor would have to play a role in that movement. And so I never went back to a conventional career, ever.

And I suffered a fifteen-year break with my father who wouldn't speak to me for all those years; he could not understand how he had created a person who went to college, got a degree, and went to Mississippi, Georgia, and Newark to work among blacks. It just didn't make any sense. So a great price was paid in terms of my own family as well as my world view. It's a price that was painful but I think it happened to a great many people. I came out of it and my family came out of it, I think, stronger and with a far richer life than if I was editing copy at the Paris bureau of the *Detroit News;* so I'm glad for it.

CHARLES MCDEW: There are so many memories that come flooding back. One memory that I have was when some of us from the Orangeburg [S.C.] Movement for Civic Improvement—great names back then—went to Raleigh for the first meeting that was to become the Student Nonviolent Coordinating Committee. The meeting was called by SCLC. Ella Baker was the coordinator and the one who called us all together. In rural South Carolina we didn't know what this SCLC was about, but everybody we knew trusted Ella Baker and so they gave the okay to go. We went to Raleigh and there were these very eloquent people from Nashville who understood the philosophy, who understood the reason behind it, who could talk about a redemptive community, and we knew in Orangeburg that we had been doing this nonviolent direct action strictly as a tactic and we learned so much. The Nashville people were very well versed. Jim Lawson, who is from my hometown, spent hours talking with us. But we still didn't have the grasp of the concept as well as people from Nashville did, and I have to say that that was a continuing sort of struggle within the organization: nonviolence as a tactic versus nonviolence as a way of life. I remember when we left Shaw College in that initial conference and going back to South Carolina State and Orangeburg and talking to people about rehabilitating white folks, and I remember an old man said to me, "It's like rehabilitating housing. How you going to *re*habilitate what ain't never been bilitated?" There were arguments that were constant about how can you make a moral appeal in the midst of an amoral society. Not immoral, mind you, amoral. A society that had never accepted us as full citizens and that was a constant. We had a small office down in Atlanta and the arguments would go on forever. SNCC meetings went on for days. Days and nights. I remember at one point we even talked about splitting the office. We had two rooms. On one side we were going to say "Student Nonviolent" and there would be a dove with an olive branch in its beak, and on the other door, we'd have "Coordinating Committee" and there would be a fist. We seriously talked about those things. As Mary mentioned, there was nothing under the sun we did not consider worthy of talking about. And if you came to consensus on something, then you would do it. Many of us bear the scars today of meetings when somebody, after four nights of discussion, would say, "We ought to go down and make a citizen's arrest of the chief of police." And we'd do it. Or try to, and be whipped and put in jail. But through it all, through all of the arguments, philosophical differences, we called ourselves a beloved community. A band of brothers and sisters, a circle of trust, and we trusted that what we ultimately would do would be for the best of us and best for the movement.

A lot of people don't realize when we finally made SNCC a working organization. We were in the beginning really just coordinating by collecting information. We decided that in order to keep it going, some people would have to drop out of school and work full time. I remember Sherrod, Charlie Jones, myself, and several others decided one of the first things we had to do was make ourselves knowledgeable about the system we were going to deal with. We raised money. The first time we raised money was to educate ourselves. We had a seminar in Nashville in 1961. We called it "Understanding the Nature of Social Change." We brought in labor leaders, historians, psychiatrists, psychologists, people from the entertainment world. We brought in everybody who would talk to us about different aspects of the system that we were about to attack. I think that's important to understand, that once we decided we were going to make our move, we felt we were making it with the widest possible knowledge and information and as I said, we talked about all sorts of things as being possible and desirable programs. We talked about taking over the NAACP. We said the NAACP was already organized. They had youth chapters. They had money. Let's take them over. I remember we went to the NAACP convention that year. We were going to try and get the votes to rule the NAACP. We talked about taking over the Southern Christian Leadership Conference. We said Sherrod can speak as well as the Lord. We ought to do that. These were serious considerations. Years afterward, I used to sit down and laugh— wow, we were really bold. SNCC was bad. And if we said we were going to do something, we would do it. Just wild things. Because we really didn't know exactly what we were going to do, but we knew we were going to change the face of America.

Another thing people don't realize generally: we said we were going to do this in five years. Back then Chairman Mao had his five-year plan for growth for China. We talked in terms of five years, for a couple of reasons. One, we felt that you only had five years to do it and we should then disband the organization. We talked about that. We said because if we go more than five years or if we go without an understanding or feeling that the organization would be disbanded, we will run the risk of becoming institutionalized and spending more time trying to perpetuate the institution than having the freedom to act and to do. So we talked about in five years, that's it.

And we talked about what are we going to tell our parents about dropping out of school? You could placate them by saying that this is going to end at a specific time, five years. Then we're going back to school. And the other thing we said was that we would have to do it in five years because by the end of that time, you'd either be dead or crazy. That you could not bare your chest to that sword constantly without its taking its toll. We were very serious and gave great thought to that. We knew. We'd seen people burn out. It hadn't been five years and we were seeing already, in a very brief time, it was getting to you. It was getting to us all. So we set a time and then we set about to put together a plan on how we were going to act.

JAMES FORMAN: Sherrod used to say, "If we could only find one person, the key is to find one more person other than yourself and then things will begin to roll." Diane Nash Bevel was responsible for the organization of a lot of us, including myself: she was directly responsible for all of the misfortunes in SNCC because she recruited me, so you just remember that. And then there's Mary King; she worked with Jimmy Carter, and that came about because registration worked and Bernard Lafayette and other people organized in Alabama and Sherrod in Georgia, and Mary King as the assistant to Julian Bond in the communications department was instrumental in the organization and election of James Carter as the President of the United States. And there are a couple of other people who are still trying to carry on, Joanne Grant and Dorothy Zellner. And there's Ralph Allen, who recruited Jack Chatfield. That's how the ripples are organized—one person takes up the responsibility and he gets another person involved.

DANNY LYON: Many different kinds of people made up SNCC. By the way, I'm flattered to be here with these people. I've run around after them, driven cars for them, taking their pictures, trying to make them more famous and more mythological. I was in love with all of them; they're great, great people, really absolutely remarkable and I'm honored to be here with them.

I recall that I had a revelation of death at that point in my life, I guess I was twenty or twenty-one years old at that time. I had a nice Oldsmobile—I should have just kept that car, I could have put one of my kids through school with it—it was a black 1957 Oldsmobile with all that beautiful chrome on the grill and I was probably going 100 miles an hour through the Delta, which is really flat, and the police were so busy beating these people up, you really didn't worry about speeding tickets, and I was flying, and I was so happy, because I had fallen into the midst of this thing. I was twenty-one years old, I had a black Oldsmobile, it was incredible! I'm completely serious. I was happy like Mozart's happy when he writes *Cosi fan tutte*, and suddenly death appeared before me and I said, "You mean I'm mortal? This is going to end?" And I was stunned. I couldn't believe it. Because in a way to understand death and what it meant, I had to understand life and what that meant.

And in a way, I think, just for myself, I decided I was going to do something with that life. Then, in the future, forever, because it would end. SNCC totally changed me as a person and that's probably true of everybody who was on the staff. I think part of the feeling of SNCC as a radical organization was that part of the struggle was won just by the existence of the movement; that was one of the things that was discussed there. SNCC workers mostly were out doing things.

When I first got to the office, I too had crossed America, hitchhiked down, took buses. I reached the SNCC office and it was closed, because nobody was there, they were all in jail. It was the summer of 1962, and someone, a neighbor or somebody, said, "They're down in Albany, Georgia, go down there."

So the office was closed and I went down to Albany. And I had a picture made of myself in front of the SNCC office, 1962. It was a barbershop, is that right? Had a barber pole in front of it. It said "Student Nonviolent Coordinating Committee," and I'm so proud of myself standing there with my Nikons and I'd hitchhiked down all the way from Chicago, and there are endless stories, really. But anyway, I ended up back up North and I took my pictures and I printed them. I hung them up in the University of Chicago as an exhibit. It was the first exhibit I ever had. And that was the beginning for me. Forman, I guess, got to know about the pictures, that I was doing something useful, and that's how I was sent down to Mississippi.

I think for the record it should be clear that SNCC had its own media. I was the media of SNCC. I was what would become a profession: a photojournalist, a film maker, an author, but I was SNCC staff. In other words, they were telling me what to do, I was fighting them off trying to do it the best I could, but the result was SNCC was turning out its own propaganda and SNCC was trying to control the media and create its own mythology and it did it. Now the word "myth" here was completely intentional. There was a legend of SNCC. These are legendary people. I'm a very romantic person. I'm an artist. And I'm somewhat detached from the struggle because I could always go to Katz's and eat pastrami sandwiches. In a way I think that's why my photographs were good, because I could step back a little.

SNCC published a book, the royalties went to SNCC, called *The Movement* [1964]. SNCC published its own posters. They were very well done. SNCC published pamphlets for fund raising and to bring people down. Dottie Miller wrote them, Julian did something—you weren't just sitting there, you must have been doing something. We told a lot of jokes. It was an incredible, exciting time.

At the beginning, television was not that important and the media didn't know about SNCC, and that's the truth. It came and went. *Life* magazine was important, much more important than television. There were very few cameras there at the beginning. The movement would appear and then it would vanish; there were Freedom Rides and there it was and then it was just gone, it didn't exist. The turning point was the photograph.

I sat down next to someone who was within twenty years of my age, a nice-looking woman, and she turned to me and said, "Is that all you did for SNCC was take pictures?" And I said, "Yes, that's all I did."

Voter Registration *Is* Direct Action

In 1961 SNCC activists met at Highlander Folk School to reassess their strategy. Two factions emerged. One wanted to continue SNCC's focus on "direct action," the confrontational but peaceful demonstrations against segregation. Another argued that SNCC should concentrate on gaining voting rights for African Americans in the South. Through various stratagems, black people had been kept from voting for decades, and disfranchisement had left the community powerless to combat the poverty and segregation its members faced. Although SNCC agreed to pursue both courses of action, it quickly became clear that in the South, the two were one and the same—trying to get African Americans registered to vote constituted direct action of the most confrontational kind. And indeed, whites responded to voter registration efforts the way they did to other direct action efforts: with arrests, beatings, and other forms of physical and mental intimidation. Nevertheless, SNCC drew volunteers from local communities and across the nation who believed in the worthiness of the struggle despite the very real threat to their lives. One center of such activity was southwest Georgia.

CHARLES MCDEW: It's important to understand how we weren't always agreed on a nonviolent, direct movement. The Highlander meeting in August of 1961 was a highlight of that, where there was a split and very heated discussion about whether or not we were going to continue direct action, that is, sit-ins and boycotting and the like, or also involve ourselves in voter registration.

Ultimately, after four days up in those mountains where the beloved community nearly fell apart because everybody was arguing so passionately for what direction they felt SNCC should go in, we finally agreed that we would do both direct action and voter registration because we concluded that voter registration in Mississippi and Lowndes County, Alabama, *was* direct action.

JAMES FORMAN: Basically, as you know, in 1619 the first slaves came into the United States. Then the Civil War was fought, ending slavery. White people from all over the United States helped to fight in the Civil War, as did black people. During Reconstruction we had the rise of the Ku Klux Klan. The Ku Klux Klan was a terror organization then and it still is, and it began to terrorize black elected officials and drove a lot of them from office.

In 1890 the Mississippi legislature decided that they were going to take the vote from the poor white people—and I stress this—as well as the black people, and they were going to do this by passing a new state constitution with literacy laws and poll tax measures, primarily. Those were the two main ways that the vote was taken away. This meant that people didn't have a right to run for office, they didn't have a right to vote for elected officials. And it was not until 1955, when Rosa Parks sat down, that extralegal challenges began. But it was the Student Nonviolent Coordinating Committee which developed extralegal tactics to their greatest degree. What we were saying was that we don't agree with these things; that these laws are unjust and that we should take direct action. And Sherrod was one of those individuals, Lafayette, and Julian; tremendous amounts of nonviolence training. And people decided that the legal approach was not working. There are people who are oppressed, they can't vote, they can't sit down in public facilities. So we must do something extra. We explored this question of nonviolent protest, and then that was carried on into voter registration. My own contribution started in Fayette County, Tennessee, when we were registering people to vote who were denied the right to vote there. There we met John Doar, who was a central figure to this. He was in charge of the Justice Department's Division of Civil Rights, as was Robert Owen who was another Justice Department official in Fayette County, and that relationship with Doar carried over into the activities of the Student Nonviolent Coordinating Committee.

Now, in one way we were pressured to do voter registration. Robert Kennedy felt that would be a safer method of protest and also it would not embarrass the United States government as much. Congressman Charles Diggs picked up on that and began to try to organize the student movement into voter registration. Well, during that time, I had been working in Fayette County and I knew that wouldn't be no contradiction. I knew that voter registration there probably would not work, and so at the Highlander meeting of August 1961, SNCC reorganized itself. There was a staff of sixteen people. Charles Sherrod was into voter registration; Bernard Lafayette, myself, we were in direct action. The direct action people insisted that I should be the executive director of the organization. My position was one of unity, because I knew that registering voters *was* direct action. I mean Fayette County was a horrendous experience. But the Justice Department under Robert Kennedy, or certainly Robert Kennedy himself, felt that students should go into voter registration, and that would be a safe method of protest.

I wasn't at Highlander, but it's my understanding that some people were objecting to that. I know in the direct action wing the concern was being expressed that we not be coopted by going into voter registration, that the movement through sit-ins and direct action had achieved a tremendous number of objectives. In voter registration, people were saying that we had to register voters, and I certainly agreed with both positions. But those were the main considerations in choosing that as our direction.

My concern was that the student movement not be coopted by the Justice Department. And I certainly felt that everything that we could do to try to keep the student movement moving, we should attempt to do. Those were the basic considerations; and of course, they made foundation grants possible. And this is one of the tragedies. The government can do a lot of things, the Justice Department can do a lot of things. A lot of voter registration money was made available through various foundations primarily because the administration wanted to register voters, there's no question about it, that's just a fact. And we attempted to get some of that money, but SNCC got very, very little money. A little money went to southwest Georgia, $5,000 went to Mississippi, but most of that money went to these other organizations. But we were still registering voters, and we should not forget that.

The foundations and the Voter Education Project did not want us in the rural counties, which was our approach. They objected to our method of registering voters. They said they'd try to get us into the cities, where we could register larger numbers of people, and so we tried to explain to them the rationale for registering in the counties. We presented that proposal and we didn't compromise on that. We negotiated, we attempted to get some funds, but there was very, very little money that came as a result of the voter registration activities for SNCC.

This raises the question of relations with the federal government. Everybody has to understand that the Student Nonviolent Coordinating Committee knew what it was doing. We were cooperating at various phases with the federal government. In Fayette County, before we went into voter registration, the

United States government couldn't act, because there were no organizers, there was no field staff. In order for the Justice Department to file these voting-rights suits, it was necessary to have field people; that is, people who were willing to take people down to register to vote. It was only in that way that you could invoke the 1957 civil rights law which simply said—it wasn't much, but it was an opening—that the federal government had to protect people who were willing to register to vote and those people who were trying to help them to register to vote. And it was that law which we used all throughout the sixties in order to try to pressure the federal government to do what it was supposed to do and that is to protect people in the exercise of their right to vote.

My criticism was not of John Doar. I point out that it was primarily the Federal Bureau of Investigation which was refusing to carry out a federal law. Now this should be discussed in further detail, because remember that everything that we were doing in terms of voter registration was basically legal activity and that the federal government was supposed to protect us. It was not supposed to let anyone interfere with our lives, but, as I said, in order to do that, you had to have staff people.

In Greenwood, Mississippi, the Justice Department was insisting that we drop our opposition to the literacy laws, that it was in favor of a civil rights act but not for the clause that says drop the literacy laws; and this is how the demonstrations started in Greenwood. Our position was that we can't compromise on this question, that if you can register to vote in Illinois just by signing your name, or in New York, we have to have that same right in Mississippi. And so the thing to do is to start demonstrating, and that's how we started the demonstrations in Greenwood around this question of completely eliminating these literacy test laws.

Now, what I can best contribute is to talk about some of the effects of the voter registration and some of the consequences. The effects have been enormous. Julian Bond was an elected official, he was a SNCC field secretary, working on communications, he was on the Atlanta Committee on Appeal for Human Rights. Charles Sherrod is an elected official; Robert Mants, who worked in southwest Georgia, became an elected official. John Jackson is the mayor of Whitehall, Alabama. These people are elected officials who were involved with the initial organization of voter registration. So just from that point of view, it's important. What does that mean? It meant that we crushed, if you want to use that term, the 1890 decision of the Mississippi legislature. We were able through successful, sustained, organizational work to overturn something that had been a barbarism in the history of American society, that is, the denial of the right to vote. And that was codified in the 1965 Voting Rights Act, and a lot of that is directly related to the work of Bernard Lafayette. John Doar came up to me in 1965 at the time of the Selma to Montgomery march and said he was very, very sad. I said, "What's the matter?" He said, "I see all this publicity that Dr. King is getting behind the Selma to Montgomery march and I know it was the Student Nonviolent Coordinating Committee that came into Dallas County, that came into Selma, Alabama, and began to register voters and began to challenge this whole process and that this circuit court of appeals is going to hand down a decision within a week which will practically"—he didn't use the word revolutionize—"shatter this whole literacy test that the South wanted to impose." Now, in 1964 the Civil Rights Act had a severe weakness; it did not completely eliminate the literacy requirement. But in 1965 the Voting Rights Act did eliminate the literacy requirements, and therefore a lot of people began to register to vote. And that's directly related to the work of the Student Nonviolent Coordinating Committee as well as allied groups. We're not trying to take away anything from other organizations, but the role of the heroic people in this organization and on this platform is usually not talked about, so I want to take an opportunity to say that.

Now, I want to talk about some of the enormous negative consequences. The repression of people who associated with voter registration intensified. We have concrete proof of the introduction of the FBI and the Central Intelligence Agency into the Student Nonviolent Coordinating Committee to destroy the organization. Why? Because of the work that it had done, because of its efforts to register voters, primarily. Because when you register voters in the United States of America you're talking about changing power relationships. You're talking about taking the ability to control the tax dollar away from some people and giving it to other people, and that's an enormous reality in the lives of any people. And that's why the organization and all of its contributors have been undergoing severe repression since 1964, because the organization was successful. We have to understand that, and SNCC's members have to appreciate that, so that we're not confused about why all of us are going through this kind of turmoil, and why some people get recognition and other people don't. But that was never our concern because we were not just interested in registering voters, we were talking about a new world, changing values, changing the values of the people of the country, and we have to try to get back to that as much as we can.

Now, another consequence was that the government organized a lot of people. I have a book here by Elijah Muhammad called *Message to the Black Man in America* [1965[. (Elijah Muhammad's organization, the Nation of Islam, is being carried on today by Louis Farrakhan, not by Wallace Muhammad, who has broken with the ideology of his father. He has said that black supremacy is the worst thing in which they could have been trained, so he is not in accord with this position expressed by Elijah Muhammad.) In this book—and we didn't know this at the time—Elijah Muhammad says to the world that if they're opposed to civil rights that the Nation of Islam will "take care" of the civil rights people. That didn't mean just the workers—myself, Bernard Lafayette, or Charles Sherrod—but it meant contributors, anybody for civil rights, as we interpreted it. Now, we didn't know that at the time, because we were interacting with the Nation of Islam and we would tell them, "We know that you're a religious group, but these laws are going to affect you; you're black and you're suffering from segregated laws, so don't worry." Had we known that this was the position of Elijah Muhammad, we probably would not have contacted him.

Now, this book didn't come out until 1965. But since that time there have been a lot of other things happening in the United States in terms of the consequences of our particular action and the actions of other people. People were talking about the revolutionary acts of the movement, and race war as a consequence. Race war got introduced as the consequence of a broad interracial civil rights movement which overturned hundreds of years of deprivation in the United States, certainly from 1891 up until 1964. All that has to be discussed.

There is a book by Don Lee, or Haki Madhubuti, after he came back from the Sixth Pan-African Congress in Dar es Salaam, Tanzania, in 1974, in which he said he was going to organize a race war. Well, we were opposed to race wars. You can see by the composition of people in SNCC that within its ranks that was not the reality of the organization. Now, a lot of the white people who were in SNCC are still confused about a lot of things, and I'm not trying to cast any aspersions, but all of this is not the problem of black people in the organization, because I talked to some organizers who were in the People's Republic of China, and they told me they came back to split the movement; they came back to organize the white people out of SNCC. And I explained to them that what you in fact did was to split the Student Nonviolent Coordinating Committee and that's an objective fact; there's no way that you can look at this other than that. And I also went to the People's Republic of China and said that some of us in the United States are opposed to race war; we've dedicated our lives to racial harmony, to a new world, and we want the People's Republic of China to know that we are opposed to race war and that we would consider any support for the race war ideology given by the People's Republic of China to any group in the United States to be something that is not in the best interests of all of the people of the world, and we discussed that. The main answer we were given was that Mao Zedong was saying that Robert Williams, founder of the Revolutionary Action Movement, was the head of the black American nation in the United States of America. That has to be further discussed.

Voter Registration Is *Direct Action*   45

Now, in terms of some of the future projections, one of the things that we discussed in SNCC was how to handle Washington, D.C. The general strategy was get the right to vote in Georgia, Alabama, Mississippi, all the other southern states and then begin to concentrate our energies on Washington, D.C. Why? Because Washington, D.C., was controlled completely by the federal government and it's still controlled by the federal government. The budget of Washington, D.C., still has to be sent to Capitol Hill. And that regulation by the federal government has enormous consequences to people all over the world. Washington, D.C., is the capital of the nation, and a few people control it, so we're trying to change that. I think that if we're able to get statehood for the District of Columbia the basic objectives of the Student Nonviolent Coordinating Committee will have been completed. Then the only thing left is the question of full equality in terms of employment for people of color and for women.

I've tried to discuss some of the effects and some of the consequences of voting rights efforts. The consequences were enormous, but we have to fight against the repression against everybody in the United States because the FBI does not hammer on just some of us.

CHARLES McDEW: I got into SNCC because I never quite adjusted. My father had the idea, as many black parents did, that you should have the black experience. You should go to a black school where you see black professionals. In Massillon, Ohio, there were maybe 3,000 black people. So when I was sent to South Carolina, to South Carolina State, I had never seen segregated anything. And I just could not adjust. By the time I went home for Christmas, I had been arrested three times.

The first time was in Sumter, South Carolina; a group of guys had been stopped by the police. I was driving, and the police pulled us over and I said, "What's the problem?" And the cop said, "Where are you from?" I said, "Ohio, why?" He said, "They never taught you to say 'yes sir,' 'no sir,' up there?" I said something like, "Man, you must be jiving me." And that's when I tipped from observer to activist, because he broke my jaw. He hit me with his night stick and broke my jaw. I tried to fight back and was beaten bloody. One of the things that I kept thinking as I was being beaten was not so much about these two cops that were beating me but the four other fellows who were standing there watching me being beaten and not helping, and I was saying, "I'm gonna kick your ass, every one of you." I could not understand why they would do that, why they wouldn't help.

I understood later, but that night, I was beaten, my jaw was broken, I was put in jail, and when they got me out, bailed me out, I was put on a train to go back to South Carolina State, still with bloody clothes on. This guy says, "Get on back to the colored car." I had never been on a train before. I'd been driven to the South by my parents. I had never been on any public accommodations, and I said, "I'm not going to ride back there with caskets and dogs and all that sort of stuff. I paid my ticket, I'm riding in the regular car." And I was back in jail. And I was calling my parents, saying, "Get me out of here. These people are crazy. I'm not going to stay." We agreed that I'd have to stay for the end of the semester, which fortunately ended in February. And before that time, a group of people came and said, "Would you join us in this movement we're going to start?" And I said, "It's your problem. You all going to put up with what these white folks do, that's your problem. I'm getting out." And as many of you know, I was reading the Talmud, and there's a part that says, "If I'm not for myself, who will be for me? If I am for myself only, what am I? If not now, when?" I gave that a lot of thought and decided, I cannot only be for myself, I cannot only just fight for my own dignity. I'm having to deal with this now, because my father didn't deal with it back then. My children will have to deal with it later, so I might as well do it now. And that was when I made the commitment.

There were all these ridiculous charges that were made at the time about outsiders and communists too. The first time I ever heard the charge of outside agitators coming in to foment dissent, if I could have turned red, I would have. I said, "Look, Governor Hollings, I will not stand here and have you insult my intelligence and insult our intelligence to suggest that we are so dumb that we have to wait for somebody to come 10,000 miles to tell us that you, the government, and every social institution in the state has their foot on our neck. It is an insult to our intelligence to say that the black people of this area do not know that they are being exploited and wronged. It is not an outside group that is agitating, although the agitation gets the wash clean. The thoughts are from people from here." And the whole thing about northerners—we used to say that it's a mistake to think that when state troops or the local police start cracking heads, they'll say, "Show me your license and if your license says Connecticut or Illinois, we'll sit you over there and we won't beat you." Once you joined yourself to the struggle, it made no difference where you came from. We faced a common enemy and a common problem. It made no difference that you spoke with an accent that was from New York or Chicago; you faced a common battle. We talked about it in the early days; it was necessary to have whites, because (1) we did not want to get into a movement that was going to polarize us and (2) we were concerned about the type of society we would create after this was all over. And we used to take the position toward communists that if you do this, you can get over. Here's what you do, Sport. You know we believe in your moral commitment, we believe in your political analysis.

Put your body where your thoughts and passions are. Bring your body down here with us and if you can in Lowndes County or Augusta sit out there and discuss the *Communist Manifesto* and get these people to organize around it, fine. But the important thing is that if you are prepared to bring your ideas, we're prepared to let you try them out. But you have to come down there with us. So I don't think in the early days there was any fear or concern about northerners coming down. We needed all the help we could ever get.

DIANE NASH: I was at Fisk University at the time that I got drawn into SNCC. And after the first three or four weeks, I guess, when the novelty of being in a new school wore off, I really started feeling unjustly limited by not being able to go downtown with a girlfriend and have lunch, even at someplace like Woolworth's or Walgreen's, and not being able to attend a movie theater in town. I was in college and I thought that this was a time when I should be expanding and growing as a human being, so I started asking people around the Fisk campus, other students, if they knew of any organizations that were trying to do something about this. I was from Chicago, which is very segregated, but the public accommodations were not segregated. And I was quite outraged when I first encountered "white" and "colored" signs at the rest rooms at the Tennessee State Fair. So I asked the students if they knew of anyone trying to do anything about it. I asked many students and they not only told me no, they didn't know of anything, but their response was along the lines of "No, and why are you trying to do anything? It's been this way a long time and it's probably going to stay." I came to the depressing conclusion that Fisk students were really apathetic. And then of course I did find out about the workshops that Jim Lawson was holding and proceeded to go to them.

Frequently today, I hear people say that students are apathetic, and I really doubt it, because I do some talking on college campuses and there are always one or two students that come up afterward and say, "I'd really like to do something meaningful with my life. You got any ideas? What do you think about the Peace Corps or something like that?" And what happened with the students at Fisk that I thought were apathetic, was that when there was a framework for them to move into, when you could say, "We're having a sit-in, Tuesday morning at 10:00, be at such and such a place," they were there. And by the hundreds and thousands. They were on picket lines and sitting at lunch counters and going to jail. So it turned out that they were not apathetic after all. And I think that if there's an ingredient that we in my generation have not provided, that I was fortunate enough to have had, it is that my generation has not provided a framework for youth today to move into and to make the necessary changes.

Rᴏʙᴇʀᴛ Zᴇʟʟɴᴇʀ: I thought that when I joined SNCC in 1961 I was joining a real going concern. I thought SNCC was the most exciting thing around. I'd been meeting them in passing here and there for a while, and now I was about to start working with them. I assumed they were a going concern. I had been told to get a room at the Atlanta YMCA which was right around the corner from the SNCC office on Auburn Avenue. I think it cost $1.50 a night. My father and some of his preacher friends had driven me over from Alabama on their way to a conference on Lake Junaluska in North Carolina. I got in my room with a little cot and put my things away and went looking for the SNCC office. I finally found it. It was just one room, a tiny room too. I knocked on the door, which was open as a matter of fact. There was one desk, and a light-skinned black man was sitting there. I asked if this was the SNCC office and he said, "Why do you want to know?" I said, "I'm Bob Zellner and I'm trying to find the SNCC office." He said, "Oh, okay. I've been expecting you. Come on in." It was Ed King, a young black Kentucky State student, who was SNCC's executive secretary, I think. He told me he was glad to see me, and then he put a briefcase on the table and said, "Here's the briefcase." I thought, "Oh, good, the briefcase." He said, "You take this. It's got everything in it." I asked him what I should do with it and he said, "Don't do anything, just keep it." He told me to be at the office at 7:30 every morning and not to leave before 5 ᴘ.ᴍ. Then I asked him what time he would be there and he said, "I'm not going to be here." I asked him where he was going to be and he said, "I'm leaving." I asked when he was coming back. And he said, "I'm not coming back. I've finished my job here and I'm going back to school." I was beginning to wonder what was going on, so I asked him what I should do and if someone else would be coming in. He said, "I've got no idea, just be here in the morning and answer the phone. Take messages." I thought that was a good idea. "If you have any trouble the SCLC office is across the street, someone will come eventually." That was it. He gave me the key, showed me how to lock up, and he was gone. I never saw him again. I don't think to this day I've ever seen him again.

A few days later, maybe as much as a week, I was still alone in the office. People were calling from all over the place and most of them wanted to know about Bob Moses. I later realized that they were probably concerned about my accent. It was very southern at that time. I was filling up a pad with messages and still carrying the briefcase with me to the YMCA every night and back to the office every morning. I kept wondering about the briefcase and about Bob Moses. One afternoon I was sitting there and suddenly, without a sound, a black man was standing at the door. He said, "Who are you?" I thought,

"Oh, good, finally a little action." I said, "I'm Bob Zellner, who are you?" He said, "I'm James Forman." He came in and I got up from behind the desk and offered him the chair. We always had that position in SNCC, no matter what they tell you about the whites taking over. Well, the first thing I said was, "Here's the briefcase." And he said, "Oh, the briefcase. What's in it?" I said I didn't know; I thought he would know. He said, "How would I know?" So we opened up the briefcase and there was every issue of SNCC's newspaper, the *Student Voice*. Copies of leaflets and the contact list. All of SNCC was in that briefcase. Oh, my God. And in a little bit, Forman went home and brought back a suitcase and a great big tape recorder and he put it on the table, put a mike in my face, and said, "I want to know everything about you from the time you were born until now." I was very flattered. But I realized later that was Forman's little intimate way of practicing security.

So anyway, I still was very puzzled about Bob Moses and I asked Forman, who was Bob Moses? He said, "He's in Mississippi." I said, "I didn't say where was he, I said who is he?" He said, "Don't worry, you'll meet him soon." So that was September 11, 1961, my first week in the SNCC office, and by October 4, the following month, I was in McComb, Mississippi, where I was beaten and thrown in jail. The first time I was ever put in jail. For the first five or six months of my SNCC tour, one month I was beaten and arrested, I got out, rested up, and didn't go to jail the following month, but the month after that I was in jail somewhere else. I remember McDew and I did some time in Baton Rouge in 1962.

But I have to tell you a little bit about McComb. Because everything in life has circles. It didn't take us long to get to McComb, because it wasn't long after Forman got there that people filtered in and I began to learn what the ropes were. My job, by the way, was that I was supposed to go and visit white campuses. I had been hired to be a "campus traveler." And so I thought, well, I had to keep up with more or less what's going on but I can't really get involved too much, because how am I going to get on southern campuses? So I asked Forman, "What should I do? I need to know what's going on." He said, "Well, why don't you come to the meeting in McComb?" I thought that was reasonable enough. But I had no idea what it would mean, because when I went to McComb for the meeting, lo and behold, we were meeting up in the top story there and late in the afternoon we heard strange sounds from far away. We heard the sounds of "We Shall Overcome," and it got closer and closer to the office, and in a little bit the students were all streaming up and got the placards and everything. They were writing out placards and they were going to march to the county courthouse in Magnolia. And so everybody was getting ready and the question was, who was going to go? And I said, "Of course I can't go. I've got to go to white southern campuses and I don't want to get arrested, because then how can I ever get on campus? Plus my parents are going to get in trouble. My mother is a schoolteacher, she'll lose her job; my father won't have a church anymore. He's a Methodist preacher, he's going to lose his job. Plus, if I go, I'm going to be the only white person, there might be more violence. I'm glad that I know that I can't go." So nobody said anything, you should go, you shouldn't go, and so forth. But there was that feeling that came over me when somebody said, "Well, it's getting dark, if we're going to go to Magnolia, we'd better go." So down the stairs they went. And all of a sudden I said to myself, "What are you doing? Here are these kids in Mississippi. They are going to go and march, the first march ever. Like that, in Mississippi. They were going to march with placards, on October 4, 1961. What's going to happen to *them*? What's going to happen to *their* parents?" And everything else paled into insignificance, and I said, "If I'm going to be a SNCCer, I've got to be a SNCCer," fell in line, and away we went. I think there was criticism later on, but I don't think I would have ever been a SNCCer if I hadn't done that. Because what SNCC was, was when it was time to do it, you had to do it.

There was one time in the SNCC office. Talladega, which was a black college in Alabama, kept calling the SNCC office. "We need somebody over here, we need workshops, we're going to go sit in," and so one day Forman said, "Zellner, go to Talladega." And I said, "What am I going to do?" He said, "Stay there 'til somebody gets there." He knew I had experience doing that. So I went to Talladega and nobody ever came. So when I went to Talladega, I *was* SNCC. They said they were going to have to start without anybody else. So we started workshops and everything and sure enough they started going down to the city square to integrate the city lunch counters and everything.

Big Jim Folsom was a great big tall Alabama guy who had been governor a couple of times. He was a moderate on the racial question. A white moderate—you know what a white moderate is? A white southern moderate is a white guy who will hang you from a low tree. Actually, Jim Folsom wasn't that bad, he was a pretty good guy. One time in 1958 he had Adam Clayton Powell down to Montgomery to visit him and he had Mr. Powell come over to the Governor's mansion, and the word got out that he had been in the Governor's mansion drinking Scotch with Adam Clayton Powell. And Jim Folsom went on television—that was when they first had television—and he said that a lie had gotten out on him in Alabama, that he had gone to the mansion and drunk Scotch with Adam Clayton Powell. And he said, anybody who knows me, knows that's not true. I can't even drink Scotch. I drink bourbon.

So anyway, we were in Talladega and we were about to have a demonstration there and Big Jim Folsom was going to have a rally right there in the city square, at the courthouse. And we said, Should we go or shouldn't we go? You know, he's not a bad guy and everything, but we decided no, if we don't go, we'll be supporting him and we can't support him because he hasn't really done anything for us so we'd better go anyway and just pretend we didn't know.

So we went, and of course the fire trucks were there and the dogs and everything. It was a terrible mess. And we had a reporter there, Per Laursen, he was in jail with us in Albany. And he went under cover of the press to find out what Big Jim Folsom thought about this whole thing. And he says, "Well, as near as I can tell, it's not really against me, but I think it's all on account of that guy Ralph Zellner, with the Christian Nonviolent Communist Integration Organization." It was almost what my father called SNCC. My father was an old southern preacher and he thought we were the Nonstudent Violating Uncoordinating Committee.

It was amazing the way we were in SNCC. When it was time to do something, you just did it. McDew said we spent a lot of time trying to figure out what we were going to do. Well one thing that we were always doing anytime we were trying to figure out what we were going to do, we were doing what we were doing. We were still doing those things.

MARY KING: When I arrived in Mississippi, half of the counties in the Mississippi Delta had not one single black registered to vote, and the protocols that were at work were essentially those passed in the 1890s, when lynchings of blacks by white mobs occurred on the average of one every two-and-a-half days. Lynching still took place. I remember clearly that after the death of President Kennedy I spent five days trying to find one reporter who would report the fact that Bob Moses had told me that the bodies of five black men had turned up in the Homochitto River near Natchez. I could not find one reporter for five days who would report that fact. Finally, after five days, Claude Sitton of the *New York Times* was willing to include that in his account.

The situation had been like that since the 1890s. Today we have a situation in which there are over 7,000 blacks who have been elected to office; more than 300 American cities have black mayors. The black mayors in Mississippi comprise the largest number in the country. Black voter turnout in 1986 was responsible for bringing the Senate back to the Democrats. In Alabama, Florida, Georgia, Louisiana, North Carolina, the incumbents were dumped because of a black voter turnout in excess of 85 percent. So we are beginning to see the full flowering of the political muscle that began to break out at the time of the early 1960s.

Georgia

MENDY SAMSTEIN: I was a graduate student at the University of Chicago when the movement was bursting in the South, and I was immediately affected by everything, the sit-ins, the Freedom Rides, the voter registration. I will never forget the day in September of 1962 that I read in the paper about things that were happening in Albany, not only about Dr. King, who was obviously most prominent, but about Charlie Sherrod and about Jack Chatfield and Ralph Allen. They were in a house, supposedly helping people to register to vote, what I thought we all accepted as a part of American life, and they were shot at, and that story moved me and touched me along with many other things.

Fortuitously, I got an opportunity when I was at the University of Chicago. There was a professor at Morehouse who had a grant to write a book for one semester and he had been a graduate of the University of Chicago, so he came up there looking for somebody to teach his courses for one semester. And when I heard of it, I leaped at the opportunity because I wanted to see what it was like. I was too afraid, much too fearful to think of going on a Freedom Ride or getting involved in any way like that, so this was a way of easing my way into it.

Chicago was very cold at that time; it was January, it was about 20 below, and I got in my car, packed up all my belongings, and drove South. I had never been in the South, and it started getting warmer and warmer. I was driving through the night, and I went to sleep on the side of a road, somewhere in Tennessee, near the Georgia border, and it was still cold, it was three or four in the morning. I woke up and I saw the South. I saw the sun coming over the horizon and it was a very dynamic kind of experience. Atlanta was no different. When I got to Atlanta, the teaching at Morehouse was no different. Everything touched me and moved me.

Atlanta was SNCC's office and its headquarters, and in the spring of that year, SNCC had one of its major conferences at Gammon Theological Seminary. I was able to attend, and I met Jim Forman and Bob Moses and Charles Sherrod and many of the other SNCC people. And I sat in on the meetings and on the discussions. These were people talking about change in this country; they were talking about creating a sense of human dignity. They were talking about human worth. Wow. I couldn't believe this. I read books, I taught Western civilization, and here people were talking about something very real, very important, and it was quite moving.

And I had made a decision I had to be a part of this. Somehow or other I would overcome my fears. I had lots of fears about staying, giving up my graduate work, but I would stay and get involved in this movement. I had some help. Jim helped me a lot, and others. And so when my time at Morehouse ended in the summer of 1963, I decided to stay on and I was offered a salary of $10 a week which I leaped at, and I was happy to get it. I think my first assignment was to New Orleans. I went with some of the Freedom Singers and some other people, Willie Peacock, and lived with them for two or three weeks at some-body's house. That was extraordinary. I was getting to know people that I wouldn't ordinarily ever have known, and I was again and again struck by the common humanity, the bonds, and the sense of acceptance. I found that quite amazing. And still do, when walking around Atlanta or Hunter or Peachtree; it felt so right, so comfortable, so much of a good place to be.

ROBERT MANTS: What I'll try to do is give my personal account of my involvement in the movement. This is my testimony, Reverend Sherrod, or as local people would say, how I got in the midst. I had the unique experience of having seen in SNCC periods from the redemptive beloved community, where we were trained in nonviolence and made a serious effort to take nonviolence on as a way of life, to the more nationalistic, much more what you would call radical phases of SNCC. I sat there in 1960, I was in the eleventh grade, mind-ing my own business, getting in the midst. Up the street in the next block was the office of the Atlanta Committee on Appeal for Human Rights, the Atlanta student movement. Our house was right there on Chestnut Street right in the midst of the Atlanta University complex. SNCC, during that same period of time, moved its office off of Auburn Avenue to Randall Street, two blocks from my house. I saw all these folk, these young folk, these young students, march-ing by my house. My curiosity led me to stick my nose in other folks' business.

At Rush Memorial Church there on Chestnut Street in the next block, again, all these students from Atlanta University were gathered, and I was wonder-ing what was happening. So I went up there, sat around long enough so that they made me the captain of the picket signs, with no soldiers. My job was to look out for the picket signs. They had these big placards. I took the picket signs when they would come off from picketing downtown, places of public accommodation. My job was to stack the picket signs neatly and orderly and pass them out. They raised my status in the sit-in movement to the manager of custodial services. They paid me $3 a week to clean the offices. Some of those people who were there at that time, I think, who recruited me and got me involved at that age, were Lonnie King, who at that time was chairman of the Atlanta Committee on Appeal for Human Rights, Ruby Doris Robinson (Smith at that time), her sister Mary Ann Smith, Herschelle Sullivan, Marian Wright, Frank Holloway, and Julian Bond, to name a few. At that time I was the youngest person in the Atlanta student movement. They were reluctant to have me involved in most of the direct action that was taking place because I was a youngster. It was a legal question. If they were going to jail, I would be separated from them and I would go to the juvenile probation thing. But I stayed around anyway and became involved in some of the sit-ins and demonstrations, and some of the other direct action campaigns.

I remember very clearly the first time I met Jim Forman. My first encounter with Jim was in a direct action campaign in which blacks were moving into white communities and there was a buffer, Jim called it the Berlin Wall, to keep black people from moving from one section of that street to another section.

I was also, during that period, a student at Morehouse College, and when SNCC moved its office on Randall Street, I started hanging around there, sticking my nose in other folks' business. And I met Dottie Zellner and some other people who were working in the SNCC office. During that same period of time I was introduced to the Nation of Islam, through Minister Jeremiah X, and to another fellow whose name was John Churchville, who raised my level of black consciousness. Here we were, here I was, a young, impressionable student, with SNCC talking about, during that time, integration, the beloved community, and here was this fellow John Churchville telling me about being black and all this stuff.

What I did to find out for myself after John Churchville kept nagging me so much, I went to the library: to the Atlanta University library, the Lowndes Public Library, and started reading black history for myself. It was through John Churchville that I first became aware of my black identity.

Some other things happened around that same time. I met Willie Ricks for the first time—the Reverend C. T. Vivian had brought Ricks from Chattanooga, dropped him off at the SNCC office and left and went on back, and Ricks has been around since that time. There were several things happening in Atlanta, but the one thing that I remember most during that early period was a conversation with Sherrod nagging me to come to southwest Georgia. Here I was, a young student, first generation to be college educated, my parents had suffered and sacrificed for me to go to college. Here's ol' Sherrod talking to me about coming to southwest Georgia, dropping out of school. One Sunday morning, I asked my dad to come on the front porch so we could talk. I told Dad that I wanted to drop out of Morehouse and go work in southwest Georgia. My dad's immediate response was, "You must have been studying too hard, you need a vacation, you got to be crazy." But something else he said to me, it was many years later before I fully understood what he meant. I was out of school, grown, married, had a family. He said to me, "If you must go, go, because it's in your blood." I didn't understand that when he said that.

I later went to southwest Georgia and I'll never forget, this is 1963, and hell had broken loose in southwest Georgia. Three SNCC workers, Ralph Allen,

John Perdew, Don Harris, and a worker from CORE, Zev Aelony, were in jail in Americus, Georgia, for insurrection. Charles Sherrod threw me, a little city boy from Atlanta, right in the midst of what I thought was hell at that time. I later learned that there were some other hells outside of Atlanta and in other places.

During that same period of time was the March on Washington. Some of us who were working in southwest Georgia at that time with Sherrod and some other people had gone up to the Justice Department in Washington to picket. Sherrod left me and others with the responsibility of organizing the people in southwest Georgia; get them on the train. We had to get people from Albany to Thomasville, Georgia, to get folks to the train to go to the March on Washington. When we hit Washington, D.C., there must have been twenty-eight coaches of people from southwest Georgia and from Florida, Tallahassee and Miami, for that occasion.

Some other things were happening during that same period. The Civil Rights Act of 1964 was passed and, again, here we were with some more direct action, because we wanted to test whether or not these places of public accommodation would allow us in. One of these same fellows who had been charged with insurrection, John Perdew, who was a Harvard student and from Denver, Colorado, came to me in Americus and said, "Bob, we need to test these places." I said, "John, let's see what happens everywhere else before we go in there."

There was a little place called the Hasty House on Highway 19. We went, there were about five of us, and a local fellow who went with us to test this place *at night*. We went into the place with all the blacks in there. I sat down. You see, I'm from the South, I grew up in the South and there are some things that we, before the movement, knew. It was inbred with us to find survival. I sat so that I could watch front and back, and the way I did that, there was glass so that I could see what was happening in front of me and in the reflection from the glass, I could see what was happening behind. That's what happens when you don't plan, and it was John Perdew's last-minute "Let's go test the place."

I was watching in the glass, and one of the local fellows who we called Kitty got up and went to ask the waitress where the restroom was. We didn't know Kitty was going to do this, and she sent Kitty around the building. We didn't know what happened to Kitty. It was the next morning after we had walked out of the Hasty House and got the shit beat out of us, that we found Kitty. I said, "Kitty, what happened?" He said, "Man, I had to use the bathroom, I went and asked that lady where's the bathroom, and she sent me around to the back of the restaurant, and I got the dog shit beat out of me back there." I said,

"Why didn't you come back and tell us?" He said, "Man, they ran me all across the bridge and up the hill, I didn't get back here 'til this morning."

We spent a good time in southwest Georgia. I remember what we called the Prayer Breakfast. Anybody who went down there and worked with Sherrod in southwest Georgia remembers the Prayer Breakfast. Every morning, over a glass of orange juice and a cinnamon roll, and the ravioli that people had sent from the North—that was my first introduction to ravioli—we would sing and pray. I'll never forget how we used to sing, "Let Us Break Bread Together." Very meaningful experience.

I do have three things to say in sincerity. First of all, what the southwest Georgia project did for me and for most of us who came from there, who later went on to other projects, was to build a sense of camaraderie, a sense of reverence for what we were about, a sense of commitment to what we were about.

I think that southwest Georgia was the proving ground for many of us and in many ways, the way in which we would go for years to come. I'm thankful for that experience. There was one other thing that southwest Georgia taught me and that was how to survive on nothing. I remember going with George Bess, may he rest in peace, over to Cuthbert, Georgia, Randolph County. SNCC didn't have any money; some people would see us coming, they'd run. We had to eat. We used to steal folks' chickens at night. Go up under the house and bury the feathers. Some people who were there during that time used to go out in different parts of southwest Georgia from Albany, pick cucumbers, squash, go fishing, so that we could eat. I remember a time when a farmer in Lee County told us that he had some wild hogs loose and if we caught the hogs, we could have one. Needless to say, that hog didn't have a possible chance, and we ate well for a little while anyway.

During the summer of 1964 in southwest Georgia there were many direct action campaigns, especially to test the Civil Rights Act of 1964 in regard to public accommodations. We were having mass meetings all over Sumter County, which also happens to be the home county of Jimmy Carter. We knew him before he was President Carter; we also knew him before he was Governor Carter. The town and the county were very tense with demonstrations. I remember the Martin Theater. We attempted to go into the Martin Theater before the Civil Rights Act was passed. Around the corner and up the back, a flight of stairs, where the colored folk sat. I remember very vividly all those nights we had mass meetings there; there was a little girl about twelve years old who used to walk across town from the south side of Americus, Georgia, and would come to the mass meetings. Her name was Sandra Gail Russell, and we would make sure that she got a ride back home after the meetings.

I later decided to leave southwest Georgia and go back to school, and I was trying to get some report on myself as to whether my activity meant some-thing, what was the significance of it, what did my participation there in south-west Georgia do, especially Americus, what difference did it make? I couldn't think of anything until I took a taxi from the Freedom House, going down the main street to the bus station to go back home on a Sunday afternoon, and I looked at this theater on the side, around the corner where the black people always went. There were some of those people who were leaders in the marches, other black people still going up to what we called the peanut gal-lery, around the back, in the back way. But I also looked to the front and there was a little girl, twelve years old, Sandra Gail Russell, with all these white people, standing in line with another little black kid about six years old, hold-ing his hand. And I said, "My God, Bob, that's your report card."

I went back to Morehouse and I took a course in public speaking and part of our semester grade was based on giving a speech, a eulogy or a tribute speech. My colleagues in our class talked and made tributes to Martin Luther King, about Dr. Benjamin Mays, Thurgood Marshall, Mary McLeod Bethune, and a little boy in the class, Bob Mants, made his tribute to a twelve-year-old girl from southwest Georgia named Sandra Gail Russell. My classmates said to me, "Who in the hell is Sandra Gail Russell?" But that experience of the movement, or what we attempted to do in SNCC in southwest Georgia, was transformed from us to Sandra Gail Russell, to that little kid that she had in line with her at the Martin Theater in Americus, Georgia.

R<small>ALPH</small> A<small>LLEN</small>: It's typical of a southwest Georgia mass meeting to get the people who were out in the field or the people who had gone up to regis-ter to vote, or the people who were thinking of going up to register to vote, or the person who'd lost a job—to get them up at the meeting. (We called them mass meetings, but out in Terrell County they were about thirty-five strong.) We'd get them up to talk about the problems that they had had so that we could all know what was going on.

Chuck McDew said that when SNCC decided to go into Mississippi to do voter registration, they decided that because in Mississippi voter registration *was* direct action. Well, southwest Georgia was not the heart of the beast, but it was one of the other vital organs. And when Sherrod decided to do voter registration in southwest Georgia, he decided that he was going to do it inte-grated, which meant that was direct action. Don Harris and I were sidekicks in Sumter County, Georgia. When we walked down the street in the white sec-tion, everybody moved over to the other side of the street, they closed up all the stores. That was direct action. If we walked down the street and we'd get in the black section, the kids would come out because it was a strange sight to see a black guy and a white guy walking down the street together. We didn't have to hunt people out of their houses to organize them, they came out because they were curious. It made the job a lot easier than it was probably in Alabama or Mississippi.

The cumulative effect of all this was that the white people began to organize. The more they organized, the worse it was for them. I'll give you an example. One night in July of 1962 when things were kind of dead in Albany, Sherrod talked to a couple of reporters who were there. He said, "Why don't you come out to one of our mass meetings in Terrell County and see what we're doing out there with the voter registration?" So we got this *New York Times* guy, this *Atlanta Constitution* guy to come out to the meeting. I was real proud that night because I had got two women who were going to go up to register to vote. Lucius Holloway, who was the head of the movement in Terrell County, and I picked them up and we were coming into this meeting and I said, "Wow, there's a lot of people here tonight. Something must have happened." And Lucius let me and the two women out because he was going to go park the car. We walked up and I realized then why there were so many cars—there was a group of about twenty local white citizens standing on the steps. I didn't think much, I just kept on going. I walked into the church. They said a few things to us as we were going in, uncomplimentary. We got inside and then they came into the church. At the time that they came in, Lucius had just finished the report of the week's activities and then Sherrod was up and he said, "If God be for us, who can be against us?" It was at that point in the meeting that we had a prayer, he was ending the prayer, and he said, "If God be for us, who can be against us?" And Sheriff Z. T. Matthews and twenty-five deputized white citizens walked in.

And the sheriff just took over this meeting and meanwhile the reporters were sitting right there writing down stuff and he says, "Hey there, boy, put that pencil and paper away. Who are you, anyway?" One of them said, "I'm Claude Sitton from the *New York Times* and I'm a native Georgian, just like yourself." And the other guy from the *Constitution*, Bill Shipp, just got the whole story—Sheriff Matthews could not have hung himself any higher if we had asked him to perform in a play or something, wrote the script for him. That was Sherrod.

PENNY PATCH: When I go now to speak in the high schools or on Martin Luther King Day in the small community that I live in, I take with me a whole stack of old *Student Voices,* and a sign made out of wood, painted shiny brown with red words, and what it says is "Colored." This sign was taken from over the water fountain in the Albany city courthouse. It was taken by three young women who were leaders of the student movement in Albany, Georgia. And I'm not talking about college students, I'm talking about high school students. I just want to say their names: Margaret Sanders, sixteen; Patricia Ann Gaines, fifteen; and Joanne Christian, fifteen.

Fᴀɪᴛʜ Hᴏʟsᴀᴇʀᴛ: In southwest Georgia we believed and I still believe that organizing is very slow work and very respectful work, and it has to start from the ground up. And maybe that's why I had planned to end my words much as Penny did. I thought I would pick at random as they occur to me the names of a few people from the southwest Georgia movement, local ground-up people, and commemorate them and just say a little bit about each one. You have to realize there were thousands, tens of thousands of people like this.

The first that I think of is Miss Corinne Watkins, who sold Avon in Albany, Georgia. When I was in jail she brought the movement women makeup, just to sweeten Laurie Pritchett's jail for us. Another one who occurs to me because she was perhaps my closest friend there is Joanne Christian, who Penny also mentioned. Joanne was a junior high school student and a great song leader of Albany, Georgia, and led hundreds of people in marches at the age of thirteen or fourteen. Another person is Reverend Samuel B. Wells, who worked as a welder at the local base. He called himself a toiler in the vineyard of the Lord, and that's really what he was. Annette Jones, who was homecoming queen at Albany State, was thrown out of school for her participation in the movement and then became an organizer. Deacon and Mrs. Bruner, who lived in Sasser, Georgia, and lived way out in the cotton fields and were undoubtedly at the church the night that Ralph spoke of. I'll stop there. There were tens of thousands if not more of people like this and this is what organizing is all about.

Pʀᴀᴛʜɪᴀ Hᴀʟʟ: There are a couple of experiences that I will never forget; the night in September 1962 that we were all in the house and Jack Chatfield was shot, I will never forget that. And then there was another time. We've talked a lot about coming face to face with death, and I think sometimes for young people that's very hard to imagine. But we did it, we had to do it every day. That meant that if you were driving down the road and a car came up behind you, if the car stayed behind you, you were terrified that you were going to be shot from behind, and if the car passed you, you hit the floor, which put you in a pretty difficult position if you were the driver. So fear was something that was real. Nobody here has ever said they were not afraid. In fact, anybody who came into that situation and wasn't afraid, we didn't want anything to do with.

Carolyn Daniels was an extraordinary woman; she was the local beautician with whom we lived, and it was her house that was shot into. And it did not move her. It did not unnerve her. She was a single mother struggling to make it but she was steel, she was strength for all of us, and she took all of us, with our technicolor selves and our strange ways and some northern and some southern and all of that, and she wasn't that many years older than many of us, but she mothered us.

One day four of us—Carolyn's son was in this group—were in Sasser, Georgia, and we were confronted by a guy with a tin badge on, he said he was the marshal; he came up to us and he wanted to know, "What are you doing?" And I said—like Chuck and Bernard, I would do that—I said, "We're registering people to vote and you have no right to stop us." And he went *mad.* I mean, really mad. And he began cursing and calling us all these names and literally foaming at the mouth. He pulled out a pistol and began firing bullets in a circle around my feet. And the only thing that I can be thankful for is that I didn't move. But that was another one of those moments when you look death in the face and you also look at the enemy, which is that evil, and the victim who is the bearer of that evil, in the face, and it takes care of the fear problem. When his gun was empty then they dragged us off to this scroungey little place that they called the jail. It was not as big as from here to that table, about half, maybe half that big. They had two cells filled with all kinds of crud and vermin and whatnot, and rather than put the two women in the same cell and the two men in the same cell, because we were a white and a black woman and a white and a black man, two blacks were put in a cell and two whites were put in a cell— just another illustration of the insanity.

I have several memories from southwest Georgia and from my time in Selma, and I want to say that I learned there some of the most important lessons I will ever learn in my life. I had been to school, I had been to college before I went South, and I've been to school a lot of years since. But the most important lessons that I ever learned, I learned in those rural counties from people who could not read or write their names.

CHARLES SHERROD: I'll just say that the southwest Georgia project still lives in south Georgia; we're still working, we're still on the case.

"In the Middle of the Iceberg": Mississippi and the Mississippi Freedom Democratic Party

SNCC's voter registration efforts took a new turn in Mississippi, where workers employed a strategy called "parallel institutionalism." Where black people could not vote, SNCC held mock elections (the "Freedom Vote" campaign) with its own candidates. The success of such efforts led to two new developments. First, SNCC decided to broaden its challenge by running an alternate slate of delegates from the Mississippi Freedom Democratic Party to the Democratic National Convention of 1964, in a project called Freedom Summer. Second, SNCC invited large numbers of northerners, white and black, to come to Mississippi to participate in that effort. The hundreds of volunteers ran registration campaigns, conducted educational programs called Freedom Schools, provided medical and other care for local communities, and participated in a myriad of other civil rights projects despite widespread violent retaliation by many southern whites. Many of these volunteers were in turn radicalized. Many became involved in other protest movements after returning to the North. A number remained in the South and in SNCC beyond Freedom Summer. And some never came back, including three civil rights workers killed at the very start of the summer: Jim Chaney, Michael Schwerner, and Andrew Goodman.

Hollis Watkins: (Sings) They laid Medgar Evers in his grave.

Before Medgar there was Emmett Till, there was Herbert Lee, after Medgar there were three civil rights workers: Goodman, Chaney, Schwerner. I mention that to try to justify the subject "in the middle of the iceberg," to let you see a little bit about the conditions that existed in Mississippi because from my understanding, if you look at an iceberg, if you're in the middle of it, you're in a bad condition. If you run into the iceberg, it's going to bring some harm and damage to you. And if it runs into you, the same is going to happen. And I think based on what we were dealing with in Mississippi, the title is appropriate. Although from my understanding and my experience, the iceberg was not just Mississippi, but more so America. And Mississippi was just one little aspect or corner of that iceberg.

I'm Hollis Watkins and I'm the twelfth child that was born to some sharecroppers down in southwest Mississippi. And I'm thankful that I got involved with SNCC, the Student Nonviolent Coordinating Committee. I'm thankful that SNCC came along and I got involved in it because as I see things, SNCC was an organization that had begun to rake up a few leaves, to gather a few sticks, putting them all together in one common pile to start a fire, to burn in the midst of this iceberg. SNCC began to get the leaves together, bring the sticks together, pour a little fuel on it, and began to strike the stones together to create a spark in the hearts of those of us who could not see the light. After a period of time we saw that spark and that spark became a blaze in our hearts and in the hearts of our brothers and sisters. And we ourselves as a whole began to add fuel to the fire and the fuel came in many, many different forms. The Mississippi Freedom Democratic Party that grew out of SNCC—that was one of the back logs that SNCC laid on the fire.

You know, as SNCC began to search for fuel, SNCC reached into the hearts of the churches and the National Council of Churches said, "I see the flame." And then they got involved and saw to it that a group of ministers and other supporters came into Mississippi and as a result of that, they created another log in the form of the Delta Ministry. And as SNCC began to pull the different parts together and people in the different communities began to see the sparks fly, they began to ignite and cause other small fires to start springing up elsewhere.

When the Freedom Democratic Party blew up, there was a big commotion, but there was a commotion even before then, in the McComb area where I went in search of Dr. Martin Luther King and found Bob Moses. When we got involved, that led to demonstrations at the F. W. Woolworth lunch counter, that led to demonstrations at the bus station, that led to students walking out of Burgland High School—that whole movement itself created the beginning of another log that was important, because as a result of that movement, SNCC set up its first Freedom School in 1961.

Because in that process, some of the students decided that they were not going to go back to Burgland High School. The principal had laid down a stipulation that said you may reenter high school if you will sign a statement saying that you will not participate in civil rights activities anymore. Many of the students and their parents didn't agree with that, because they had seen the light, and they didn't sign those statements. And as a result of that, SNCC set up its first Freedom School in McComb so that these students that had walked out in protest of their fellow students not being able to come back could continue their education. That broadened SNCC's relationship that reached on into the A.M.E. Methodist Church, because J. P. Campbell College in Jackson finally opened its doors and said, "We have a little more space, we'll make room for them, bring them here."

So the sparks began to fly. They began to spread. And as they began to spread, more things began to fall in place. Now I think we need to set the record straight about COFO, the Council of Federated Organizations, set up in 1962. COFO, for the most part, was a good-conscience effort that we made to show a sense of unity and harmony, especially to try to prevent the conflict in fund raising. It was hard at that time to raise money, especially when in Mississippi you had the NAACP going after the money, SCLC going after the money, CORE going after the money, and SNCC going after the money, and in Mississippi we know SNCC was doing 'most all of the work. So we also know that most of the work that was done under the name of COFO, SNCC was the one that was doing it.

One of the things that was so important about SNCC as it began to pull the pieces together, not just in Mississippi, was being able to educate, motivate, and inspire people from different areas to get up and do something and take some initiative upon themselves. And as a result of that, when we looked at the SNCC staff as SNCC began to spread and reach out from McComb, after a very short period of time, most of the SNCC staff in Mississippi were Mississippians. When we looked at the SNCC staff in other areas, we saw that it was that handful that had begun to motivate and encourage and inspire others to do something from those areas. When we came into Hattiesburg in 1962, we had reached the level of being a SNCC field secretary, proud, determined, prepared to take on the world if necessary. Had a little money in our pocket: SNCC gave us $50 to go to Hattiesburg and set up a three-month voter registration project. Things were just that tough. And when it came to the situation where we got in jail, the bond situation was even much more devastating, because in Mississippi, for almost everything you got arrested for, you generally had a $2,000 bond set. In Mississippi at that time they were not accepting property bonds, neither were there any bondsmen in Mississippi that were willing to work and cooperate with SNCC. That's why those that were in charge of the direct action would tell you that if you're going to jail, be prepared to serve your sentence out. After a while they told you to be prepared to serve at least thirty days in jail because they knew and we knew that it was not easy.

And there were many things that helped to spark more people into the whole process. As we moved from the McComb area into Hattiesburg, into the other areas of the state and especially into the Delta area, into Greenwood in 1962, there was another important figure. Dick Gregory led an initiative in the fall of 1962 with the help of Harry Belafonte and a few other people to do some fund raising. In addition to that they brought in food and clothing into the Mississippi Delta, while we were trying to get people to go down and register to vote. And one day, just before we were getting ready to give out food and clothing, we had all those people gathered there and Bob Moses made a little speech. He said, "You know, it would be good if we could really begin to move toward truly impacting on the situation that causes us to not have food, that causes us to not have clothes." To make a long story short, that was directed toward becoming registered voters to elect the kind of people that were going to see that that happened. And as a result of that we got our first large demonstration in Greenwood, Mississippi, in 1963, which really broke things open for us because from that point on Mississippi had really begun to get a lot of attention.

So SNCC began to really pile on the logs that have impacted on what is going on today. At one point during Freedom Summer there was the creation of the Medical Committee for Human Rights in Mississippi, that had an impact upon medical clinics throughout the world today. The creation of community centers in Mississippi spread throughout the South and the country.

SNCC was the beginning of many of these things. There was another time leading up to Freedom Summer, as it's called by some, the Mississippi Summer Project, as called by others. There was a great controversy over whether it should or should not be. And for many different reasons it prevailed that it should be, and it did come about, in 1964. I remember at the training sessions in Oxford, Ohio, people would ask some of us, "What should we expect when we get to Mississippi?" And some of the ones in the training session would tell people: "If you're going to Mississippi, you should be prepared for at least three things. You should be prepared to go to jail. You should be prepared to be beaten. And, ultimately, you should be prepared to be killed." All three of those are real possibilities which we found to be true even before the orientation sessions were over, because the word came that some of those that had left early, Goodman, Schwerner, and Chaney, had been killed in Nashoba County. But SNCC, through all of its efforts, began to build that fire, and it grew larger and larger until in the midst of all of that growing, it finally melted completely through the iceberg where a little air came in; not enough to put it out, but just enough to rejuvenate the flames that were burning.

A lot of us know about a lot of the progress that was made during the 1964 Summer Project; however, there were some other things that were negative about the project. One of them was that it retarded the growth of individual initiatives on the part of many Mississippians. And as a result of that, it enabled someone to put a lid on the small hole that had been burned through the top of the iceberg. But because of the size of the flame, even though the lid was on top, it was not able to put it out because you saw where blacks were continuously registering people to vote and getting elected and participating in the democratic process. And that process continued to go on and lo and behold, Jesse Jackson in 1983 saw the lid and he reached down and grabbed the lid and he threw it off the little hole, and the fire immediately began to blaze out more vigorously once again. People knew that there were new signs of hope in a more unified national movement that was in the making.

And as he was running for President in 1984, as he began to pump oxygen through that hole, where he had raised the lid, people in Mississippi participated in the caucus process in Mississippi to the tune that they had never participated since the Freedom Democratic Party's effort in 1964 that gave life to the Mississippi movement. And through that effort of him running, we had a tremendous number of blacks that began to get elected as mayors of little towns. We had a tremendous impact as people began to get elected to the board of supervisors. We began to use the legal process to break down some of the barriers, changing the form of governments, getting people elected as councilmen, as aldermen. And we see us today continuously expanding those initial efforts. We begin to expand those efforts as we begin to elect blacks to larger cities as mayors such as Vicksburg, Mississippi. We expand the effort through electing black women as mayors of some of those smaller towns.

For those that may not know or understand, the removal of the literacy requirement for voting that was once in Mississippi was not just removing a requirement but actually a stripping of power, because before that literacy requirement test was taken out of the process, white men in Mississippi, most of whom had less than an eighth-grade education, had the power and authority to say to well-educated blacks, including schoolteachers, doctors, and lawyers, that you don't have the knowledge of how to interpret a section of the Mississippi constitution, which is what you had to do to pass the requirement. So it was a transfer or a removal of power.

The thing that is most important is that we understand that the movement which encompasses many organizations of which SNCC was one, is still going on, was going on before SNCC, and will continue to go on in the future.

And we as organizations, we as individuals in those organizations must understand that, and work to make sure we do our rightful part. If a people feel that it does not have a movement, that's very self-defeating. And we should make sure that we understand the fact that in a movement we do not have a leader but we have many, many leaders. That's the way it always has been and that's the way it will continuously be until and even after we completely bust apart and completely destroy this gigantic iceberg.

LAWRENCE GUYOT: To me, SNCC was the most intellectual feast available to this country. It was a meritocracy with none of the limitations of a meritocracy. There were some very brilliant people in SNCC, but there were some very active people, one of them in particular, who had the IQ of a four-year old. I won't name that person but I worked with him for four years and didn't know that. And I say that to say the contribution of the Mississippi Freedom Democratic Party pales in comparison to what SNCC created. SNCC created the Free Southern Theater. I watched the Free Southern Theater present *Waiting for Godot* in the Delta of Mississippi and in New York. And the astounding thing is there wasn't very much difference in the reaction. I watched the battle over who makes the decisions in SNCC, and that battle flowed into the MFDP.

I want to discuss the question of how do you use parallel institutionalism to prove what Ernst Borinski taught us all, that some institutions are functional only in their bifunctionality. That is exactly what we did in very simple and pragmatic terms in Mississippi. We took the regular Democratic Party and turned it on its head. The law did not require party registration, you simply went in to register to vote. And the party didn't have to hold precinct meetings because there was no need for them; they were going to support the Republican candidate, Barry Goldwater, anyway. So we adhered to the letter of the law. And we went through that process and we brought about some changes, the likes of which some of us still don't quite understand. We changed the regulation so that never again would a segregated delegation ever be seated; 50 percent of each delegation had to be minorities. (In 1968 some of our previous enemies used very effectively the modification of that rule to make sure that the minority was defined as female. So as Julian Bond has pointed out, the women Democrats who sit as delegates owe that to Fannie Lou Hamer, Victoria Gray, and those of you who made the Mississippi Freedom Democratic Party a possibility.)

Not only did we move to reapportion the state of Mississippi before the Freedom Democratic Party; we filed that suit. Peggy Connor, who was the secretary of the Freedom Democratic Party, filed that suit as a plaintiff in 1965. We added the organization as a plaintiff later. It took us until 1979 to redistrict the state of Mississippi to put seventeen black members in the state legislature. If any one of them has the nerve to dissociate their ability to sit in the state legislature from the Mississippi Freedom Democratic Party's reapportionment suit, I want to hear about it.

Not only did we assist in passing the 1965 Voting Rights Act, but I worked at the Lawyers' Committee for Civil Rights Under Law to monitor the Voting Rights Act because Section 5 of that act says that any submission that may have the potential of diluting the black vote has to be submitted to the attorney general and has to pass muster in administrative hearings. Not only did we work to administer it, but the first case that opened up the constitutionality of Section 5 was a court case, *Whitley v. Johnson,* filed by who? The Mississippi Freedom Democratic Party. Once Section 5 was declared constitutional, annexation, the abolition of election of offices, the moving of polling places from a church to a cemetery—anything that could be used to dilute the power of the black vote—was now under legal attack. We did that.

Myself, Armand Derfner, and Harry Bowie got $12,000 from a foundation. We held a meeting at Mary Holmes Junior College of people all across the country who were working on voting rights, and we worked to extend that. And we had a bill passed by two senators, Dole and Kennedy, to extend the Voting Rights Act.

I attended the meeting with the leadership of this country and the decisions went along the lines of "We can't win. We're going to simply ask for removal of the literacy requirement." And a couple of people prevailed, that we have *got* to win. And let us look at what we won. Senator J. Bennett Johnston of Louisiana, no flaming liberal, called together ten southern senators in 1987 and he said, "I want to tell you something. All of you are going to vote against the Supreme Court appointment of Robert Bork," and someone said, "This old man must be senile." He said, "Okay, get a pencil. You got 10 percent of the white vote, maybe 12, who do you think sent you here?" It was the black voters that put them there and could take them out. Columnist David Broder wrote that there are several southern senators who were rated higher, more liberal, on economic issues than at least 65 percent of their colleagues. Now, did this happen because of some Christian revelation? Did nonviolence work by some miasmic cold force? It was raw, creative, beautiful political power.

The question comes—what do we have to do now? I think what we have to do now is make sure that political parties and political activity goes to the heart of the immediate questions of people: homelessness, how do we deal with the redefinition of work? How do we deal with the people who created small factories that hired 1,500 people, who now send that money to Taiwan?

Let me just mention one other thing about gains. The Mississippi legislature before it was integrated passed a bill called the County Consolidation Law in 1966, which gave to the state legislature the right to consolidate any two adjoining counties with the express purpose of diluting the black vote. The Mississippi Freedom Democratic Party took it into federal district court and it was overturned by the Supreme Court in 1969 in *Allen v. State Board of Elections.*

I want to make a final point. MFDP was a good PR program but shouldn't be considered seriously, politically. Bayard Rustin had written his *Commentary* article in 1965 on the difference between protest and politics ["From Protest to Politics: The Future of the Civil Rights Movement," *Commentary,* February 1965: 25–31]. Martin Luther King, speaking at Howard University, had established that. Columnists Rowland Evans and Robert Novak had already red-baited SNCC and raised the question of who were Maoists in SNCC [see, for example, "Danger from the Left," March 18, 1965, and "A Long Look at Snick," April 9, 1965, both in the *Washington Post*]. And some of the good white liberals in the South, specifically Charles Morgan of the ACLU, had done the same thing to SNCC. While SNCC certainly was key in the organization of MFDP, it was Moses's position that the MFDP should be discontinued after the Atlantic City convention. There were other forces who continued it. I think it's important that we understand also for the sake of historical clarity that the good people of McComb had come out against the Vietnam War in 1965, before SNCC did. SNCC came out in 1966, before Martin Luther King in 1967, but not before the MFDP.

CHARLES McDEW: We decided at the Highlander meeting in 1961 that we would have a program. We called it Project MOM: Move On Mississippi. We were going to move on Mississippi, in direct action and political education and voter registration. And with those thoughts we headed to McComb. I remember when we first went to Mississippi, Sherrod was in the car, myself, Charlie Jones, and we stopped at the border and there was a big sign that said, "The Knights of the Ku Klux Klan welcome you to Mississippi," and we grew silent and we all were very afraid. And we knew that we were about to walk into the heart of the beast. With the memory of Emmett Till's bloated body still fresh in our minds—everybody at the time knew where they were when they saw the pictures of Emmett Till's body. We knew what it was like in Greenwood and to further underscore what we were walking into, we stopped for gas and Sherrod foolishly went to the bathroom. As I recall, the owner escorted him out with a pistol. And we felt we are here . . . we are in Mississippi. We are in the heart of the beast.

When you made a move on Mississippi, one of the things you had to do was come to grips with your own mortality. It was a clear understanding that this ain't fun and games. This is not going to be big demonstrations with lots of television cameras with people around watching. When we went to McComb and when we went on those highways in the middle of the night and it was dark and you were frightened, you had to think that you would never live to see your home again. And once you dealt with that, it was a very freeing sort of situation.

I remember I dealt with it in McComb the day they beat Bob Zellner up. We had a demonstration. It was October of 1961. There we were down in Mississippi educating people to vote. Hollis Watkins and Curtis Hayes, high school students, Brenda Travis, were asking us, "Do we have the right to go to the train station?" We say sure. So they went. They were arrested. Kicked out of school. The other kids said that they had to support them. Went on a march. We went along with them, and we were arrested. And I remember the police and the mob were beating Bob Zellner, because Moses and I tried to cover him. And later they took us down to a cell in the basement. And we didn't know what was happening. That was one of the first times I thought that Bob was dead. One of several times I thought that they had killed him. They would come and take you out of the cells, one by one. Take you upstairs. And we'd all say good-bye to each other.

And I remember being taken out of the cell in McComb, and taken upstairs and I was sitting on this bench, thinking, "What am I doing here? I don't want to die. Is this really going to make a difference? Maybe I did the wrong thing? I hope I can be courageous when they do this." And as I was sitting there— there were about two hundred white men in the hall in McComb. I suddenly snapped out of my thoughts because there was somebody hitting me with a rope, slapping me across the face and saying, "You son of a bitch, you son of a bitch . . . you'll never marry my daughter, you'll never marry my daughter." And I thought, "Oh, man. These people are really serious. This man is prepared to hit me with a rope, is prepared to kill me about somebody I have never known who probably isn't my type and they *will* kill me." And at that moment, I thought, these people have been so corrupted by their own beliefs that they are sick and I too; we all have an obligation to make them well. As well as ourselves. And after that point, I was really never afraid to face dying in the South again. Sort of freed me up.

That was good because that very next day, they arrested most of our people. Most of the SNCC people. We were all down there on this big Move On Mississippi project, and we decided we had to leave McComb but we had to leave a symbolic presence. We worked by consensus. The consensus was, "You're

the chairman, it would be best if we leave the head of the organization there."
I stayed. Everybody else left. And I remember going to the SNCC office the
next morning, and there was a big sign that said, "SNCC Done Snuck." I took
the sign down and sat in front of that little grocery store in Burgland where
we had the office and said we were open for business, and we were registering voters.

It was always very important to us that we not give people the sense that
we had deserted them. The night the kids were killed, Goodman, Schwerner,
and Chaney, the first thing we did was send field workers back to Mississippi.
And I can remember driving with Dorie Ladner and George Greene back to
Natchez and how that felt, how good it felt that we left something behind. For
years I felt that we failed. But now I really believe that we overcame a lot of
things.

JOANNE GRANT: Reading Mary King's book *Freedom Song*, I was reminded of Mendy Samstein's injunction sometime in the early 1960s. He said
that if you were in a Freedom House and you woke up in the middle of the
night with a feeling of foreboding, you should quickly wake up everybody in
the house. One night when I was in Greenwood, I woke up with that kind of
feeling. The feeling had been creeping up on me all day long, I think, because
I had driven from Jackson with Victor Rabinowitz and Barbara Dane. And Victor, in a typical New York white man's fashion, had pulled into a gas station in
Greenwood and asked for directions to the SNCC headquarters. Consequently,
we were tailed to the headquarters and he was arrested later in the day for
passing a stop sign; we had a lot of other incidents during that day but, anyway, that night I woke up in the wee hours of the dawn with a very funny feeling something bad was going on, and I woke up Sally Belfrage whose bed I
was sharing and I said, "You know, we're going to be killed." She crawled to
the window and looked out and then she said that the kid in the house was
being picked up to go on his newspaper route. So I felt like an idiot, but when
I stayed in Meridian a couple of weeks later, the lady of the house did stay up
all night on guard and they took turns every night staying up, so it wasn't really
a false injunction, but I did feel like an utter fool that one night in Greenwood.

To say that I was frightened most of the time that I was in Mississippi is a
bit of an understatement. Yet, as with all of us, it was the best time in my life. I
felt that we were building something new, I felt we were changing the world,
and we really were. I'm terribly impressed by the changes that we all helped
to bring about and I don't want any of us or any of them to forget it.

I went to Jackson for the twentieth anniversary of the sit-ins, to a conference that was sponsored by Tougaloo and Millsaps colleges, and we were all

picked up by our hosts, a black student and a white student. And we were standing around reminiscing and Barbara Dane and I were talking about the fact that when we had driven around Mississippi in the sixties, if there were a larger number of black people in the car, then the white people rode on the floor, and if there were a larger number of white people in the car, then the black people rode on the floor. And these students just opened their mouths, they gaped in utter astonishment and they said, "Not in Mississippi." So changes did take place; we know that. Some of them were visible changes; you see black people working in banks, you have integrated public accommodations. But there are a lot of changes that still haven't taken place. We have a long way to go.

TOM HAYDEN: I was with Paul Potter who was the National Student Association president; we went down to Mississippi in October 1961 because there were phone calls coming from the SNCC office that indicated that some killings and some mayhem were at hand—police and rabid segregationists were trying to get into Mr. Ernest Noble's Cleaners on DeSoto Street, which is in McComb. Bob Moses and these other people were hiding in among the clothes and trying to call out, and Paul and I had this idea, which was approved by SNCC, that we should try to go to Mississippi and do a quick report and take it to the Justice Department and try to write something for the national press to get protection. So we went down and we tried to go through this role of being reporters. So we stayed at the Camellia Motel in McComb, then alternately we would go to see George Guy and Oliver Emmerich, the police chief and the editor of the local paper, and they would rave and rant to us about these SNCC workers McDew and Zellner, who they wanted out of town, or worse, and then we would go to meet with McDew at night. You'd have to hide in the back of a car and be driven to a gas station and then switch to another car and go to a house with curtains pulled and blankets nailed over windows so that nobody could see that there was a meeting about voter registration going on. Because the house would be blown up if they saw this.

And when those students that McDew was talking about had that march from Burgland High School, Paul and I followed in a car and to make a long story short we were ripped out of the car and beaten up by this guy, Carl Hayes, who was a local electrician. And a photographer took these pictures of my being beaten up. I'll never know him, but he saved my life because he came up to me after the beating and he whispered, "Get out of your motel, they're going to come there tonight"; and at the same time, with a quick gesture, he took the film out of his camera and put it in his socks. He just put it down and, sure enough, the police confiscated the camera. And he sent the photos out, and they appeared on the national wire all over the country the next day. And we were taken down to city hall and told that we could stay in jail a long time as vagrants or we could leave, so we left because we were going to try to go to Washington to the Justice Department.

Just a few years ago I went back with Casey, who was my wife at the time, down to McComb because I wanted to retrace the place, and McComb has grown from 10,000 to 14,000 and the ghetto was still there and Mr. Noble was still there. He still spoke fondly of the SNCC workers and he still had the cleaner's and everybody in town was registered and the school, Burgland, which was the segregated school for blacks, is now the only integrated school in the town.

I went to see the chief of police to see if he was still alive, and he had died, and so I said, "I'd like to see the new chief," and this fellow comes out all decked out in military accoutrements and I said, "I'm Tom Hayden, I had the hell beat out of me twenty-five years ago down here and I just wanted to see if things had changed and what happened," and he said, "Oh yeah, yeah, the church bombings—that doesn't happen anymore." And I said, "Well, good." And he said, "That was all caused by those Yankees." And I said, "Well, you're looking at one right now." And I said, "I just want to know one thing: is it a fairer system now than it was?" He said, "Yes." And I said, "Does that make your job easier?" He said, "Yes." I said, "That's all I want to know," so I left.

And just on leaving town, we tried to call Carl Hayes, the guy who beat me up. I knew he'd be in the phone book and I called up and Carl wasn't in. I called back, kept leaving messages that Tom Hayden wanted to see him. And finally, I had to go. So I said that I'd call him the next time I'm back in Mississippi, but I'm sure that he would remember me and that I'd like to have a word with him. And that's where it was left.

Now Robert Kennedy was an important figure in all this. He had gone from the anticommunist legal counsel of Senator Joseph McCarthy in the mid-fifties to his brother's attorney general to negotiator with the Freedom Riders, telling Diane Nash to please cool it and call off the Freedom Rides, and with his brother telling the black leadership not to have the March on Washington. On the other hand, they were destined to be linked to us. They did make phone calls. They did work through the night on many occasions trying to mediate or get people out of jail. We had a very complicated relationship. When I was beaten up with Paul Potter in McComb, Mississippi, in 1961, the next day I was in Washington at the Justice Department. I met with Kennedy's top aide, Burke Marshall, and after we recounted how horrible it was down in Mississippi, he said that he and the attorney general had a request of me and I asked what that was, and they said, "Could you persuade the SNCC workers to leave Mississippi?" I said, "Why?" They said, "We can't protect them; they'll be killed."

I said "I know they'll be killed but this is the United States government, we have the Constitution that goes border to border—you're telling me that the Constitution can't be enforced in some parts of the country?" And he held up his hands and said that while I was right morally and in principle, the fact was they couldn't enforce it and their advice and their request was that I try to urge the SNCC people to leave the state. Well, imagine urging Chuck McDew, "Chuck, I was talking to the attorney general's office and they want you to leave the state." It's impossible. But it was a relationship in which the Kennedys, particularly Robert Kennedy, grew in their understanding. And after John Kennedy's death, I think Robert Kennedy was spiritually radicalized, and came to see the nature of fate and the nature of tragedy, and the nature of commitment, and began to be curious about people who are willing to sacrifice their lives for social justice whether it was in South Africa or in Mississippi.

I'd like to just end with one other thought. One thing I noticed that shows a legacy is that when Robert Bork was defeated for the Supreme Court in 1987, there is no doubt that the one and only reason for his defeat was the voter registration drives and the civil disobedience of thirty years ago which enfranchised blacks in the South, which made it necessary for politicians of all parties to seek black votes, and which made it inevitable that they would cast a no vote on Bork who stood for rolling the clock back on all those years of progress. So it takes a long time and it comes in surprising and unexpected ways, but there are long-term results from these efforts of a few relatively invisible people.

VICTORIA GRAY ADAMS: I've called this "Mississippi, the Closed Society," which, of course, did not originate from me, or "The Origin and Formation of Turning Points in the Life of a Christian Activist."

On January 9, 1861, Mississippi seceded from the Union and thus began the intentional journey of a state into a stance of regression that would earn it the reputation of being the worst of these in almost any area of civil and human rights that you wish to consider. This journey into regression could and did lead only to the stagnation and death—mentally, physically, morally, and spiritually—of many if not a majority of the inhabitants of the state of Mississippi. On November 5, 1926, at one o'clock on a cold Thursday morning, I'm told, a baby girl was born to Mack and Annie Mae Ott Jackson, their first born. That baby girl was Victoria Jackson. With this event, a unique conscientious objector to the closed society became a member of the family called Mississippians. I trust that no one hearing this statement will misread the declaration because I promise you it is not one of arrogance.

The first incident that I consider a turning point took place when I was very young. Following a visit of my aunt's white employers, I said, "I sure wish we were white so we could be rich." I remember clearly sensing that I had said something that got their total attention. Thus began my education on the importance of the richness of being what and who God created you to be.

The second turning point came when I was five or six years old. I had attended the baccalaureate service of the graduation class of the DePriest Consolidated School, and upon returning home from that event that Sunday evening, I recall sitting on the edge of the wood box that sat next to the fireplace. And sitting there on that wood box, I saw Victoria marching up that aisle in that auditorium as I had observed that graduating class do that Sunday afternoon. And I knew beyond a reasonable doubt that at some point I was going also to march up that aisle. Indelibly implanted in my mind at that point was the vision, the dream, the intention of marching up that aisle. Now, probably most of you will think, what's so big about that? Well, in the part of the country that I grew up in, even in 1945, which is when I graduated from high school, my high school class numbered fifteen. Now, we started out like any other group of children entering the public school system; the room was full of children. But very, very few of them completed high school. And I emphasize this because I think it is of the utmost importance. The ability to envision what it is you want is of the utmost importance. Because that is the beginning of what's going to be happening in your future. Never downplay the importance of dreaming, of visioning, and then believing in that and latching onto it.

I was a rather controversial child, I guess. I frequently disagreed with my peers and fell out of favor with my elders in the classroom and elsewhere and I guess it had something to do with the fact that I was keenly aware of the contradictions around me, and I didn't have a lot of reservations about sharing that fact.

One other thing I need to share with you is that I was told many, many times, directly and indirectly, that I was called to do important things in the community. That I must be prepared to give leadership to the people in my community. But I was also told that I would probably self-destruct quite early, and I was told that fairly frequently also. However, I feel to my credit that I was far more impressed with those whom I called "the prophets" in terms of who I would become than I was with the negative predictors, and in fact those negative predictions really strengthened my resolve to go with the expectations of the prophets.

My next turning points came in my late preteens. First I spent a year in Detroit with my parents—my father and my stepmother, Louise McKeller Jackson. My father had gone north seeking employment, simply couldn't find any there at home, and was for the first time exposed to an open society and that was quite an experience. And I know there are loads of you who wonder, what was so open about that, but you didn't know anything about the closed society in Mississippi in which I had lived all my life up to that point. And there I was introduced to a whole new kind of a life. Who ever heard of black and white kids going to school together? I didn't know anything about that; never even thought about it.

On returning from Detroit a year later, my mother and I were riding the Greyhound bus and when we got to Louisville, Kentucky, we had to change buses. So we came off the bus, we went in the bus station, we sat down to wait for the next bus or whatever, and this very lovely little old white-haired lady came over and wanted to know where we were coming from and my mom told her and then she wanted to know where we were going, and my mom told her. And then she invited us to the other waiting room. And you know, the walk out of that waiting room into the other waiting room was really traumatic, even after one short year. The turning point that took place in my life at that time was nobody is ever going to convince me that I'm less than anybody else—that was a decision that I consciously made at that time.

And the other came a little later when I was back home in the black school with the black classmates and schoolmates and teachers. As I said earlier, I frequently didn't get along too well with my peers, and was told that some of the teachers felt threatened by me. So, to make a long story short, I was a misfit in that community that I was born in and grew up in. As a result of that I frequently got my name taken for things that I didn't do and, of course, when you got your name taken, you got punished for that. I remember very vividly the last time that I permitted that to happen. I was called up for something and I asked what was my name on the list for, and they said, "You were talking, girl." I had not been talking, I had been sitting there reading, and so I said, "I wasn't talking." She said, "Come on up here, girl." So I went on up there and she said, "Put your hand out." And I said, "I wasn't talking." She said, "Put your hand out, girl." I had been taught to obey, so I put my hand out. She had a big board and she hit me in my hand and she didn't do it tenderly. And I took my hand down and she said, "Put it back up, girl." So I put it back up and she hit it again, and I took it down. She said, "Put it back up," and I said, "I'm not putting it back up. I'm not ever again going to allow anybody to punish me for something I didn't do, I'm going to resist." I didn't say that to her, but that was what I meant, that's what I did, that's what I said to myself, and that became another turning point in my life—not to passively cooperate, to allow people to punish me for that which I did not do. Well, there's much more, but I really must move on.

In the interim, I fulfilled the dream from the wood box, I finished high school, I entered college, but that process was aborted by a lack of funds for me to continue. I got married. I entered the teaching profession briefly. I lived in other areas of the country, traveled and lived outside of the country for a while, became a mother, returned to this country, and had to seek employment. At this point, I knew that I had to have employment but I wasn't willing to leave my small children on an eight to five basis and so I became a businesswoman, and that gave me flexibility.

And this is where I was when the civil rights movement came into full bloom. I was at this time living in Mississippi. I had my own business and was really enjoying it because I was able to recruit and encourage people to participate in financial freedom, and I thought we were doing a great job. It was very fulfilling to help people break loose from the kitchens and the yards and the other places where they labored simply because there was nowhere else to labor.

And then a couple of young men, really teenagers, came to Hattiesburg. Those young men were very dear to my heart, Hollis Watkins and Curtis Hayes. And there was a meeting called in my area. This meeting took place at the St. John Methodist Church. Now, the St. John Methodist Church was probably the least of these. When these young men came into Hattiesburg I think they came into Hattiesburg fully expecting a great welcome, with the churches open to them, where they could go out and share their mission with the people in the community and all would go well. Well, the only thing that opened up to them was the St. John Methodist Church, which I happened to be a member of. That night we gathered there at St. John's and the Reverend Ponder prepared the audience for what was about to take place. Then he introduced these two young men, who shared their mission with the people there, and then offered the altar call, the invitation for people to come and participate in seeking first-class citizenship. I saw Reverend Ponder's hand go up and then my hand went up, and the few brief moments that it took for me to get my hand up, I had another vision, another turning point. Because somehow intuitively I knew that my entire life was going to be changed as a result of this. I knew that I might even lose my life because of raising my hand, but I knew that I had to do what I had done, and that brought the most important turning point in my life. And as we began to go on this new journey, this journey where we were seeking that most basic of all freedoms, I felt like I had come home. There was the fear that you've heard mentioned time and time again, absolutely, scared stiff many, many times, but in no way did I ever consider turning back. Some other conscientious objectors were also in Mississippi: Hollis Watkins, Curtis Hayes, Lawrence Guyot, and many others, and, of course, some others had made it prior to my time and these all came together for me there at St. John's that night when I raised my hand.

Another turning point that I'd like to share with you came one night at the Starlight Baptist Church. COFO was in the midst of really opening things up in south Mississippi. The call had gone out to the religious community of the country to come and make their witness there and so we had expected twenty-some ministers to come in, and to our surprise, by the end of the day I think we may have had something like a hundred plus there. And, we didn't have anywhere to put them because at this point people were not yet liberated enough in our parts to be willing to open up their homes, and we didn't dare put them into the motels or hotels. So most of these people stayed in either Victoria and Tony Gray's home or they stayed in the home of relatives of Victoria Gray.

We would all gather around at night to share our experiences of what had happened during the day. And even though these people had come in for a very short time, a one-shot commitment, after the first day many of them realized that they couldn't just walk away. We're at the Starlight Baptist Church this particular night and I was feeling the pressure myself knowing that many of these people needed to be leaving but were reluctant to go and yet knew they had to go and I was saying to myself, "More local people have got to become involved, because these people can't stay here and march for us: we have to march for ourselves."

So I was up talking to the people in the Starlight Church and I was telling them how wonderful it was to have these people come and share our journey and fight with us and for us and all that, but trying to say we too have got to do something. And then all of a sudden I remembered someone else who had preceded me in this stance, in the scripture from Isaiah. "In the year that King Uzziah died, I saw the Lord," and further down it says, "And I heard him say, 'Whom shall I send, whom can we send and who will go for us?' And I said, 'Here am I, send me, I'll go'" (Isaiah 6:8). And all of a sudden I found myself standing there saying that and realizing that it wasn't what somebody else said; at that moment it was my word of truth. And so I said to my fellow citizens there in Starlight Church that night what I now say to you: "I heard the call, 'Who will go?' And I said, 'Here am I, send me, I'll go.'" And so it was and so it is, and so shall it ever be. What happened as a result of that decision on my part I think is representative of the many other decisions that were being made across Mississippi at that time, in the same way and in the same manner.

C<small>ASEY</small> H<small>AYDEN</small>: I did the research for that voting rights challenge. We were organizing people to go to precinct meetings. I took those calls when they came in from the precincts, the white Democratic Party precinct meetings. It was a very, very dangerous thing to have done, and everybody who went knew that it was. Many people suffered at those meetings physically. It all sounds comfortable but it was a very courageous activity on the part of so many people, of whom Victoria was one.

JAMES FORMAN: The question of the Mississippi Summer Project keeps being debated, and there are some factors about it which should be discussed so that people can be very clear. There was a meeting in Greenville, Mississippi, in 1964 and a majority—or some part—of the Mississippi staff took the position that we should not have the Mississippi Summer Project of 1964. The project envisioned the organization of a lot of people from northern states and the organization of a lot of whites. Bob Moses was the project director, and there was a lot of disagreement with the decision that was taken—I wasn't at the meeting—not to have the Summer Project. Plans had been made, and so forth. Moses came to Atlanta, to the Executive Committee of the organization, and he discussed this question, what were we going to do. He took the position in Greenville that he didn't want to be part of a racist organization— he considered a decision to exclude Mississippi Summer Project volunteers because of their race to be a racist position. And he explained this to the Executive Committee and we decided that the Summer Project should go forward. It was a unanimous position that it was in the best interests of everybody in the United States of America, the entire population, not just a few people in the Student Nonviolent Coordinating Committee, for the project to take place.

Now, during the Summer Project, Bob Moses called me from where they were training volunteers in Oxford, Ohio, and said, "Look, Allen Dulles, former director of the Central Intelligence Agency, would like to meet with some of us, with Guyot, myself, and you." I said, "Why do you want me involved? You're the Mississippi Summer Project director." He said, "Well, the staff at Oxford insisted that you be at the meeting because they felt that if you were not at the meeting that they would be sold out." And so I said okay, if that was the position of the staff, then I would come to the meeting. We met in Mississippi. Allen Dulles said, "President Lyndon Baines Johnson wants to help the Mississippi Summer Project and he wants to know what it is he can do. He asked me to come out of retirement to meet with you and to give him some kind of assessment as to what he should do." So we discussed this problem of Mississippi, we discussed the historical terror. We discussed 1890, we discussed what had been happening with those literacy laws and what this was doing all across the South, not just in Mississippi. And how people did not have the right to vote. There weren't any elected black officials in Mississippi or across the South in 1964. So we said the thing for you to do is to tell the President of the United

States—and we did all this in a very amiable fashion— to try to pass the Civil Rights Act of 1964, an act which was to reverse seventy-five to eighty years of power-taking by the Mississippi legislature, of denying people their right to vote, of instituting segregated laws.

There were certain things that occurred in the Mississippi Summer Project. One of the things we decided to do was we said that every project director in Mississippi had to be black. And every summer volunteer who was interviewed had to answer the question, "Would you be willing to go to Mississippi and serve under a project director who was black?" And interviewers were instructed to pay very careful attention to that question, because that would determine perhaps more than anything else whether you should accept this person to work in the Summer Project in 1964. And every summer volunteer was asked that question.

There were certainly issues about initiative—I remember Dickie Flowers in particular. I said, "What's the problem, Dickie?" He said, "I am the project director; I'm black. And one of the things that has happened is that a lot of the volunteers have come in and I have found myself saying I went to Morehouse when I *know* I didn't go to Morehouse." And I said, "That problem can be resolved. That problem occurs in every situation." There were other people who may have felt that their initiative was stifled. In any situation there are going to be some excesses, some casualties, but we have to look at the overall good. We have a mayor of Vicksburg, we have other mayors all across the South— that could not have come about without the 1964 Civil Rights Act, and we have to be very clear about this. We have to try to get over this feeling that some people's initiatives were crushed. This is no reflection on anyone. But there was an overall consideration that had to be analyzed. Even the sanctions on South Africa—how could we have passed sanctions on South Africa without having black officials? How could we be doing what we are doing in Mississippi? Ruby Doris Robinson was instructed to go out and try to make every effort to recruit black people for the Summer Project. We made all sorts of efforts to do this so that people would not get the impression that there was an invasion of volunteers coming in who may not have been the same skin color as the majority of the people in Mississippi. The 1964 Civil Rights Act made it possible for black people to register to vote and for black officials to get elected. There are now over 7,000 black elected officials in the United States and in 1964 there were fewer than 500, and that is a tribute to every Mississippi summer volunteer and every member of their families regardless of their race.

And all the volunteers were not white. There is no need to be apologetic about this particular matter. People laid down their lives—there were people killed. The only people killed were not black; there were white people killed.

The only people killed were not white people; there were black people killed. Everybody knew that that was probably imminent for all of us.

But there was an overall good. We can all nitpick. Let's look at Bob Moses. Where was Bob Moses and his position on whites after 1964? He went to Africa in 1964 and again in 1965. Right after the Summer Project the organization asked, how can we relate to the peace movement? We made a decision in our Executive Committee that Bob Moses and Courtland Cox were mandated to work with volunteers to try to develop a peace project that would include the volunteers so they would not be isolated if they did not feel that they had anything else to do in terms of civil rights. The Assembly of Unrepresented Peoples was led by Bob Moses. Then he said he's stopping all contact with whites; no more whites in the organization. My position was, "Where did you get this line?" He said he decided in Africa that SNCC would be better off with no whites in it and said, "I'm breaking off all contacts with white people." There are a lot of contradictions here, and I think we should debate it.

LAWRENCE GUYOT: Both of the meetings regarding the project were held at Greenville. Dave Dennis chaired the first one at which the decision was made that there would not be a Summer Project. Bob Moses came in on the second day and threw his mantle in support of the Summer Project and reversed the staff's position—there are tapes of both of these meetings. As to the Mississippi visit with the CIA director, Allen Dulles; Aaron Henry was at that meeting, a lot of people from MFDP were there, a lot of people from SNCC. It was not a meeting with Moses, myself, and Forman. That meeting with Moses, myself, and Forman took place in the attorney general's office with Arthur Schlesinger, Burke Marshall, and John Doar. Hollis Watkins nominated me to make sure that there was no compromise, and the SNCC staff in Mississippi supported me and him in that position. All of this could be documented.

Now I supported white involvement in the Summer Project. And the reason I did was because I saw how the FBI followed around white volunteers in the Freedom Vote in 1963. We could not move unless we bumped into an FBI agent as long as there were white people involved. The political justification for the 1964 Summer Project, as Moses stated it, we agreed, was to bring the country into Mississippi. And we did that by bringing the wives, daughters, sons, nephews of the Binghams who were in Congress, the Rockefellers who were elsewhere, into the Freedom Houses of Mississippi; the Mario Savios who cut his political teeth in Mississippi then went on to Berkeley. We also got Andrew Kopkind in *New Republic* magazine, who pointed out that a SNCC volunteer or SNCC organizer could be seen in the fields of Mississippi by day and in a meeting with people who had congressional contacts in the evening, so the national base and the national reaction to atrocities were always spreading. Parents of volunteers came to Mississippi every Wednesday; they became known as the "Wednesday group." They flew in from across the country to see what could they do, what kind of data they could get and take back and mobilize around. There would be have been no way we could replicate that; it was right at the time and it's right now.

And Moses is the last person who should be attacked by anyone at any time, especially in his absence.

One other point needs to be made. We must understand that SNCC's later position as it relates to the removal of whites was totally independent from what happened organizationally in Mississippi. I think it's very important that we look at all of the forces at once.

MENDY SAMSTEIN: I met Bob Moses when I was in Georgia, and the possibility of going to Mississippi emerged; that was terrifying to me. I thought that if I did go I would die. I tried to ward that off for a while but the power was just so enormous, the people, Bob Moses, all the others that I began to meet like Willie Peacock and Sam Block. All these people were touching me and I responded to them and finally the Aaron Henry Campaign was launched in 1963 (this was the concept of bringing in large numbers of volunteers, putting a spotlight on Mississippi). This was an opportunity for me to slide in with others so it wouldn't be so terrifying. I got to Mississippi and I stayed. I stayed and I managed to survive. I met a lot of extraordinary people.

Let me try to share a little bit about what it was like for me being in Mississippi. There was a lot of fear because it was dangerous and we knew it was dangerous, and there were people who had been hurt and we knew that threat existed, but there was also a sense of community and movement that in a sense isolated you from that fear and kept you going. The political dimension of Mississippi was the people. Not just the SNCC workers, because we were primarily college students from wherever, Howard or from southern colleges, but the people of Mississippi I began to meet like Fannie Lou Hamer, and Victoria, and other people.

Now, I was at the Greenville meeting about the Summer Project, so I went through it, I experienced it; it was painful. But it didn't alter in any way my involvement nor did it seem to alter at that time my relationships with people. I could understand what was being said and what was being articulated and it was, and still is, a very ongoing issue. For instance, in the New York school system the question is: a lot of the administrators are white; is that the problem? Is that why black children are not learning? Some people think so. And it may contribute. But I personally don't think it's the whole story, because it's more complicated.

To put it back into history, into Greenville in 1963, there was the question which the leadership and the staff were dealing with: How do you not only gain certain goals but how do people change? How do you help people who have one image of themselves develop another image of themselves? That's what was going on, and there were those who felt that the question of leadership and the question of the role of whites was significant in this regard. And yes, Bob was decisive at that time, there's no question. And probably, if there was a vote, maybe it would have gone the other way. But I don't think it was that simple. There was a lot of back and forth discussion and I don't think it can be thought of as a cut and dried thing. The question for me has to be, how do we create a society in which the human factor is predominant. And I learned that in the movement.

Anyway, I did some organizing for the Mississippi Freedom Summer, so I had to travel around and meet people to get people to offer their homes and set up Freedom Schools and libraries and things like this. And the response and the feeling of acceptance, and seeing the sense of humanity and dignity that I met everywhere, to go into the churches and to hear the singing and to see what existed there among a people was incredible because the thing that was so dramatic about the civil rights movement in the time we're talking about was that it was also a movement of people, a broad-scale movement. Thousands and thousands of people were touched and transformed by that movement. And seeing it, walking onto plantations and churches and talking to people and meeting people in that way was so special.

I just wanted to conclude on an aspect of Mississippi called the Freedom Schools. The Freedom Schools were probably not as dramatic or well known as the Voter Education Project, the Aaron Henry Campaign, the MFDP, all of which were of crucial and great importance to everybody, but something happened there. We got the idea of organizing the schools. I don't know exactly who came up with the idea, maybe it's not important now, but the idea was a profound and important one and it's one that still has to be kept alive. It's the idea that you can create schools in which something profoundly different than what we are used to seeing happens to people who are traditionally a part of those schools. So we brought down all these people and it was the whole gestalt of the Freedom Summer. We saw some amazing things happening. We saw kids getting turned on to reading, to doing math, we saw relationships being developed, burning relationships. It was quite an extraordinary thing. I think the Freedom Schools changed—started to change because it's a very slow process—started to change the children's images of themselves.

P<small>AUL</small> L<small>AUTER</small>: I want to expand on the Freedom Schools: two more sparks in Hollis's fire. It wasn't just the Freedom Schools, it was the form of education that was empowering and was conceived of as an empowering form of education that in turn changed the teaching practice and the educational practice of literally hundreds and ultimately thousands of teachers across the country, and that fire is still very much alive. That curriculum is still absolutely wonderful and it is still one of the most effective teaching documents and ways of teaching that has ever been put together.

Second form of fire: I worked in Natchez in 1965 and went over to McComb at one point and there was an MFDP leaflet being circulated at that point that said, "No Vietnamese Ever Called Me Nigger." And it went on to talk about how black people in the South should not be serving in the military fighting against other people of color. As far as I know, it was the first public urging of noncooperation with the military, publicly issued and circulated. There was a lot going on about conscientious objection; in fact, that fall SDS issued a pamphlet about conscientious objection. I wrote it. That pamphlet was inspired directly by the fact that the people in McComb had begun to circulate that "we won't go" statement. You were at that point subject to penalties of five years in jail and a $15,000 fine, as I recall, for urging noncompliance with the draft; that's what they were doing. Another fire which began there in Mississippi, in this case, in 1965.

When the history of social movements in this country gets written as it is in the process of being written, I think we will see more and more clearly that in area after area the changes that have come about are rooted in the fire that Hollis Watkins was describing. And I think that everybody who had a part in that has the right and, indeed, the privilege of being proud of creating that fire and spreading it throughout this country and through the world.

D<small>ANNY</small> L<small>YON</small>: I was sent down to Mississippi to find Bob Moses in the Delta. Harry Belafonte, I think, gave somebody $300 to buy the ticket and they sent me down there. I was still a student at the time. And I found him, and I'll tell you a funny story. I'm going down to Jackson. And you are scared to death, you come and see these "Colored Only" signs and you're supposed to take a picture of that. Again, I'm a white guy in a black neighborhood and people tell you you can't take a white cab, he's not going to take you to that address, you've got to take a black cab. You go to a black guy, he doesn't want you in the cab.

So I get to the Freedom House in Jackson, knock on the door, people peep out. They say, "You're at the wrong house, it's next door." Knock on that door, they didn't let me in there either, they said, "They're up in the Delta, Bob Moses, Greenwood"; the guy gave me an address.

I took the bus up there and I took the address, somewhere on Magnolia Street. I get off the bus, I'm walking down the street—you walk through these towns, people notice you. And I go to the address, Magnolia Street, knock on the door, a white woman opens the door and says, "That's in the colored part, that's in the nigger part, that's in niggertown, what are you doing here anyway, you're in the wrong part of town, that's North Magnolia Street, this is South Magnolia Street." I had to go all the way back through the town again, I'd gone the wrong way. There are railroad tracks and SNCC's constituency was always across the railroad tracks, and there I was walking back through this town convinced everybody was looking at me. I got through it and I reached the office and did take pictures of Bob Moses and they're sitting around in their pajamas. I said, "I came down here to take pictures." And the next day a squad car pulled up.

He said, "Come on." He put me in the squad car, took me down to the city hall. He says, "Go in there." I go in there and there's a sheriff sitting there. He pulls out the book and he shows me a paragraph that says to do the practice of photography in Greenwood requires a photographer to post a $2,000 bond. I said, "You want a check for this?" He says, "Well if you practice photography, it's right here." It was a very civil exchange. I said, "That's all right, I'll be back in the morning. But I'm not setting up a studio." It was for liability insurance. I don't do that kind of stuff.

Well, anyway, I walked outside and this cop was waiting for me. Now I've always told this story with the guy having his gun out. It's hard to believe that a man would actually stand there with his gun out, so maybe I imagined that part. I didn't imagine the rest. He came up to me and he's shaking. In Albany, Georgia—because they arrested me there too—in Albany, Georgia, I was surrounded by a group of policemen and the policeman said to me, "You're shaking now, boy, wait 'til we're done with you," and I *was* shaking. That was in Albany. Here I am in Mississippi, this guy's coming up and he's really agitated, he's shaking. He said, "I'm going to blow your fuckin' brains out." I said, "Now?" I mean, the sun is shining, we're standing in the parking lot in front of the police station at ten in the morning. He said "I'm going to blow your fuckin' brains out—what are you going in the nigger part of town for? We don't do it that way down here."

And then, SNCC training, right? You know how they train you, someone says, "If this situation comes up, here's how to handle it. You're Jewish; just say you're colored." Great. 'Cause you see that's the problem, the mixing of the races, so if you just say you're colored, well, the problem is solved. So I said, "Well, as a matter of fact"—and here I really blew it because the key thing is to say that your mother or your grandmother was black, that's crucial, see? I said, "Excuse me, but my, my grandfather was black." That wasn't funny. I left town on the next bus.

So there were SNCC workers whose courage was a little lower than the others, who wanted to live to fight another day. I'm still alive.

I think SNCC taught us all that it's possible to have power way beyond your numbers, that being pure does pay off, that you cannot compromise on certain things that you believe in. And part of the power that came from SNCC was an extreme, radical, and uncompromising position. I'm sure that in reality there were people who had more power or did make compromises, but it was a very uncompromising group and in a way I've applied that to my whole life and to my work.

JUNE JOHNSON: Growing up in Mississippi I never had the opportunity to have a summer vacation. My vacation was either cleaning some white person's house or going to chop cotton in the Mississippi Delta—that was the gist of my summer activities before my getting involved with SNCC. And it was a sense of frustration growing up. We heard about the Emmett Till situation and really didn't understand a lot of what happened other than the fact that a black boy had been castrated, murdered, and thrown into the Tallahatchie River. There was not a lot of conversation based on our parents' fear—they wanted to continue to live and survive within that community. And I saw additional things happen, not just outside of my family but directly to my family, my mother in particular (who was, by the way, very active in SNCC and kept everybody very healthy—I think Guyot and Julian and Judy Richardson and Dorie and many others ate pieces of her corn bread because she was the cook for SNCC). And I think as a result of my going to jail in 1963 in Winona, and coming out, learning that Medgar had been killed, after being beaten very badly in the Winona jail and having to suffer and see the suffering of Mrs. Hamer, I made a commitment to myself from that day; I didn't care what happened to me, I was going to be free or continue to be a part of a struggle to fight for the freedom of people of this country. And when I walked out of jail in 1963, I knew nothing else, and I have not done anything else in my life but struggle from the time that I got involved in the movement in Mississippi. And one of the biggest enjoyments that I've ever had in my life is to have met those persons that came to my hometown and taught me to become a first-class citizen. And I take this opportunity to say to each of you, I am appreciative of that and I'm glad that you taught me how to fight for the rights of those who cannot fight for themselves.

CASEY HAYDEN: A lot of people makes power. In Mississippi, the mass character of that movement is what created a completely new power base where there was no power before. And what happened there was that a completely new set of power balances were created, because of the activity of thousands and thousands and thousands of people in very risky situations. To me, that's the main thing that happened. The other thing that happened was that in splitting that culture open, many questions were released, very provocative questions; the questions which are still at the root of social problems in this culture.

HOLLIS WATKINS: I stayed in Mississippi. I still live in Mississippi. I feel that I am, ever since 1961, and forever will be, as much a part of SNCC as anybody else was a part of SNCC, and I'm saying SNCC did not leave Mississippi. Certain people of SNCC left Mississippi and certain people at certain levels in SNCC left Mississippi, but SNCC after 1961, as far as I'm concerned, stayed in Mississippi and is still in Mississippi alive and well. So I think we have to look at things in the proper context and at the proper level so we can keep the record straight.

"Ordinary People": Alabama and the Lowndes County Freedom Organization

In Alabama, voter registration projects proved especially difficult and dangerous. Anti–civil rights violence was widespread and occasionally deadly. Nevertheless, SNCC workers set up a project in Selma in 1963 and built on the successes of a local black group, the Dallas County Voters League. In 1965 SCLC decided to make Selma a battleground as well. Jimmie Lee Jackson was attacked during a protest and later died; in response, SCLC called for a protest march from Selma to Montgomery on March 7. Met by state troopers on horseback at the Edmund Pettus Bridge, marchers were brutally attacked, earning the event the name "Bloody Sunday." Unbeknownst to the marchers, including SNCC members, Martin Luther King, Jr., reached an agreement to hold another march but to turn around at the bridge, which he did, to the disgust of many. A third march was finally held, with federal protection (although it did not protect Viola Liuzzo, who was killed by Klansmen that night); these marches helped convince Congress to pass the Voting Rights Act. In Lowndes County, SNCC tried a different strategy for gaining voting rights: a separate political party they called the Lowndes County Freedom Organization. Its symbol, the black panther, became an icon for protesters fed up with white resistance, and its ideology helped establish a basis for the next phase of the civil rights movement: Black Power.

B ERNARD LAFAYETTE, JR.: There *was* a split in SNCC and there was an ongoing debate about direct action and voter registration, and I think that

Charles Sherrod probably epitomized that debate because he was one of the people who was part of the direct action wing and who believed that nonviolence is a way of life, but when we had the opportunity to get some financial support to do voter registration, we jumped right at it.

The spring of 1962, I was off raising funds in Detroit, Chicago, and St. Louis, because Chuck McDew and Bob Zellner and Dion Diamond were in jail in Louisiana on conspiracy charges, conspiracy to overthrow the state of Louisiana because they were trying to get people registered to vote. And I think the bail was about $10,000 each; they were only accepting cash bail. And we didn't have that kind of cash, $30,000. I had come down to work in a project, but Jim, who was executive director, said no, we need you to go raise funds. Go out and organize Detroit. I didn't even have a pair of shoes. I ran into a cousin I didn't know I had in Detroit and he bought me a pair of shoes. But, anyway, Elizabeth Hirshfield and some people who had been on the Freedom Rides and who had been supporting efforts in the South were there, so he sent me there to raise funds. Jim always had great ideas, so he said, "I have a great idea, what we'll do is get Diane Nash out of jail and have her come up there and speak." You see, she was in jail and she was pregnant, about eight months pregnant. Her father lived in Detroit and was a well-known dentist; she was a well-known freedom fighter from the Nashville movement. So he sent me this eight-month pregnant woman to help raise funds in Detroit. It was a close call. I got her on the plane that afternoon, the next day she was in Albany, Georgia, and she had the baby.

I don't know how much money we raised, Jim, I never did find out. Well, I'm only saying this because I was late getting down to Atlanta to take on a project and so when I arrived, Jim Forman said, "We could send you to some places in Mississippi with Bob Moses, we could send you over to Arkansas with Bill Hansen." I said, "No, I'd like to have my own project." I was a young guy, maybe twenty, twenty-one years old, and I wanted to do my own thing. So, he said, "Well, there's only one other place left, and that's Selma, Alabama, but we've scratched that off the map." We'd sent in a SNCC staff person and the only people he could meet that had organized themselves was a group called the "12 High"—and that's because they stayed high all the time. This is true. They were organized and very serious. I mean, you never caught them sober; it was their policy. You got kicked out of the group if they ever caught you sober.

The other problem was he felt there was so much intimidation in Selma, and that black people were just afraid. The last organized effort they'd had was an effort to desegregate the schools, and they had about ten people who had signed a petition. That was the method for desegregating the schools in the

South: ten people from the community would sign the petition and they would send it to the school board demanding that the school be desegregated. They would be systematically rejected by the school board, an all-white school board, and then that would precipitate a suit from the NAACP. And then they would file a suit that would go through the courts. In fact, it's still in court; it's been in court for the last thirty-five years. That was the slow approach to desegregation. But some great results have come out of this kind of effort.

But what happened in Selma is that the White Citizens Council and the Ku Klux Klan systematically forced all the people to withdraw their names from the petition, and they did some very unscrupulous things—I mean besides shooting in their homes and discouraging them in that way and intimidating their children—one fellow's mother-in-law was fired from her job, and he had to leave town because of that. They used various forms of intimidation until all the people withdrew their names except one person that was a postal worker, a fellow who worked as a mail carrier in Selma. So they didn't go very far with their desegregation suit. The point I'm making is that Selma had had some very serious experiences, so there was a reason why people were very much afraid and intimidated and slow about getting involved in the movement.

Well, this staff person had decided that we had to go some other place because Selma was a little too rough. So I said, "That's great! I'd like to take that place." Jim said, "Well, if you want to go down there, you can check it out and see what you think." This was back in the fall of 1962.

There was always a lot of pressure on the staff people because Jim Forman would call people on the phone: "What's going on down there? I don't see anything in the newspaper. You all sleeping or what?" In Selma he didn't expect anything because everybody assumed that place was so backward. So I thought that was a great place for me to do some serious social science work, so I said, "I'll take Selma." There was a fellow named Jack Minnis who had done some research on the hidden power structure and the economics of the South. I took my time and I went down to the library at Tuskegee. Before even going into Selma, Alabama, I did research. When you can take your time and really do a thorough job, it pays off, and I found this over and over again. It doesn't make sense to rush. And the older I get, the slower I get at making decisions, and talking, and walking—it's great! I mean, wait till you get old and try it.

So I stopped at the library in Tuskegee and read all of the newspapers of the White Citizens Council. I wanted to see what happened in Selma in terms of lynchings and stuff like that, so I got a chance to read, and study all about the banking and finances. It was fun, I enjoyed it, it was very exciting. Armed with all of this information, I decided to go and start talking to people in Montgomery who had experiences in Selma, Alabama, and in Dallas County.

I talked to Mr. Rufus Lewis who had been an NAACP organizer, and since I mention that, I should tell you it was no coincidence there were so many movements in Alabama—the Montgomery movement, Birmingham movement, Selma movement. You see, during the period when SNCC went in, the NAACP was outlawed; they had banned the NAACP operation from the whole state. Teachers had been fired from their jobs simply because they had membership in NAACP. The NAACP could not operate. So that created a gap and a void. And as a result of that, we were able to do some things. Now the other reason is that when SNCC moved, it mainly moved in rural areas for voter registration; there was no competition. The SNCC people were in places where only angels dared to tread. You're talking about the bodacious thing.

Going into Selma meant we were going into a big void that was created by a lot of things that happened earlier. My first work in Selma was to focus on the leadership. What SNCC people really did was to become full-time volunteers for community groups. We became the staff of community groups. I began to work with the local organization, about thirty people. When I got there only about three hundred black people were registered to vote in the whole county. The literacy test was a problem. So we tackled the problem exactly where we found it.

There was Ms. Marie Foster and Mrs. Amelia Boynton, and there was Attorney Chestnut—a few people around who were not afraid and they were willing to stand up. So we worked with those few people. As Sherrod said, you find one other person interested in doing it. I found about four who were interested in doing this thing. We set up office and began to start the movement.

Well, a couple of things happened. The first mass meeting we had in Selma, Alabama, was in May 1963 at a memorial for Mr. Boynton, who had passed. He'd been the head of the Dallas County Voters League. I stayed with him in the hospital to relieve his wife at night while he was dying, and I realized this was a great man who had made a tremendous contribution. His son was the one who filed the suit, *Boynton v. State of Virginia* [1960], that desegregated lunch counters at the bus stations, and there was a whole lot of strength there.

I always stayed open to learn from the local people, and I learned a lot. If you want to know how to organize people, what you do is ask them to teach you, and they will teach you how to organize them and to educate them. I asked the people to teach me how to organize them and they did. They were concerned about outside people coming in, taking over the leadership. So what we did was help them to organize a movement against me. We got all the people who wanted to be leaders, and I got somebody else to organize them. I didn't want to be the leader. I had already had my head cracked. Coming from a mass meeting one night, June 14, 1963, one of the local white gentlemen waited for me. I was unloading some leaflets in the back of my car, getting ready to go into my apartment, and this huge tree on the side of the little apartment where I lived shaded the streetlight, so it was dark. I had already observed a car parked there across the street when I drove up. When I was bent over in the back of my seat of the car for the leaflets, I heard some footsteps coming behind me, the cracking of the leaves. There were different periods in the movement when we thought it was going to be all over, and that was one of the periods that I thought that was it. We knew the day would come at some point, and I thought that was it. And then I heard this voice, it said, "Buddy, how much do you charge me to give me a push?" I was so excited, he only wanted a push, I volunteered right away, I said, "I won't charge you anything, gladly give you a push." Well, he had other plans, I learned later. I had this 1948 Chevrolet; Julian Bond had gotten me this car in the movement. Everybody else had a new car; Jim, you didn't ever give me a new car. Gave them to all those other people and they wrecked the cars and I took care of mine. I just want the record to show, Julian's contribution to the Selma movement was to get the staff person a good car to last, and it made it. Well, so much for that.

So I had this high-bumper car, so it would be no problem pushing the car that was supposed to have been stalled. And what happened was, the fellow said, "Maybe you ought to come out and take a look at this to see if the bumpers match, so the bumpers wouldn't get stuck." I was wondering what the problem was. I hopped out of the car and bent over, and then he clubbed me with the butt of a gun. I fell to the pavement and I stood up again. Well, the significant thing here is in terms of nonviolence. The most important thing is to be able to face death, and when that moment comes, the question is whether you have the courage. But one of the things you have to do is first of all is give up life. It's only when you give up life that you really and fully embrace life and really appreciate it. And at that moment, I had no thought of what would happen to me. And I stood up and I watched this man, and he clobbered me again; in fact, he hit me three times in the head. Each time I would stand up again and there was blood dripping down on my shirt as I stood there and watched him.

Now, that was unexpected behavior. And unexpected behavior sometimes can have the impact of arresting the conscience of your assailant, because they don't know how to respond to you. They expect you to run, they expect you to plead for your life, they expect you to fight back. I did none of those things; as I was trained in the movement, I simply confronted him and looked at him. That upset him, unnerved him. He began to back away and I was afraid that he would shoot me as he got into his car, so I yelled up to my neighbor, and my neighbor came across the banister upstairs—we called him "Red"—with a shotgun. And then I really got terrified because if he had shot that white man down in Alabama, there was nothing I could have done for him. So I said, "Red, don't shoot, don't shoot"—I started screaming and hollering, "Red!" Part of the account is in Howard Zinn's book *SNCC: The New Abolitionists;* he never talked to me about it, so he didn't get the full story, but it's okay.

That was the same night that Medgar Evers was killed. The reason I didn't know Medgar Evers was killed that night was that I was in the hospital. And I learned later from the FBI that there was a three-state conspiracy: they were going to get Elton Cox over in Louisiana, Medgar Evers, and myself.

As a result of that experience, the people in Selma really began to rally. When we had the first mass meeting, we had a memorial service for Mr. Boynton and on the leaflets it said, "Memorial Service for Mr. Boynton and Voter Registration." And that was the thing that caused people to come out. Jim Forman was our first mass meeting speaker in Selma, Alabama, and he gave one hell of a speech that night. A mob came in front of the church with baseball bats and big table legs to break up the meeting. The only thing that saved us was the high school coach, who had some influence, because the sheriff was just out of it.

The other thing about Selma, Alabama, is there's tremendous history there. Reverend D. V. Jemison (whose son in Baton Rouge, Louisiana, desegregated the buses in 1953), Tabernacle Baptist Church was the church where he pastored. He was the president of the National Baptist Convention, USA, Inc., before Dr. J. H. Jackson—early on we're talking about. I think that history has to be resurrected.

When we look at history, we begin to see that there are sediments of things that are already there. It's an opportunity for us to bring those back together, but the seeds of resistance were there before. It was a matter of rearranging those and replanting those in a way that would cause new life to grow. Well, that's a bit about what happened from the beginning. The main thing that happened in Selma, Alabama, was that we took the time to develop local leadership and to bring them together in a way that they were able to sustain themselves through the struggle.

SILAS NORMAN: There is a song called "Ordinary People." "God uses people, ordinary people, like you and like me, to do His will, no matter if you give Him your all, no matter how small your all may be, little becomes much when you place it in the Master's hand." The story of SNCC and the story of Selma is a story of ordinary people. And if there is anything that we need to remember, it is that thousands of ordinary people made this movement.

There's been some talk here about connectedness, and I want to talk a little bit about connectedness. Connie Curry was at Paine College where I went to undergraduate school. She was a representative of the National Student Association during a conference which we used to have annually in the spring. It was an unusual thing for Georgia, but there were white students from all of the schools around Georgia as well as black students coming to the Methodist school that I attended for the spring conference. And during that conference—it was the early days of the sit-ins—we decided on that Saturday afternoon that we would give them a new experience. We took young southern white students and young southern black students on a demonstration downtown. This was a new experience for them. Let us just say that their parents went crazy. By Saturday evening, Sunday morning, many of the parents of the young white students from around the state came to pick them up. We were criticized and applauded alternately about our involvement in that activity, but that was our way of saying we understand some of what is going on in the South, and we were taking steps, organizing in ways we thought we needed to organize to deal with the problem.

I'm the first of five living children of working parents in Augusta, Georgia. The connectedness doesn't just start there. Augusta, Georgia, has a rich legacy; some of the significant personages in black history lived and moved there. At Paine College during that time we knew about Mr. Lawson in Nashville, some other personages like Harry Ashmore, a white activist and journalist in the South. We were influenced by the Atlanta Committee on Appeal for Human Rights very profoundly. I got to go to Atlanta as a leader and meet Benjamin Brown, who was a contemporary of Julian Bond, and to meet Ruby Doris and others. And later when I would go to graduate school in Atlanta, at Atlanta University, we would be in the same class. In fact, Tom Gaither from CORE and I were in the same biology program. We learned much more about each other's history at that time. So the history and the connectedness were very important. I was vice president of the state of Georgia youth and college chapters of the NAACP, a very, very supportive organization to us in those early days.

I left Atlanta University and went to the University of Wisconsin and became president of the Student Council on Civil Rights. I got connected with other activists at the University of Wisconsin. If you know anything about the University of Wisconsin, you know that there were student activists there of many persuasions. I remember being called into the dean of students' office, and he explained to me that being from Georgia, perhaps I didn't understand that I was associating with the wrong people. It was from that place that I was recruited by Mary Varela, now Maria Varela, to participate in the Selma literacy project. This was in the summer of 1964. I'm not sure how Mary found me, but through that connectedness, through her knowledge of people at the University of Wisconsin, I was recruited to the Selma literacy project.

I had considered going to the Mississippi Freedom Summer. Ivanhoe Donaldson and the Freedom Singers had come to the University of Wisconsin; the Freedom Singers were late and Ivanhoe Donaldson talked for about two hours, and I knew at that moment that I had to go back home and I had to follow Ivanhoe. And so I was going to the Mississippi Freedom Summer, but then Mary Varela recruited me for the Selma literacy project.

I, along with James Wiley from Gary, Indiana, Carol Lawson from New York, and Karen House from Washington, D.C., made up that project. Bernard Lafayette has told you about what was happening in Selma up until 1963. At the time we arrived in Selma, Selma was under what they called the injunction. There was an injunction against mass meetings, against voter registration action, against anything, so at the time we arrived in Selma we were supposed to be undercover, because there were not supposed to be any gatherings. We lived and worked in the Good Samaritan Mission, a Catholic mission there where the priests and the nuns lived; that's where our offices were. Mary lived in the white community and we lived in the black community, because we didn't want anybody to know what we were doing. And our meetings at the black churches, in the homes of the people of Selma, were supposed to be secret. We were told very specifically that in order to do our jobs, we couldn't be in jail. And Mary made it very clear that we would stay clear of the SNCC people, because if we got involved with the SNCC staff we'd be in jail and we couldn't do the literacy project and it was important for us to do the literacy project.

We must have lasted about two, two-and-a-half weeks, because on July the 2nd, 1964, the Civil Rights Act was passed and we heard on that day that some of the old SNCC staff was down at the office, which happened to be across the street from the jail, cleaning it up and getting ready to move into action again.

We decided during lunch that in spite of Mary's warnings that we would go down to the SNCC office and we'd help them clean up. However, on the way to the SNCC office we decided since the Public Accommodations Act had been passed, part of the Civil Rights Act, that we would stop at a place called the Thirsty Boy, a white drive-in restaurant. At first we decided we'd drive in and we said, "No, we don't want to drive in, we'll park across the street." So we parked across the street and we went into the Thirsty Boy. We went up to the counter; they wouldn't serve us. So we decided, well, we'll sit down. That's when I met Jim Clark—the sheriff of Dallas County, Jim Clark. I will never forget, I was facing the door; he entered without a word, accompanied by a number of other white men in various kinds of uniforms. It seemed like a number of cars pulled up out there. He didn't say a word. He walked over to me, and that was my first experience with cattle prods, and let me tell you, it worked. I was trying to decide *which* car to get in, not whether we were going to jail. That afternoon, after people heard about our arrest, the demonstrations started again in earnest.

Now you need to know that the staff in Alabama, before the influx of other SNCC staff from Mississippi and Georgia, was made up primarily of people from Alabama, primarily of people from Selma. I won't forget some of the names; high school students from Hudson High School who had been in the vanguard of that movement. People like Terry Shaw, Cleo Hobbs, the Roberts brothers—Willie C. and Charles—Betty Fikes, Eugene Pritchett, Avery Williams, Sammy Williams, James Austin: any number of persons were responsible for organizing that movement. And it was the indigenous staff that was in the office on the day that we got arrested. They decided after we were arrested that they would then go to the movies in downtown Selma. For the next eleven days, as we sat in the Dallas County jail, hundreds of people filled the jails. About eleven days later we were released on bond, which had been sent down from the North and through the many other channels that SNCC usually used. That was the reopening of the movement to some extent—it was the summer of 1964.

At that time I was not a SNCC staff member, I was on the Selma Literacy Project. I was supposed to be underground, but our cover had been blown. So Mary Varela introduced me to Jim Forman, and he allowed me to join the SNCC staff in Selma. The first project director who returned after then, the return of action, was John Love. And at that time, in the fall of 1964, our actions consisted of getting ready to move in mass action again. What we would do, since we were still sort of undercover: the SNCC workers would go out to homes of members in the wards, in the various parts of the city, who would allow us to come. They would invite in their neighbors, and we would go into the homes and talk about voter registration. We started to get ourselves ready to move into action again. We felt that it was very important that we were knowledgeable and prepared because we were going to move to break an injunction and we were going to once again incur the wrath of Jim Clark and his cronies.

We continued to involve ourselves in that way. Also, you must understand that one of the active organizations in the community was the Dallas County Voters League. That is the organization to which Mrs. Amelia Boynton, who has been mentioned earlier, was a part. Her husband had been a part before he died in 1963; later councilmen like Reverend Reese, Mrs. Foster, other very active community persons were in the Dallas County Voters League. The Dallas County Voters League decided sometime in the fall of 1964 that they wanted to invite in Dr. King to spark the movement. And so in January of 1965, in the midst of our preparation to move again, the Southern Christian Leadership Conference was invited to Selma. Needless to say, there were a lot of discussions and philosophical and procedural differences with the organization, but that was mediated by the fact that by then Diane Nash Bevel, who had originally been in SNCC, then worked for SCLC; James Bevel, who worked for SCLC, had previously been a SNCC organizer; Bernard Lafayette who had previously been in SNCC, by then was in SCLC, and those individuals helped us to bridge the gap.

So immediately we got together and we decided that we would work together in Selma, in terms of organizing in the wards. We assigned an SCLC person and a SNCC person to each ward. For the ward meetings, we would go to the meetings together and we would essentially try to check each other and try to make sure that we were all working in the same direction.

People have been talking about grass-roots organizing. We felt that that meant we had to be in the communities, living with people the way they were. We had to be with them. Large demonstrations were not necessarily productive; the hard work of organizing was sitting in those small groups and preparing to move in effective ways. So for example, there was some disagreement over the march to Montgomery in March of 1965. In fact, SNCC voted not to participate in the march from Selma to Montgomery, but as always, there were individuals in SNCC who participated in that march because we had freedom of conscience, and people were free to participate in any way they wished. So there were members from SNCC who participated in the first march on Montgomery. You will remember the pictures, you will remember seeing Hosea Williams from SCLC, you will remember seeing a picture of John Lewis with a knapsack on his back going down under the batons of the state troopers.

At that time, after that incident, I decided that I could no longer sit back and philosophically be opposed to participating in the march. On the second march on Montgomery, I emptied my pockets and I prepared to offer my body as a living sacrifice. We started the march across the bridge for the second time and as we got to the end of the Edmund Pettus Bridge, state troopers lined up on every side. I noticed they were not moving toward us, and I will remember that Dr. King—he was a row or two behind me—said, "Let us pray." We prayed. And then the march proceeded to turn around. Well, Jim Forman was close to me, we were all sort of baffled. Jim was saying, "What's going on, let's go ahead," and as we turned around and headed back across the bridge, there were hundreds of people behind us asking, "What's going on, what's happening?" We had no idea. We were to discover later that there had been some agreements with Robert Kennedy, with the government, that that march was not to proceed. Personally, I did not participate in that march again. I felt that we had been betrayed, and I no longer wanted to participate in that. I felt that I could best spend my energies working with people in the movement in small groups in Selma.

Now, about that time, SNCC staff had started to arrive to support us from the Mississippi staff, from the Georgia staff. When I first arrived in Selma, one broken-down Jeep was the vehicle. By that time we had one car. SNCC members will remember that we used Plymouths with radios in them, large antennas. Hollis Watkins had painted these hands on the side of his car. One day I looked up and Cynthia Washington and a number of other people had come over from Mississippi and Georgia to support us. The sight of these eight to ten Plymouths coming in front of Brown Chapel was quite a sight to see. At that point we were deciding what we were going to do in Alabama. We decided that it was not productive for us to fight with SCLC. So members of the staff then decided to move out; we decided to move to places where we decided they would not come.

Accordingly, there were members of the staff here who moved out to Wilcox County; Cynthia Washington went to head the project in Greene County; Annie Pearl Avery went to head a project in another town, I can't remember, in Hale County; and then finally there were staff members who went to Lowndes County: Courtland Cox, Stokely Carmichael, Bob Mants, Judy Richardson, Ruth Howard, Jennifer Lawson. There are many other names, but that's the way we got to Lowndes County. The decision was that Lowndes County was so bad that nobody would come in there showcasing, that it was only going to be serious work there, and so we would not be bothered and would not be in conflict. So we decided to decentralize the movement.

In Selma, as elsewhere, staff members had an opportunity to devise any projects they wished. The basic project, of course, was voter registration, but later as we began to move in Selma, some folks had started a unionizing project, and so we decided to unionize the Coca-Cola Company in Selma. And so in the midst of all of this there was union organizing going on at the Coca-Cola plant, there was the voter registration and some of the other things.

R<small>OBERT</small> M<small>ANTS</small>: Let me tell you very briefly how I got involved in Alabama. I had left southwest Georgia and had gone back to school at Morehouse. James Bevel came to Frank Smith and myself, who were students, and said, "We want you all to go down to Alabama because there's an effort in the United States Congress to bring about the Voting Rights Act." Frank and I both refused Bevel, said we had been out there, got our licks, and we wanted to go to school; we wanted to get a college degree. Not long after that, in the next few days, Frank Smith went to Mississippi and I went to Alabama. I went to Alabama with John Lewis, again, another spur-of-the-moment thing, to participate in the march in 1965 from Selma to Montgomery.

I never will forget how the leadership of that Selma to Montgomery march on "Bloody Sunday," the first march, was selected. Some of us who experienced this in other places had gathered at Brown Chapel, and then we went into the parsonage at Brown Chapel. Some of those people there were Andy Young, James Bevel, Hosea Williams, Albert Turner, myself, and others. Dr. King was not there that day. They were trying to decide who would lead the march for SCLC. Andy, James Bevel, and Hosea Williams flipped a coin to decide who would lead the march for SCLC. I guess I'll always believe that Andy and Bevel, having worked longer together in the movement, playing odd man, put the stuff on Hosea. John Lewis volunteered to lead the march for SNCC. Albert Turner volunteered to lead the march for SCLC, and here I am with no other choice but to march behind John Lewis.

It was during that period, the first attempt to march, that some of us decided to go back to Alabama. It was during that time that Stokely Carmichael, as he was known then, came from Mississippi, I came from southwest Georgia, and we and SNCC there in Selma decided this was the opportunity for us to capitalize off the motion of the march to go into Lowndes County.

Now Lowndes County had had a very long history of being the most violent county in Alabama. Folk there told you that they would kill you in Lowndes County, and there was no question they would kill you. I remember the first time we went into the county. Stokely Carmichael, Scott B. Smith, Judy Richardson, and myself went into Lowndes County. The people there, some of the people that we were able to talk to at first, including John Jackson's father and others, told us this is a very dangerous place. Highway 80 that runs through Lowndes County was notorious. I remember one evening, a prominent black doctor in Selma, at almost sunset, her car stopped on her and I asked her if I could help her, she said, "No, boy, just give me a ride into Selma and get me out of Lowndes County." Lowndes County was a proving ground for many of us.

It was also during that same time when we went to the Lowndes County Training School. Remember that during those days black folk were trained, and most of the schools in that area, especially Alabama, were called training schools. We went there capitalizing off the motion of the Selma to Montgomery march in an attempt to organize people there in Lowndes County. We went to the Lowndes County Training School, where we were passing out leaflets about the march coming through Lowndes County. It just so happened that the school was letting out for the day and we were passing out leaflets around the school and on the buses. Although most people dodged us, didn't want to take the leaflets and stuff, there was one young fellow there who kept begging for us to give him some leaflets and some SNCC buttons, and that was the first time I met John Jackson, now mayor of Whitehall.

Carmichael, Judy Richardson, and myself were at the school. As we left the school the sheriff and state troopers came to us and pulled us over, saying, "Come on back to the school. Don't you all know that you all ain't got no business passing out leaflets and stuff on the school campus?" And this was the first time and only time Carmichael probably ever used his head. We were all there shaking, perhaps with the exception of Judy. We had these two-way radios in our cars with long whip antennas. Carmichael picked up the two-way radio as if he were talking to the base in Selma. The problem was that we were out of range, but nobody knew that. He told them—he was talking and the sheriff and state troopers and other folks could hear—that if we weren't back at a certain time, what to do. That perhaps saved our lives at that time because what happened was, they let us go.

It was from that point that we were able to begin to organize in Lowndes County. I would suspect and I still suspect very strongly had it not been for that incident at the school it would have been at least two, three, four months before we moved into Lowndes County to organize it. But what happened was, when the teachers and students were getting out of school, the word had spread around the county, them civil rights folks was in here. And we knew that. The next morning we roll back out, people waving, "You all all right, you all all right?" And once they had seen this incident at the school, we knew we had to be *bad* then. We were back out there the next morning.

I want to say something related to the formation of the Lowndes County Freedom Party, as it was called; the press called it the Black Panther Party. There were some people who you might not ever hear of, if you listen to some people, who were involved in that process. Without a doubt, central to the formation of the Lowndes County Freedom Party, and the emblem of the black panther, was Ruth Howard. The Alabama law required that any political party have an emblem. The Alabama Democratic Party had had the white cock; we wanted the black panther. Courtland Cox was also involved in that project.

I always marvel at how the public perception is of these great thinkers who sit around and carefully plan and strategize things. Most of the things that have happened in my experience, happened sporadically, spontaneously or freak of nature, or some other reason.

I think, in conclusion, and this is my challenge to young folks today, if you don't want to get in the midst, don't stick your nose into other folks' business.

JOHN JACKSON: Lowndes County, Alabama, straddles Highway 80 between Selma and Montgomery, where it's further distinguished as being the place where the marchers camped on the way to the Voting Rights Act of 1965, and the one which the Ku Klux Klan chased down Viola Liuzzo to kill her that fatal night when freedom refused to take a back seat to fear.

It was in Lowndes County where the Black Panther political party was formed. Its real name was the Lowndes County Christian Movement for Human Rights. And its purpose was to allow poor black people to exercise their constitutional rights as U.S. citizens by accepting the nonviolent constitutional means of registration and voting. This is the American way. Not murder on the highway by night riders, and church bombings, and bus burnings, and standing in the schoolhouse doors, but the patient, fearless, Christian method of education, enlightenment, and conversion of enemies to our just cause. Don't you believe Bob Mants when he tells you I was begging for him. They were so afraid in Lowndes County till they was begging for us. And I was crazy enough to stop my bus and take some of the leaflets. And I went home and I talked to my father about it. We had an abandoned house that my brother had just left, and I said to my father, "Them boys are going to get killed trying to make it back to Selma, and George Wallace is going to hang them if they keep going into Montgomery. So they need a place to stay." My father met with them, and I think he kind of liked those fellows or he was about like me, half crazy. So he said, "Hey, boys, you all could take this house over here, there's nobody staying in it." They were kind of glad, because they used to have to get the hell out of Lowndes County before dark.

So they began to stay in Lowndes County and we began to work. I was driving a school bus, sixteen years old, making $50 a month, and of course the week after I took the leaflets, I was fired. And of course Bob and Stokely assured me that I could be hired with the Student Nonviolent Coordinating Committee. But the only thing about that was I never got a chance to get with Jim Forman. I wanted to have an executive meeting with him; I never got a check yet.

And to make matters worse, after I lost my job, the large landowners during that time financed the sharecropper, and being one of thirteen children and a son of a sharecropper, we never had no money that year to plant a crop. I was kind of glad, because I didn't want to pick no cotton nowhere. After that, my sister was a schoolteacher in Lowndes County, she was fired and, of course, SNCC said, "We'll find you a job too." Neither one of us received a check yet. My father was supposed to be getting rent on the house, I have not seen *that* check yet. And the white folk in that county called my father in and said, "Hey, you ain't got to be in that mess, you don't need those folks staying there" and, clearly, I remember his words: "If we are not for ourselves then who can be for us?" And we continued to work.

Then, I don't know what happened to me, I graduated, I got a scholarship to Tuskegee, and I would come back every summer to work with the movement, I was just so excited, still hadn't got no check. Ed Geffner, a great friend of mine in Michigan, sent for me to come to Michigan to work in the Ann Arbor Friends of SNCC office that summer. I had never been on a plane before, and I'm without a check yet, but I worked in the SNCC office in Michigan that summer. Then he fooled me the next summer, to take a trip to Russia, I believe; that was long before Nixon or any of them thought about going to Russia. And then when I come back I couldn't get back into my school; they said I was a communist. Still hadn't got a check yet.

But one thing that we did, SNCC did for us in that county, they aroused us, getting up off ourselves to do something to help ourselves. And we were really committed, after being shot at seventeen times—seventeen bullets went into the car—and seeing Samuel Younge, Jr., laying down in Tuskegee because he wanted to use the restroom and Jonathan Daniels being forced out of jail, and Gloria was standing by his side, he was shot and killed, and seeing him lay on the ground three or four hours before anybody came to get him. We made a total commitment ourselves. We also offered ourselves up as a living sacrifice.

Every member organization has four kinds of bones. There's a wishbone—folks who sit around and don't do nothing and wish somebody else would do all the work. You also have a jawbone—there's a lot of jawbones in SNCC too—folks who sit around and talk and don't do nothing else. Then you have the knuckle bones—folks who knock everything you do and don't do anything else themselves. And lo and behold, you have the backbone. If I could say anything about SNCC, they were the backbone of the movement. SNCC was the kind of organization who got under the load to do the work.

When they came into Lowndes County, they were different from a lot of other young people. They did not come in there telling us what we needed to do. They came into the county asking "What are the problems? What can we do to help you?" And I remember very clearly, I don't know whether it was Stokely or Bob, but they asked the question: "Can these bones live?" And I was confused about that because I'd always read in the Bible about the dry bones in the valley (Ezekiel 37: 1–14) and I thought that was just a bunch of bones out there laying with nothing on it, you know, and the preachers used to preach the sermon about the bones connecting. And I was confused about that; I didn't realize you could be living, asleep, and be dry bones in the valley, but that's the way we were in Lowndes County. No registered voters, no black people owning their own homes, denied the right to go into the Republican Party to run for office, denied the right to put our name onto the roster.

A lot of people don't understand why we chose the black cat as an emblem. There were a lot of our people could not read and write. And when we did petition to get on the ballot, they typed the name so little we couldn't see it. So we had to have something that people could identify with. I want you to know that when we did petition to get on the ballot, that cat gave that elephant hell and picked all the feathers out of their chicken.

I could hear the old sister over the corner, Mrs. Jackson and all the old sisters used to sing all those songs. When they asked the question, "Could those bones live?" that sister said, "Yes, these bones can live." And then we looked around as we began to get on the ballot and rattle those dry bones in the valley, I began to see Charles Smith move and become first black county commissioner. Then we looked around and saw the head bone begin to move, and we elected the first black superintendent of education. Oh, my goodness, those leg bones began to move, all the way into Montgomery, Alabama, and elected the first black representative and the first black senator from Lowndes County. Then that chest bone began to jump and we elected the first black sheriff of Lowndes County, John Hulett. Oh, we began to rattle those dry bones in the valley.

One thing SNCC taught me is that time does not change things, men change things. When you act, something would happen. If you don't act, won't nothing happen. I'm mayor of Whitehall, Alabama. We've got problems that face this nation that don't discriminate. And I want to challenge you to get involved. Because as SNCC rattled those bones, they challenged us in Lowndes County. They challenged us to dream—a little bit before Dr. King started dreaming, I believe. They challenged us to dream of a community, a city, and a county full of love instead of hate. They challenged us to dream of people who were concerned about the human race, not the dog race. They challenged us as a people to bury our weapons and serve the human family. SNCC challenged us as they rattled those dry bones in the valley. SNCC challenged us to dream of teachers who would teach for life and not just for a living. SNCC challenged those ministers and preachers who would preach and prophesize instead of profiteer. SNCC challenged us to dream in Lowndes County, to dream of lawyers who were concerned about justice and not a judgeship. SNCC challenged us to dream. To dream of the coming elected officials who would become public servants and not politicians. I challenge you to dream today; to dream of a people who will love one another and who are motivated and obligated to serve the human family. I challenge you today to dream—and when you dream and when you act, something will happen. And when you do that, no greater love than this than a man who will lay down his life for his friend.

G<small>LORIA</small> H<small>OUSE</small>: Courtland Cox told me that I'd better not say how I was in awe of all the other people here with me, but I'm going to say it anyway, because I am. I have a great deal of love, admiration, and respect for the people I came to know and love in SNCC. I did then, I still do. I still feel about them as if we are a beloved community even after these years. So yes, I am in awe.

I went south to Selma, Alabama, from Berkeley, California, where I had been a graduate student in the Comparative Literature Department. For a few years I had been watching the southern movement, and some things had happened in the South that were just so horrible that they preoccupied me and kept a hold on me. One of them was the murder of the four little girls in the Birmingham church; the other was the killing of Goodman, Chaney, and Schwerner. I remember walking home from campus one day from the library, picking up a newspaper, and looking at a photo of Mississippi policemen dragging bodies onto the shore of the river and putting them into huge, black sacks. And there was a thud in me. I was horrified. I felt then that we live in a country where the ruling class, the power structure, will allow genocide against us as a people. I wanted to be a part of changing this. Meanwhile, something happened at Berkeley that kept me there for a little bit longer, the Free Speech Movement. I'm going to get back to a theme that Silas brought up before, the connectedness of the movement at this time and students who were involved in the movement.

The Free Speech Movement was a struggle against the university administration who had told us that we did not have a right as students to mobilize and to raise funds to support the struggle in the South. And we said, "We do have the right and we will go on." And we had set up tables at the entrance to the campus there, Telegraph Avenue and Sather, and we were collecting money. One of the people who was instrumental in the leadership of the Free Speech Movement was Mario Savio, who had himself been in Mississippi the summer before and had come back with a great deal of enthusiasm and commitment to work to support the southern movement, even though he was still in school.

As a result of this determination on the part of students to go on collecting funds and politicizing people and talking about the movement in the South and engaging in boycotts and pickets right there in the Bay Area, the administration decided this had to stop. When we couldn't get the administration to negotiate any further with us, some students decided to stage a sit-in in the administration building. I was not one of those students who decided to stay overnight, but I remember coming to campus early the next morning and being shocked to see that there were police forces. National Guardsmen, every armed body they could find from all of the neighboring cities in the Bay Area, were there on the University of California campus lined up for blocks. As we stepped onto the campus we could see policemen dragging students down the marble staircase in Sproul Hall.

Those of us who were outside immediately started to organize. I can remember students sending us messages out of the administration building. Since they couldn't get out to talk to us, messages were dropped out of the windows. As a result of this mobilization, we carried on a major general strike at the University of California that changed the relationship between university administrations and students, I think, once and for all. Students sat on the University of California Board of Regents. Students had a say in government, and teaching assistants and graduate assistants organized the first labor union for graduate students ever in an American university. We learned that a few people unified around an objective, trusting each other, could require even the most powerful institutions to change, and we were of course very exhilarated by that.

By the time the Free Speech Movement was over, I learned that a group of students from San Francisco State were collecting books for Freedom Schools in the South and were planning to go to Selma and set up a Freedom School. I thought, "Aha, now is my chance finally to go South." We all got together and we drove south. We rented a house right on the edge of the housing project, I can't remember the name. In the center of this housing project was Brown Chapel, and Brown Chapel was a central organizing place for the Selma movement.

The first night in Selma, people who were there in the Freedom School house encouraged me to come with them to a mass meeting at Brown Chapel. And who should be the main speaker at Brown Chapel but Kwame Toure. I was introduced to Kwame after the mass meeting and, of course, fell in love with him immediately, but that's a different story that we won't take on.

I went on teaching at the Freedom School in the mornings and working with the children. By the way, when I first came into Selma, in 1965, the two things that impressed me most were the energy and enthusiasm of the children and the incredible music of the movement. This kept spirits very high. Resistance was very high in spite of the Edmund Pettus Bridge and all the accommodationist policies that you've already heard Silas talk about, SCLC and all the things that we were outraged about in terms of how *they* organized in Dallas County and the neighboring counties. The people's spirits were still high.

I worked in the Freedom School in the mornings and Kwame invited me to come into Lowndes County and meet the families that he was working with and to come to some of the mass meetings that took place on Sunday evenings in the churches in the county. I started to work with a group of people in Lowndes informally at that point. Kwame had also invited a young seminarian, Jonathan Daniels, from the East—he was studying at an Episcopal seminary, I believe, in Boston—to come into the county too and to be involved in this work.

A few weeks later, during the summer, a group of us agreed to go with some local youngsters to picket a store in Hayneville, Alabama, which was the Lowndes County seat. We picketed the store and, of course, we were arrested. We were all hauled onto a big garbage truck and taken to the county jail, which was almost as filthy as the garbage truck. There were puddles of refuse on the floor. There were three sisters, three women—myself, Ruby Sales, and Joyce Stokes, I think was her name, a local sister from Lowndes—several teenagers from Lowndes County, and Kwame and Scott B. Smith and a few other Lowndes County organizers. We agreed within a few days that we should get Kwame and Scott out and they should try to raise money so that bail could be paid for the rest of us.

Meanwhile we sang and tried to keep ourselves together. It was while we were in jail there in Hayneville that we heard the news of the Watts rebellion in Los Angeles, and we all had the sense we were living in a very, very important time. All of us there in the jail had that feeling, that wow, things are beginning to open up, move; we're part of something very important.

I think we may have been in jail for about eight days when all of a sudden the guards just came to us and said, "Okay, you're going, we're releasing you on your own recognizance." Of course we were suspicious of this. No one from SNCC had been in touch with us. We had not been told that bail had been raised; we had no information from anyone, and we thought, this doesn't sound right. But they forced us out of the jail at gunpoint. Being forced out of jail at gunpoint—you know something worse might be waiting for you outside, so you sort of hang onto that jail. Well, we did. We were standing around outside the jail and they forced us off the property onto the blacktop, one of the county roads, again at gunpoint.

Since we had been in jail and really hadn't had anything fun to eat or drink—we had been eating pork rind and horrible biscuits and whatever—some of us thought, "Let's walk to the little store here and get a drink, have some ice cream." We headed to a corner store. Just as we turned onto the main street of Hayneville, gunfire broke out, and we realized the gunfire was coming in our direction. The youngsters, of course, started running everywhere, and some of us just fell on the ground. Ruby Sales and I had been walking with Jonathan Daniels, and we fell there on the ground. Jonathan was hit and we think he must have died immediately. Father Richard Morrisroe, the only other white member of the group, was also hit. He did not die, but he moaned and groaned and moaned and groaned in a horrible way that none of us who were there will ever forget. It seemed to me it was hours before anyone appeared on this road in Hayneville. Everyone had been informed, of course, that something was going to happen, so this curiously deserted main road was silent because that's the way it was intended to be. We thought we were all going to be killed.

We later learned that the targets were Jonathan and Father Morrisroe, the two whites in the group, and that a marksman had been hired to kill the two of them, and had been deputized for that purpose. This man got off scot-free after the trial. Most of us returned to the county for the trial and watched him get off scot-free.

Well, I was scheduled to go back to Berkeley to resume work as a teaching assistant in the French Department, which I did. I stayed for about three days. I remember going in to the chairman of the French Department and saying, "I'm really sorry to inconvenience you in this way, I know that now you're going to have to find another teaching assistant, but I'm leaving." And he said, "What's the matter and where are you going?" And I told him and he said, "Oh, I understand completely, I'm Algerian, and I have been involved for a long time in revolutionary struggle."

So I came back, and I was hired by Silas as a field secretary and started to work in Lowndes officially. I have to thank people like Judy Richardson and all the others who had worked there long before I showed up; I was like the rear flank. The staff at that point was Kwame, when he was not off doing speeches and tours (because by this time he had been elected chair of SNCC), Courtland Cox, Bob Mants, and Janet Jemmott, whom I miss a lot today. As has been said frequently, our job was to do what the people said we should do, to help them move the struggle forward in the ways that they thought it should be moved forward. There were already some very strong activists in Lowndes County, the Jacksons, for example, who gave us a Freedom House, a place to live, and other families who were not afraid to take a stand and who were ready to cooperate in the work.

Jack Minnis had discovered in the Alabama code that it was possible to get an independent political party on the ballot in Alabama if you met certain stipulations, so that gave us immediately a way to get in and organize people independently. The Democratic Party was still the party of white supremacy. That rooster that John Jackson talked about was about white supremacy. People knew that that party wasn't something that they wanted to be involved in, so it wasn't difficult for us to talk about independent organizing. What was difficult was to make clear the process by which this kind of operation had to be undertaken, and that was our job as SNCC workers, to inform people, to make that clear.

There was also some literacy work to be done. Many people in the county could not read and write. Also there was some teaching of history, because we learned very early in the work that it was our own sense of identity as a people and our own sense of historical continuity that gave us the strength to do the kind of work that we were doing, and it would also empower the people that we were working with.

R̲OBERT ZELLNER: What got me into SNCC in the first place was Diane Nash. I had never met Diane Nash. But I had watched her on television. And John Lewis, I had met him, because he came to Montgomery on the Freedom Rides and I visited him and William Barbee and Jim Zwerg and so forth in the hospital in Montgomery. I was a civilian then. And I couldn't believe the level of fury that was coming from my people and what was happening. I could not *not* get involved.

I remember another thing that brought me to SNCC. There were the Freedom Rides and there were the sit-ins. I remember when the Freedom Rides came to Montgomery, I went down with some students from my college and the thing that sticks vividly in my mind now about the Freedom Ride was that after they entered the city, everybody was beaten severely. Some beaten nearly to death. The crowd gaily swept up the clothes and the books and burned them in the streets. And I remember that right near the bus station in Montgomery there was a construction site. There was three-quarter-inch plywood as a fence there. And in that plywood were imbedded bricks. Bricks were stuck in the plywood. They had been thrown with such fury and such force, like a tornado. I saw this happening. And I either had to completely give up or I had to join them.

So the first very timid thing I would do was I went to an integrated meeting in Montgomery, where some SNCC people were. And as a result of going to that meeting, the Klan burnt crosses around my dormitory. I was called into the office of the attorney general of the state of Alabama and he said, "You've fallen under the communist influence." And I remember saying, "You mean there are communists in Alabama?" This is MacDonald Gallion, he wasn't too smart, but he said, "Well, they don't live here but they come through here." So he gave me a list of names and he said if any of these people contact you, you let me know immediately. And he gave me a list of names. Anne and Carl Braden were at the top of the list. Clifford and Virginia Durr, other people. And when I found out that they actually lived in Alabama, I laughed. A little while after I was put in the paper and asked to leave school for going to this integrated meeting, I got a call from Anne Braden. And I said, "Oh, here's the communists." And I got an invitation to come to dinner at Virginia and Clifford Durr's house in Montgomery. So for the first time I'm meeting people that are on the right side. I said, well, if the attorney general is against these people, they must be all right. But anyway that's what brought me to SNCC and brought us all to SNCC. A necessity, a need, and you did what you had to do when it had to be done.

COURTLAND COX: I'd like to talk a bit about Lowndes County, the Lowndes County Freedom Organization, because I think probably it's one of the most important things that SNCC did. John Jackson and Gloria House referred to the rooster. I just happen to have a copy of that document, and on the top it says, "White supremacy," and the bottom says, "For the right." The official slogan of the Democratic Party of Alabama.

I think that what we were trying to do was to pose the question that was very important after the Voting Rights Act. The O'Jays sing this song: "Now That We Found Love, What Are We Gonna Do with It?" Our view was, now that we have the vote, what are we going to do with it? I think it was very important for us that if we had the vote and we looked at the situation in Lowndes County, we develop a strategy that would move us forward. In 1965 Lowndes County had a population that was 80 percent black, yet only 4 percent of that population was registered to vote. All the elected officials were white, and the people of Lowndes County, like the rest of the people in Alabama, faced a number of conditions. They faced police brutality; they faced poor housing; substandard education; poor health facilities; very low ownership of land; a hostile and arrogant courthouse which had a tax assessor, tax collector, and probate judge that cared nothing for their views or their ideas.

I think what we were faced with at that point was do we complain and protest about these conditions or when you have a situation where the community is 80 percent black, why complain about police brutality when you can be the sheriff yourself? Why complain about substandard education when you could be the Board of Education? Why complain about the courthouse when you could move to take it over yourself? There was a certain logic to that position. That is to say, in places where you could exercise the control, why complain about it? Why protest when you can exercise power?

I think Jack Minnis, who was probably one of the smartest people that SNCC ever had, looked at the law and raised the issue of putting together in each county a party that would be responsible for carrying out the wishes of the people. One of the things that we did is we took the law and we broke down the responsibility of the sheriff, tax assessor, Board of Education, tax collector in comic book style, that people could see and read, and if it was difficult reading, at least through the pictures they could get a sense of what was being talked about. Because educating the population, not just manipulating them, was very important to us.

So we felt that as we organized the Lowndes County Freedom Organization, three things were stressed. The first is organization itself. Second, that people had to understand what the responsibilities and duties were, and three, that local leadership had to come from among the population and had to be supported by the population.

MARTHA PRESCOD NORMAN: I don't think anybody who spent more than a second in Lowndes County didn't know the Jackson family, John Jackson's family, and respect them for their courage and their tremendous dedication. They have given everything there was to give. I met Bob Mants in 1963 when he was making that transition from being a student activist in Atlanta to moving into the Black Belt, community organizing, and he's still there. So impressive. And, of course, my ex-husband, Silas Norman, I thought so much of what I saw of him in Selma that—this is a true story—two years after he left Selma, after no letters or phone calls or anything, he almost literally showed up on my doorstep one day and asked would I marry him. And I said yes.

"Oh Freedom": Music
of the Movement

"Freedom songs," a combination of spirituals, popular music revised for the occasion, and new creations, played a crucial role in SNCC. They created energy, kept spirits up, and provided a sense of linkage with the history of African-American struggle. Although generally led by song leaders and even turned into a fund-raising mechanism in tours by the "Freedom Singers," these songs could be—and were—sung by everyone: during meetings, on marches, in jail. So moving and unifying was the power of music that the participants at the SNCC conference broke into song every chance they could.

BERNICE JOHNSON REAGON: (Sings)

This may be the last time,
This may be the last time
This may be the last time
May be the last time, I don't know.　　(Traditional)

Now if this was a Black event, I would not have gotten through the first line. For an event to be a Black cultural event, you have to practice Black American culture. And when there is singing, you don't have to see who is singing, you need to hear; and then before they get through the first line, join in, so they don't feel stupid that they've started a song.

Now, you are not born knowing how to practice Black American culture.

You can be born Black and not be able to execute any Black American cultural expressions. It is not in your blood; you have to learn it. And this country is culturally Black in terms of mainstream culture. I don't care who you are, if you grow up in this country, you spend a lot of your time and energy trying to be Black.

Most people learn about what is Black from the commercial industry, which does not want you to know what I'm going to talk about tonight, which is that Black American culture is participatory and you don't go *buy* Black American culture, you have to *create* it. (Sings)

> This may be the last time
> This may be the last time
> This may be the last time
> May be the last time, I don't know.

That song is sung with the understanding that you could be dead in the next moment. So it then does not remain a song, it names the quality of the gathering. Everything then becomes special, because you are actually voicing something you understand about your mortality—that this particular thing that we are doing in this moment might not ever happen again. And then everything you do comes out of that awareness and everything you do becomes precious and everything you do becomes sacred, and when you sing that song out of that understanding, everything is just a little heavier and you can feel it in the song, you can feel the weight of understanding that you are sitting in a very precious moment in your life. Any gathering with other human beings can be raised to that level just by declaring it's so. (Sings)

> I don't know, Lord, I don't know
> May be the last time, I don't know.

The last time I saw Danny Lyon before today was 1979. He had just come from Central America and he had made a film in Bolivia or someplace, then he had made a film about some bicyclists or bikers or something, and now he has just come back from Haiti. And it was nice to find that the years had passed and he was talking about doing the same thing as he had talked about when he took the pictures of the Freedom Singers in 1961 and 1962 in Chicago, Illinois. (Sings)

> May be the last time, I don't know.

Now, one of the things you have to do in order to learn about music in the movement is to understand that most of the work has to take place inside of you. And you have to go places most people who are not Black and develop or practice Black American culture never speak to in their lives. Most people who don't have access to Black American culture die and never go to the place you have to go in order to do Black singing. You don't even know it's there. And so what you have to do if you're going to know what this is about is to go and find it.

Now, when you look for it, because you're used to looking for things outside of yourself, I see you cutting your eyes around. And I'm asking you to come up with something, and so you try and find out where you're going to go get it. You don't have to look no place. Sometimes if you avert your eyes and look down—some people close their eyes—it shades external things enough so that you can quiet down and sometimes that opens the door that has to be open if you're going to know what singing in the movement was about. (Sings)

> This may be the last time
> This may be the last time, children
> This may be the last time
> May be the last time, I don't know

A lot of times when we get together like this, people say, "Let's sing some freedom songs." And sometimes you think if you get together and you sing some songs you can get back to that place that's itching that you need to scratch, which is why you said, "Let's sing some freedom songs" in the first place. But the songs are only a vehicle to get to the singing, and the singing cannot be understood as executing melody, rhythm, and harmony—although it helps if you can execute those things. But if all you do is hold the tune and get the rhythm and the harmony, you have not done what it is you say you want when you say, "Let's sing." Black people use songs to get to singing. Singing is an organizing experience. Now, I'm not saying you use singing to organize somebody—that's not what I'm saying. But you cannot create a song within the Black American cultural experience if you're not an organizer. You cannot create a song if you're not willing to be organized. You have to hear, you have to be willing to lead, you have to be willing to follow, you have to be willing to experiment and move around the basic themes.

So every time a song is raised—and that's what you do, you don't *sing* Black songs, you *raise* them, which means they don't *exist* before they are sung. And when I sing the first line of a song I have not done anything but made an announcement about a possibility. I raise the possibility and it's up to somebody else whether or not it will fall flat and empty. There are no soloists in the Black congregational song style, there are only song leaders. A song leader only leads a song. I'm not doing a lecture on Black American song genres, so don't be going around saying, "Bernice Reagon said there were no soloists in Black American singing"—I didn't say that. In the congregational style, there are only song leaders. (Sings)

I was standing by my window on a cold and cloudy day —

What do you do if I'm starting a song and you don't know it? You hum. You tap your feet. You rock your body; you just help me out. Don't let me be a fool. (Sings)

Will the circle be unbroken—

There's not enough harmony in here. You can tell, right? By now you should be over helping me out. You should be growing this piece. (Plays tape of a SNCC staff meeting:)

> What do you want? FREEDOM!
> Freedom, oh freedom
> Oh freedom over me . . . ;
> This little light of mine
> I'm gonna let it shine. . . .
> FREEDOM! Yeah!
> FREEDOM! Yeah!

Okay, you probably can tell the difference between the energy in this room and the energy that was present in this recording of a 1964 SNCC staff meeting. And we had done some work before I put that tape on. And "Circle Be Unbroken" had some power in it, didn't it? Now, when I stopped singing, some of you weren't finished, were you? What were you supposed to do? You're supposed to keep going. Just because I'm up here does not mean I determine when a song ends. A song leader only does what? Start and announce the potential. And then the piece continues based on the needs and the power not of the song leader, but of the people in the room. Now, it takes courage, for those of you who sort of hummed, then it got stronger, right? It takes a lot of courage. That's why I talk about creating a song as an organizing experience, because you have to stick out. I promise you that if you cannot sing a congregational song at full power, you cannot fight in any struggle. Because at some point you have to always be covered by somebody. And in a congregational song, you cannot get cover. It doesn't matter what your voice is like and what some kindergarten teacher told you when they told you to clap your hands or gave you the bell to ring. When the song was raised, there wasn't anybody in that room who was not singing at full power, which is why it had such intensity.

Now, all of those people were not what you'd call great singers. All of those people were people who were risking their lives, and that's what it takes to raise a congregational song: you put yourself at total risk, you go all the way out. You, in fact, invite your voice to totally crack up. And even in the crack there is freedom. The voice teachers will tell you that there's no problem with the voice that breaks clean and free. (Sings)

> Guide my feet (oh Lord)
> While I run this race (oh yeah)
> Guide my feet
> While I run this race (oh Lord)
> Guide my feet
> While I run this race
> Lord I don't want
> To run this race in vain.   (Adaptation of traditional song)

Now, you hear all the stuff that goes in between? Well, you have to put some in. And if you get this song on a piece of paper with notes—"Oh Lord now"—that's not going to be in there. But if you don't put it in there, it's not a Black song.

Now, I still see people when they hear something coming, somebody else leading, you be trying to see who it is. And you see in a room like this with everybody sitting down, if it's somebody in a row, you can't see who it is. I know it also comes from coming out of another culture which sees singing as performance that is to be observed. So that if you can't see where it's coming from, if you can't see who's doing it, you actually are anxious, or you feel like you're not quite getting it. So seeing the person who's doing it is crucial. Well, if the leader is in the back of the room and you're in the front, you got to stand up and turn around—you could stop the whole song. The person who's gotten the courage to come up with that line just might not be able to face you standing up and yoking your neck around. What you do when you hear something coming from someplace and you can't see it, is go deeper in yourself to give it strength and grounding. Instead of trying to see it, hear it and expand it.

And what I'm talking about is something that has nothing specifically to do with the Civil Rights Movement, it has to do with the culture that evolved in this country by a very, very important group of people, and this stuff was there when we decided we were going to try to do something about our lives. And this was part of the way we did everything anywhere. Many of us who started had never even understood this culture as being a culture of struggle. If it's something you're born with, especially if your grandmama does it, she can't read—how is that supposed to have something to do with you fighting White people and racism—which sometimes is the same thing? And it's not until you put yourself in a particular place and then you try to find your voice that you will select out of your repertoire those things that will allow you to stay in this new place.

In Albany, Georgia, when I walked around City Hall for the first time, it was only the second time I had ever been on Pine Street in my life. That was a new place. When we got finished—we circled City Hall twice, and I don't think Black people had ever in that number circled City Hall since the city was created—Cordell Reagon and Charles Sherrod and Charlie Jones didn't know what in the world they were going to do. Where do you go when you can't go back to Albany State College campus where you came from? Where do you go in the Black community when there is no place to go? A lot of radicals in this country are totally out of order when it comes to their dealing with Black people and our worship traditions. You can see them trying to understand it and piece it together and use it for the revolution and they don't even know what they're talking about.

When you circle City Hall twice, the only place in Albany, Georgia, you can go to that will hold that many people is Union Baptist Church, which thank God was on the corner just across the bridge. We did not plan it that that church should be there, but if that church had not been there, I am not sure where we would have gone, because once you do something that is that new, you can't walk too far. You really have to stop walking real fast. So this was a new time and a new day; I had never done anything like this before in my life.

So we get to this place, Charlie Jones looks at me and says, "Bernice, sing a song." And I go (singing):

> Over my head I see—   (Traditional, adapted by Bernice Johnson
>   Reagon)

Wait. First, you notice, I go to an old song. I'm doing this new thing, ain't never done before, he says, "Sing a song," I go to "Over My Head." And what is the line to "Over My Head"? Usually the first line you do: "Over my head, I see trouble in the air." Now, if I had understood what trouble in the air meant, I would have sung it, but nobody had taught me, and I'll tell you that story in a minute, but right now (sings) "Over my head I see freedom"—by the time I got to "trouble" I didn't feel any trouble and I knew I could not sing "trouble" and also I was given permission to mess with a sacred song. The permission came because I had walked around city hall. And if you're bad enough to walk around city hall in Albany, Georgia, you can change the words to this old song.

And as people go around they try to think up new words to old songs. You have to lift up new words to those songs; you have to take a stand and then you can sing

> Over my head, I see freedom in the air
> Over my head, I see freedom in the air.

Now, let me talk about that trouble. I thought trouble was something you were supposed to stay out of. It's an interesting thing but you can grow up in a Black family in these segregated communities and they really drill in your head that you're supposed to stay out of trouble. So trouble was a negative word. I never knew you were supposed to go and get *in* trouble. But the truth of the matter is, if you take a song like (sings)

> Wade in the water
> Wade in the water, children
> Wade in the water
> God's gonna trouble the water.   (Traditional)

You see, there's that trouble again, right? Well, you say what does it mean, telling you to wade in the water and promising you that it's going to be rough? And, of course, you go there because you don't want to be where you are before you go into the water. You have to really be ready to never again see the "you" that you are, standing before this trouble. And really the "you" that you are dies. You have to say goodbye to a part of yourself. You have to really be ready—oh, you don't have to be ready, you just have to push yourself. But trouble is the only way you achieve change in your life. And I was not taught that in my Black home. I was taught that you were supposed to stay away from it, and they would say things like, "Stay out of trouble, stay away from the police." They didn't want me to get killed, because they knew that if you got into trouble you were risking your life. And that is true. This trouble that you're supposed to get into can *kill* you—but it does not always, as I stand before you tonight, having gone through the trouble.

But there are those of us who are not here now because they went into the trouble and it *did* kill them. So you are at total risk and you feel you're at total risk, but if you wanted to kill the "you" that you are, you still had to go through it. And there is a promise that you will be different on the other side. Guaranteed. But it's like stepping off a ridge when you can't see the bridge. And since you decided you don't want to be on the ridge any more, you just step off. And you know if you survive you're going to be fighting all the way. That's what the Movement was like. I am describing not reformation, I am really describing a revolution that takes place inside of you, if you do it.

The transformation that takes place inside of you when you grow a song is a mini-symbol of that revolution, but you really have to risk losing where you are to do it. And I know some people when they start to sing or even when

they listen to powerful singing, they get a little nervous and they start holding onto chairs, like, "Let me tie my body down because I have no idea what
it's going to do if I let it go, and at least I know it now and if I let it go, what in
the world will it be?" And this whole thing of congregational singing is like a
socialization process that just really works you up and down, in and out through
change. You cannot raise a song and not *feel* yourself change; you can feel it.
You're cool, the song starts, and you get flushed, your body gets flushed and
it gets hot—that's when some people get ready to turn off all the circuits, but
you're supposed to go right through it, follow, and what you have to do is turn
up the burners; turn up the burners by making a greater commitment to the
song, and just be willing to follow it everywhere it goes.

And what happens on the other side is you never forget it and you can't
wait to get back to another one, which is why you come to these meetings and
say, "Let's sing some freedom songs," because you want it again, because it's
very sweet. There's something unforgettable about transformation. And I'm
talking about transformation that you can have some role in creating, but it is
very, very risky business. And this singing stuff is very, very crucial to it. And
you find people who are just weathered in it; they can go through more singing, gunning through song after song; everybody in church falling out, they're
still going with the singing. They've been doing that stuff all of their lives.

Now, as I describe this phenomenon, I am not saying that the people who
can create congregational song are radicals within the society. You get the lesson and you get the training; application is a whole other thing. So that it is
not enough to know these old Black songs. (Sings)

> When He calls me, I will answer.
> I'll be somewhere, listening for my name.

You can sing that until the church opens up, and the revolution will not come.
So I don't want you to get confused. In addition to this something else has to
happen before you get the freedom songs. There has to be some decision that
you will break with the status quo, whatever it is.

Prathia Hall was talking about Carolyn Daniels, who was doing hair in Georgia. You have to visualize that. In that day the good hairdressers charged $1.25
a head, and they did that for twelve hours a day. And you just fry the hair—
straightening the hair—you're curling it and frying it, and curling it and frying it. What makes you decide that it's all right for you to let these people stay
in your house, which is going to get your house shot up—you're going to lose
most of your business, because who's going to come to get their hair done if
people are shooting in your house? And it means the house you live in, the
check you get, the car you have, the education you're getting: everything you

have goes right on the block with the risk, because you found something more important to reach for.

And when you get that, and when you begin to walk in that way, it is very different from going to Mount Early Baptist Church on the first Sunday and singing these same songs. Mount Early Baptist Church may not even let you in to *have* a mass meeting. You have to have a mass meeting in Mount Zion Baptist Church, which is the high Baptist church which wouldn't be caught dead singing "Guide my feet" because that was the high church, it was the church that teachers were the members of. They sang Randall Thompson's "Alleluia." I am now talking about class too, within the Black community.

But some of those country churches wouldn't let you in; some of those churches who did the style I've been talking about wouldn't let you in. Mount Zion let you in. What do you do, you go into Mount Zion and do you sing "Alleluia"? No! You sing the thing that symbolizes transformation. And you jerk that material out of its holding place. And it's in Mount Zion Baptist Church, which would never sing like this, that you hear "We Shall Overcome" delivered back into the full range of expression of the Black choral tradition for the first time. And it's not Mount Zion, it's not the cultural atmosphere of that membership, it is that that church is now hosting a movement which is by people who then speak their own language. And these songs are the voices, these songs are the statements that they make. Therefore, things like "We Shall Overcome," "We Shall Not Be Moved," "This Little Light of Mine," "Guide My Feet," and those songs, some of them with the changed words and some with non-changed words, sit right next to "A Charge to Keep I Have," "A God to Glorify."

In Montgomery, Alabama, they sang "Onward, Christian Soldiers" until they couldn't sing it any more. I had sung that song in school; I hated that song. I never *heard* the song until I heard it in the context of the Montgomery bus boycott. And everybody who is anybody who cared, remembers when that boycott started, especially if you didn't live in Montgomery. If you were Black, you were convinced Black people can't keep nothing together. There was no way those people were going to stay off them buses. First, in the South only the poorest people in the community used public transportation. If you're a little above the poorest, you had a car; you wouldn't be caught dead on a bus. So the Montgomery bus boycott was poor people. The people preaching had cars! Jo Ann Robinson had a car. The people who were supposed to stay off the bus did not move in the same circles as the preachers and teachers under normal circumstances. Somehow those people were supposed to somehow get together, stay off the buses, and we knew it wasn't going to happen.

So every day you went home scared to turn on the radio, to pick up your paper, to look at the TV to see if they were still walking. Damn, if they didn't walk for a year! Now, by the time they did that, day after day, something happened to you because suddenly you were being taught something nobody had told you, and that is: Black people can get together and stay together even though they don't like each other. Because you know sometimes those people in the Montgomery boycott were fighting each other, 'cause you got all of them people mixed up. How are educated people like the ministers with degrees going to keep them people off the buses and all of them don't like each other? So you *know* it's a mess. And somebody told you when there was a mess you weren't supposed to execute nothing. So the first lesson you learn is, ah ha, I could have a movement and it could be a mess!

So whenever people come and ask me about what friction between organizations destroyed the Movement, I have no idea of how to respond. Which friction? There was never *not* friction! I've never lived in a Black community and not heard Black folk talking about each other. I think, though, sometimes the Movement looked like there was no friction. You see all these Black people and we're singing together, it looked like we had erased all the friction—that is a facade. That is not what the singing does. The singing suspends the confusion and points to a higher order, sometimes long enough for you to execute the next step. Therefore, singing will not set you free, but don't try to get free without it.

So the idea that there could be a Movement and that Black people could walk for a year totally destroyed lots of things we had been taught within our past through our own people about what was possible. And once you understood that you didn't have to get it right to start, all you had to do was start, it was over.

And all of the songs were not church songs. Because all of the people in the Movement were not church people. So the songs came right off the radio and the most popular person who delivered songs to the Movement was a man named Ray Charles. I don't think he knew he was delivering songs to the Movement, but Ray Charles represents a synthesis of what was happening in the Black community. It was an important thing to happen. My mother heard Ray Charles for the first time singing "Drown in My Own Tears," she was upset. She was as upset about Ray Charles as she was about Rosetta Tharpe. Every time Rosetta Tharpe would cross back into the church, my mother would be upset—she loved Rosetta Tharpe, but Rosetta Tharpe would sound so bluesy. You couldn't tell whether she was singing a church song or a real, and you were supposed to be able to separate the two musically; you were supposed to know whether it was church or blues. Ray Charles started "Drown in My Own Tears," it sounded like gospel. Well, what is he doing? Is he singing blues? Is he singing reals, or is this gospel?

So we done walked around this building in Albany, Georgia, two times, where did we go? After the march we go to the church; come right out of the street, into the church. I think Charles Sherrod talks about this better than anybody I know, about how the church had to go to jail. Now they told us about going to jail in the Bible, you get all these Bible stories about (sings)

> Paul and Silas bound in jail
> And no money for to pay their bail
> Keep your eyes on the prize, hold on.   (Music traditional; words
>   adapted by Alice Wine)

You ought to read the Bible sometimes about Paul and Silas organizing in southern Europe; that's where they were. They got put in jail; they sound like SNCC workers. And this woman, Lydia, was the person who would let them stay in her house after they got out of jail. They had to have someplace to go, there's Lydia, she lets them in her house. She's the first woman converted—there's Carolyn Daniels, Mama Dolly, or somebody in these places that let these SNCC workers in.

But you know in the Black church, even as we were being passed these songs that had these transformation lessons, nobody told us we had to go through trouble and nobody said that going to jail would be a good thing. They would preach about it, but they preached about it like Paul and Silas were so special, so unique, incredible. They were in jail and they sang until they walked out. Now, once you go through the Civil Rights Movement and you're in these cells, rocking these cells with these songs, and the jailers let you go because they can't stand it no more, Paul and Silas ain't got nothing on you. And all of a sudden, you understand Paul and Silas.

Nobody told you in church that Jesus on the cross had nothing on Black folks because we've been lynched. That we had a real, immediate relationship to the cross, all the time. How come they were talking about Jesus like that was so bad? I guess it was the part about Him getting up three days later that made it different, but they should have related Jesus in the Black church to lynchings. The preacher should have said something about that. And then you really could sort of understand what Jesus was doing. And then you put some pressure on the preachers, you see, 'cause then you could be like Jesus if you wanted to, because then you'd have to threaten to get put in jail and get lynched, which is the position people in the Movement took.

The songs wrap themselves around us, all the meetings, marching, all of this dancing and all of this activity so there is no place you go where there is not a song. There was a song that went (sings)

> I know we'll meet again.
> And then you and I
> Will never say goodbye
> When we meet again.   (New words by James Bevel and Bernard
>   Lafayette)

It takes that kind of love song—and it's a song that comes out of the Parchman Penitentiary, where these people had been in jail and were parting—it is that kind of love song that makes you understand something about love songs. Makes the little love songs you hear on the radio sort of light.

Little Willie John had a song that was called "You'd Better Leave My Kitten Alone"—guess who the kitten was? A woman, right? When the Movement took the song, and this usually happened with all the secular songs—the church songs, they would maintain the same structure, so you would lift "trouble" out, put "freedom" in: "I'm on my way to Canaan," lift out "Canaan" put "freedom" in. Nothing else had to change. But with secular songs, positions had to change in order for the song to deliver the message, and I'm still working on trying to understand why that was, but this Little Willie John song, talking about leaving something alone. When the freedom people got the song, they said (sings)

> You'd better leave segregation alone
> Because they love segregation
> Like a hound dog loves a bone.   (Words by Bevel and Lafayette)

The interesting thing is Willie John is saying "Leave this thing that's mine alone." The freedom song is saying "Leave that thing alone that is poison to you." And the song is talking to *Black* people. You can't have segregation unless *we* participate.

One of the hardest jobs of organizers was addressing Black people. A lot of times people think that organizers spent their time confronting White people in the community. You did not have to go directly up against White people. You would be talking to Black people, Black people who were terrified, and just trying to get Black people to find it within themselves to consider whether they wanted to separate themselves from that system was a confrontation of all the White people in the power structure. There are these songs that do that. It's pushing, and the organizing is aggressive and it's hard and you harass people. You make it so that everybody in that community believes that if they're going to live, they have to go to jail. That going to jail is the hippest thing going. And if they arrested people today and you went into school and took your test, you just thought you would die if the arrests stopped before you got a chance to go to jail.

That is what happened with the Movement. It's not like being nice; people were coming to you and saying, "Do you want your freedom? What you doing sitting around here?" This woman talks about her son who harassed her daily about why wasn't she going with him to jail. And she says finally the cobwebs started moving from her brain.

So, when you organize, you *bother* people. You bother people so they don't even sleep. You knock on their doors to get them to register to vote, till they decide, "Well, if I don't go, this person is just going to be here the rest of my life. So, let me go so he will leave me alone, so she will leave me alone." And there is an element in the organizer that's slightly harassment.

They don't talk about that a lot. Those folks who are trying to organize on their campuses and trying to find this proper way of doing it, so that the people they're addressing don't feel anxiety. You create great anxiety in the people who need to be free and that in itself will create anxiety in the people you need to move against; but you must stir up the people you're organizing.

This song was sung more than "We Shall Overcome." Many times it went several times a night, and I think it went several times a night because it was very important to understand that you don't get a group if you don't get some individuals. I always worry about that word "we." I don't know what "we" means. When somebody tells me "we," I want to know, "Well, where are you going to be?" "We" is a way to avoid testifying your personal stance. Now, if I say where I'm going to be, you say where you're going to be, then the "we" is understood, and we will all know what's going to happen. Progressive White people in the Movement changed "I'll Overcome" to "We Shall Overcome," to correct it grammatically, also because they believed "I'll Overcome" to be an individualistic statement. "I Shall Not Be Moved" became "We Shall Not Be Moved" for the same reason because in Western culture you must name the state. But I'm glad that this did not happen with this song, because this song says if you wake up in the morning and you are alive, you ought to position yourself so somebody else who walks past you feels the intensity of your heat. (Sings)

> This little light of mine, I'm gonna let it shine
> This little light of mine, I'm gonna let it shine
> This little light of mine, I'm gonna let it shine
> Let it shine, let it shine, let it shine.
>
> Everywhere I go, Lord, I'm gonna let it shine . . .
>
> Light's gonna shine for freedom, I'm gonna let it shine. . . .
>   (Traditional)

SPARKY RUCKER: I'm from down in Tennessee. You know, music has always been a way that people have been able to express the problems that they've been having and a way to join together. Music is the glue that holds us all together, something that makes us feel not afraid anymore. Many times during the movement, we were able to sing together at the mass meetings and on the line. But it wasn't the first time we started singing these songs. Some of these songs started way back. Let's go back a couple hundred years. Let's talk about people heading north to freedom by way of the underground railroad.

One thing about these songs is they were meant to be sung together. (Sings)

> Get on board, children, children
> Get on board, little children
> Get on board, children, children
> There's room for many a more.
>
> Gospel train is coming . . .
> There's room for many a more.
>
> You know the fare is cheap . . .
> There's room for many a more.   (Adaptation of traditional song
>   by Sam Block and Willie Peacock)

You know a lot of us learned our musical trade during those times. I know a lot of my experiences came from being on the picket lines in my hometown, Knoxville, Tennessee. I spent some time down in Atlanta and over in Nashville during the freedom movement, working with groups like SCEF and SNCC and the Southern Folk Cultural Revival Project—boy, ain't that a mouthful? Some of the people would come south from the North to sing some of the songs, and some of the people from the South would sing the southern songs. Let them know you didn't have to go get Pete Seeger, you could just get old Reverend Brother Brown down in Americus, Georgia. He's the man taught me how to play this old bottleneck guitar. A lot of those songs that we sang were songs that were the old slave songs, but we had to change them around a little bit. Songs like "Paul and Silas." The old song used to say, "Keep your hands on the plow and hold on." We said, "Shucks, man, they've been trying to keep us down in the fields all this time, maybe we'd better keep our eyes on the *prize*." (Sings)

> Paul and Silas were bound in jail
> Got no money for to go their bail
> Keep your eyes on the prize and hold on.

Hollis Watkins: People talked about the threat of being killed and facing death. Every day we knew that was a reality. And one of the things that we used to help us face that in a more positive way was the songs that we would sing, because through the songs we would motivate ourselves, we would generate the spirit; through those songs we would throw off all of the weight that was holding us down, and we became more energetic, we became more vigorous.

We also used song to give the message to those that were not working with us. Many times when we gave the message, we said it verbally. And as all of you know, many times we gave the message in songs. One of the songs that we sang asked a question, "Which side are you on?" And we made some special verses and it goes like this. (Sings)

> Which side are you on, boy, which side are you on?
> Which side are you on, boy, which side are you on?

Now in Mississippi, this is what we said to the people. (Sings)

> They tell me in Mississippi, no neutral have we met.
> You'll either be a freedom fighter, or "Tom" for Ross Barnett.
> Which side are you on, boy, which side are you on?
> Which side are you on, boy, which side are you on?   (Original
>   lyrics by Florence Reese; additional lyrics by James Farmer.
>   Copyright 1946 by Stormking Music, Inc. All rights reserved.
>   Used by permission.)

Ross Barnett was the governor that vowed that it would be over his dead body that all Blacks would enter into White schools in Mississippi. Now there was a similar verse, and it was sung for folks down in southwest Georgia. There was a chief of police down in Albany, Georgia, that was beating the civil rights workers, and when we went to Albany we said this. (Sings)

> They tell me in Albany, no neutral have we met,
> You'll either be a freedom fighter, or "Tom" for Chief Pritchett.
> My Lordy, which side are you on, boy, which side are you on?
> My Lordy, which side are you on, boy, which side are you on?

I want to direct this question to you. I want to ask you which side are you on and you let me know in regard to whether you sing this song along with us or not and I'll know which side you're on. (Sings)

> Which side are you on, boy, which side are you on?
> Oh Lordy, which side are you on, boy, which side are you on?

Don't listen to Ron Reagan, don't listen to his lies,
For he will have those bombs falling all in your eyes.
My Lordy, which side are you on, boy, which side are you on?
Which side are you on, boy, which side are you on?

CHARLES SHERROD: (Sings)

A charge to keep I have
A God to glorify

and everybody would say (sings)

A charge to keep I have
A God to glorify

and again the guy would line (sings)

A never-dying soul to save

and everybody would be singin' by then (sings)

A never-dying soul to save
And fit it for the sky.   (Charles Wesley)

I speak very softly and sweetly.

PRATHIA HALL: The song that Sherrod was singing was an extremely powerful song, and in every sense, every mass meeting was a prayer meeting and every statement and every report was a testimony. So whether you called yourself religious or not, it was about the struggle of the powers of life against the powers of death, and that's religion. And when we would walk up to the churches, coming to the meetings, the people would already be there and the church would be rocking with "A Charge to Keep I Have." The last verse of that old, old, old hymn is

To serve this present age
My calling to fulfill.
Oh may it all my powers engage
To do my Master's will.

BERNARD LAFAYETTE, JR.: One of the key things you look for in any movement is whether or not people are able to develop their own songs, songs about their local conditions. When you see people develop songs about their local conditions and make up verses about what's happening to them and their experiences, then it simply means that they have internalized the movement. And once a people internalizes the movement then the movement continues to move, because they are not just simply part of the movement, the movement is a part of them.

Like in Montgomery, Alabama, the boycott was no longer just a tactic; people had gained such a sense of dignity until they could never go back on those buses and sit in the back anymore, because they would rather walk in dignity than ride in disgrace. There was no turning back once people internalized the movement. That's the difference between a protest march or demonstration and a movement. Protest marches were temporary; demonstrations are simply dramatizing a problem; a movement is designed to change the conditions and there are no timetables on movements.

MENDY SAMSTEIN: What it was all about for me personally—I realize how we all came to this movement from different experiences and different places—was that I felt, and sensed that other people felt, that when we got together there was something special. I thought as we were singing today, where do you see singing like this? And how is it that you get singing like this? And the answer that always occurs to me is that the singing is not something that has to do with the way people usually sing; that the singing is rooted in something, an experience, and also a bond. Because I think for me, personally, there were bonds, very powerful bonds that were established then, and still exist between me and people.

The extraordinary thing was that these bonds were for me personally a kind of transformation. I came from my own personal ghetto and so when I got involved in the civil rights movement, I was coming out of my own ghetto and immersing myself in humanity, because that's what it seemed like when I got in the South. I felt, yes, I'm in a black movement, I'm in a civil rights movement, but not just that I'm in a civil rights movement and not just that I'm in a certain struggle at a specific time, but I felt I was joining the human race, and this was what was so moving and continues to move me.

SNCC Women and the Stirrings of Feminism

One of the most contentious historical arguments over SNCC has been the role of women in the organization and SNCC's impact on the feminist movement. Some have argued that it was sexism in SNCC that made many (mostly white) female activists question the role of patriarchy—if SNCC challenged oppression based on race, these women began to recognize their own oppression based on sex. As evidence, these scholars cite a position paper prepared by Mary King and Casey Hayden for SNCC's Waveland conference in November of 1964, called to reconsider the organization's direction. At the time, the paper was generally derided as off the subject. Many observers and participants, however, including King and Hayden themselves, have insisted that SNCC was more progressive than the rest of society on questions of gender roles, and that it was the empowering nature of SNCC's style and structure that enabled these strong women to ask the same questions and employ the same strategies in the feminist movement that they had learned in the civil rights struggle.

MARY KING: SNCC was important. We could get to see any member of Congress that we wanted to see, any senator. We had former CIA directors flying in to meet with us. The eyes of the world, in a sense, were on us through the television media. We, being the big, big we, all of the thousands of people, the armies of unnamed people involved in the movement, had made it irrevocable for the 1964 Civil Rights Act to be passed, and the deaths of our three fellow workers had in large part focused the legislators on that point so there was no return to the status that existed before.

But we also were not sure of ourselves as an organization; we did not know exactly in which direction we were going to move. And as we pondered all of the possibilities that were open to us, the call went out from Jim and a committee in Atlanta inviting all of the staff flung across the South, from Arkansas to the Eastern Shore, to a staff meeting to take place in Waveland, Mississippi, in November 1964. And each of us was invited to prepare a position paper on anything we wanted to write about. In SNCC's radical egalitarian tradition, we could say anything we wanted to say, write about any topic, challenge the staff to anything we wanted to challenge them to. And these position papers were gathered and mimeographed in Atlanta and sent out. There were, as I recall, thirty-seven position papers as we convened for the staff retreat. These papers were not to be the central defining question on the agenda, but they were to inform the overall environment of the meeting.

Casey and I had been talking amongst ourselves for at least the two years before that. We had been reading together and studying together at night, long discussions. We had begun to talk about ourselves as women, and as the staff pondered the question of what would be our vision now and where would we go, how would we develop a structure to support the direction in which we were going, how would we determine where we were going—because process questions always underlay content in SNCC—we decided to raise some things that were bothering us about the subordinate status of women in some projects, about the reflexive use of male organizers as spokesmen, and a potpourri of other concerns. I remember talking with Ruth Howard, with Muriel Tillinghast, with Jean Wheeler Smith, with Dona Richards, with Theresa del Pozzo, with Emmie Schrader during that period. And I started to gather examples from bulletin boards and staff meetings and memos that were coming across my desk and so on. And I put together a memo and I showed it to Casey and she said, yes, she would go along with me on it, but we decided we'd better do this anonymously. I was sure that if we put our names to it, it would be greeted with nothing but a wall of laughter. And to show you how much has changed since then, when Amy Carter read a manuscript of my book *Freedom Song* [1987], she couldn't believe that part. She said, "You weren't really afraid of ridicule, were you? I mean, you had come to grips with your own death and everything; you were afraid they were going to laugh at you?" Yes. We who had come to grips with our own death, we were afraid of what our fellow SNCC staff members were going to say when they read this position paper about women.

When we finally got it distributed, we were right, basically. There were one or two people who stepped forward but they were noteworthy, they distinguished themselves in supporting it. The women I have already mentioned, of course, were supportive, but among the men there weren't too many. I remember Bob Moses and Charlie Cobb being very supportive, in particular. But very quickly people figured out who it was. And it was out. It was out there on the table and the genie never went back into the bottle.

I'm going to do something that I ordinarily would never do; I'm going to read a segment from my book *Freedom Song*, about something that happened after that paper was circulated.

SNCC always worked extremely hard. It was nothing to work twelve hours a day, seven days a week. We were exhausted half the time. I remember one night that I passed out at 3 A.M. when the telephone rang in the Freedom House in Tougaloo. I went to answer the phone and on the way back to bed, I just passed out, I fainted I was so tired. Well, we always worked hard but we also partied hard. And that night a group of us started drifting down to the pier of Waveland, and it was Stokely Carmichael and Mendy Samstein and Carol Merritt and maybe about twenty of us. And we went down to the pier and Stokely, whom we had "called Stokely Starmichael the summer before in Mississippi because of his natural celebrity," started cracking jokes.

Cracking jokes one after another, he usually made fun of himself and the people of Trinidad more than of anyone else. It was the same this night. . . . Several . . . of us were beginning to mellow after the traumatic meetings. We were soothed by the gentle Gulf winds that were still warm in November, the lapping waves, and the wine. The moon was bright enough to read by.

Stokely started one of his monologues. He led slowly and then began to warm up. One humorous slap followed another. We became more and more relaxed. We stretched out on the pier, lying with our heads on each other's abdomens. We were absorbed by the flow of his humor and our laughter. . . . Stokely got more and more carried away. He stood up, slender and muscular, jabbing to make his points, his thoughts racing. He began to gesticulate dramatically, slapping his thighs and spinning around, thrusting his arm, silhouetted against the moon like a Javanese shadow puppet. . . . He made fun of himself and then he dressed down Trinidadians. He started joking about black Mississippians. He made fun of everything that crossed his agile mind. Finally, he turned to the meetings under way and the position papers. He came to the no-longer-anonymous paper on women. Looking straight at me, he grinned broadly and shouted, "What is the position of women in SNCC?" Answering himself, he responded, "The position of women in SNCC is prone!" Stokely threw back his head and roared . . . with laughter. We all collapsed with hilarity. His ribald comment was uproarious and wild. It drew us all closer together, because, even at that moment, he was poking fun at his own attitudes. [*Freedom Song*, pp. 451–452]

Now, that is my version of an account that has been widely reported as a serious comment and was picked up by a great deal of the feminist literature that followed, and I wanted to take this opportunity to set the record straight as I remember it, as Casey and others who were there remember it, and if you ever meet him, ask him what he thinks. But that's the true story as I saw it.

I think it's important to say as well, though, that because all of this occurred in the context of a debate on SNCC's future direction and its structure, that part of what Casey and I were doing in writing that paper was not addressing the concerns of women as a gender statement, so much as it was a belief that if the movement was all that we believed it to be, if leadership was what we believed it to be, then it was appropriate for there to be opportunities to address our agenda too, or for us to raise the things that were of concern to us.

We were concerned that SNCC move in the direction of increasing democratization. I've already discussed the deep gulfs, the ravines that SNCC straddled, questions of decentralization or centralization, of a more authoritarian approach or a more democratic approach, questions of the highly charismatic leader or of leadership from the bottom. There were so many issues, so many polarities that SNCC was constantly grappling with. And in that context, in talking about women, Casey and I were arguing that SNCC should return to the earlier vision of the sit-ins, the period when one acted on one's beliefs, because of a belief that one *was* what one believed. And so in a sense what we were doing in introducing that paper on women was broadening the debate in favor of a more decentralized and democratic SNCC, one that implicitly would be able to address our concerns too, and we were also asking SNCC, will there be room for us as women to act out our beliefs as we had with the early vision of SNCC with the sit-ins.

About a year later the issue had moved along, it was no longer so sensitive. Casey and I went to Virginia and we wrote another paper; this time it was no longer secret, we signed the paper. And the foment on SNCC's structure had deepened by then, so we were, again, basically posing those same questions. We were calling for a return to the basic values of the sit-ins and the early vision of SNCC.

This paper we sent across the country to a group of forty women organizers in some of the other peace and civil rights organizations, the northern student movement, Students for a Democratic Society, others who were organizing. And we talked about a common-law caste system in the larger society. And we said that subtle attitudes forced women to work around or outside hierarchical structures of power which excluded them. We were no longer talking about SNCC, we were talking about the entire society. I've already mentioned that one of the things we got to do in SNCC was to ask questions with astounding implications, and this is what we were doing again.

We also pointed out that many men wanted to join our dialogue but that others found it hard to respond nondefensively, and we concluded that the problems between men and women functioning in society as equal human beings are among the most basic that people face. We've talked in the movement about trying to build a society which would see basic human problems, which are now seen as private troubles, as public problems and try to shape institutions to meet human needs rather than shaping people to meet the needs of those with power.

I remember years later Barbara Raskin came to see me and she said, "Oh, Mary, I'll never forget the day that your memorandum arrived in the mail. We organized a group here in Washington, a consciousness-raising group it was called later, and we studied that memo and we restudied it and we passed it around amongst ourselves and finally the thing was so dog-eared that we could no longer read it." So that memo sent to those forty women across the country was one spark, one piece of tinder, in the modern women's movement. A year later there was a first women's caucus at the SDS convention in Urbana, and when a group of women walked out of that convention, the ironic thing was that the only man who stood to support them—this was a group of women who had been studying that memo—the only man who rose to support them was Jimmy Garrett, who was the SNCC staff member who ran the Los Angeles office.

Well, the women's movement in the modern sense was clearly the successor movement to the civil rights movement and, of course, there are civil rights issues at the core. It's an error of historiography not only to fail to recognize the role played by SNCC in the civil rights movement, but also not to realize the role of the civil rights movement in building a larger concern for the rights of women in our society. And I want again to point out what was so unique about SNCC was its openness to these questions, that it could nourish Casey and me and others to ask these questions, to write these papers, to pose these things. SCLC was priestly, patriarchal; these questions could never have been raised and there were not the women in the organization to raise them.

I think the last thing that I would like to point out is the incredible synergism that occurs between movements. I agreed completely with Guyot when he pointed out that women who are now half of the delegates of the national Democratic conventions have the challenge of the Mississippi Freedom Demo-

cratic Party in 1964 to thank for it. That is absolutely historically correct. So
there is an ongoing impulse from the movement that has taken us from one
movement to another.

CASEY HAYDEN: I had to get a book to find out what "feminism" meant.
So I went and bought this book of essays called *What Is Feminism?* In the last
essay I read, the author said that feminists don't know anymore, either. So I
figured I was on the cutting edge again.

What I'm going to talk about is the roots of feminism in the redemptive community. I came to feminism raised by a single-parent mother, where I learned
what it meant to be poor and matriarchal. I came through the YWCA at the
national level, where I learned that roles of men and women were being re-
defined, and I came through a heavy Christian existentialist background and
a college education.

In April of 1960, Connie Curry and Ella Baker were the first advisors to
SNCC. Two women, one white, one black, were our first advisors. Connie got
invited to be an advisor because she paid the phone bill. Julian would bring
her the phone bill and she would pay it out of her grant money for a whole
other project. She came through Austin, Texas, and she recruited me, telling
me about the sit-ins, and we sat in this café and cried, and little did we know
I'd be sitting up here crying now. But I'll be fine.

The sit-ins happened in Austin and because I was living in the only integrated housing on campus, I got involved. And what I got involved in is what
Diane Nash described, and I want to run through that again. She said that what
we were into at that time was the redemptive community, that we were into
healing and reconciling. We were not into gaining power. We felt that what we
were doing was more efficient than violence in the struggle for liberation and
would achieve liberation for all people more rapidly. She talked about the transition from Gandhi to Lawson to us. Dr. King, of course, was part of this also.
I feel that in claiming our victories, we need to claim the great influx of Eastern thinking into this country, which is often associated with hippies and drugs.
The sit-in movement is where I first met that thinking, the path I followed. Many
people have been political; I have not been political, my path has been a spiritual path and this is where I hit it.

She talked about truth and love. She talked about everything being a series of means; it's not really ends and means, it's always means. She talked
about how the enemy is never personal, that the systems and the attitudes of
racism, sexism, and so on are the enemy. She said oppression always requires
the participation of the oppressed and the role of the oppressed is to withdraw

cooperation. Now this was not Western nor was it masculine; it was basically Eastern. It was basically, in my opinion, feminine; it had to do with where you put your weight. If you didn't have much force you had to figure out how to throw yourself around to catch the other guy off base. You couldn't confront it directly, not while you're still creating mass—which is what we did in Mississippi, we created mass. But at first, you couldn't do that, you had to do this other kind of thing.

I got onto the SNCC staff in the process of getting involved in activity based on these very radical notions of what one was going to do with one's life: transcendent, if you will. You kind of got a new self created. A lot of the old self-definitions fell away; they weren't appropriate anymore. You really stopped thinking about yourself in terms of the limitations of sex or class or race. What you were doing was being a participant with other people in the creation of something, of a movement—there's no other word for it—of a movement, based on these kinds of notions.

There we were doing this. Then we started doing it full time. We created a profession for ourselves. We actually created a profession and it had a name: "organizer." We funded it, and here we were having dropped all these notions of who we were, which were the ways society would have defined us. To be an organizer was very asexual—we were a community of organizers. Whatever you could do, you'd do it. There really weren't any limits. So there we were doing this, and we didn't have any definition then in terms of the general culture. What we had was each other, because we could see ourselves in this new way. That's how I saw the people I worked with. I saw them as my tribe, my family. We lived communally. We lived off the same money. There was no hierarchy in the distribution of that money. We all got a little bit of it.

When I first came to the SNCC conference in the fall of 1960, the three people who were doing the organizing work for that conference were women. It was Connie Curry, Ella Baker, and Jane Stembridge. Jane was another white southerner who Ella had recruited to come be executive secretary for SNCC. Ella, I think, was the main person responsible for the nonviolent ethic, the essence of what we were doing. Even though later a lot of things changed, that place we came from, to me, was always the essence. Our style was how we nurtured that. Because if you're not being seen anywhere, if there's no mirror for you, you've got to see yourself in your family or in your community and that's what we were to each other. I think that's what people mean when they talk about the style of SNCC, the way we were to each other. Every member of the family was equally valued, just like a mother would value all her children. We even had to redefine time. Time was how long it took us, for everybody, to be able to get into it. When everybody was into it, then we could go do something. Program wasn't an external hierarchical thing. We really remolded what time meant.

Leadership: I thought of it as soft essence but hard politics. Take the idea of turning up leadership. Ella had been through so much and she had seen so many sell-outs that she knew that as soon as somebody got power and authority they were going to rise up into another class. And once they were in that other class and in a certain relation to power, they would no longer be able to represent the interests of the class they came from and they'd be lost. Hey, it happens. We've seen it happen. But it was also that this was the way we had to view each other, because if we didn't view each other that way, we didn't have the sustenance to keep functioning. We couldn't go on if we didn't give everybody the space to talk and get to where we were all comfortable with what we were going to do. We couldn't ask each other to risk our lives.

That was very nurturing, that wasn't patriarchal, wasn't masculine, particularly. It was really new, very nurturing, very loving, and it really was the beloved community. My sense of what we were doing is that we were just trying to bring more and more people into it. And to me—and I was on one wing of this thing, I know I was sort of out in left field—but to me, what we did was a technique to get everybody into our community where we were living in the communal, egalitarian, sexually equal way, this new way. And what I wanted was for everybody to be in there with us, just expand the whole thing. Then we'd have a new society. I read Nadine Gordimer recently, and she says that the reformer is always practical but that the initial impetus is always utopian. I think we were utopian, and maybe for that reason we couldn't go on beyond where utopia meant something. When it got to reformist politics, maybe that's where we floundered.

The other thing about that was the sense of a clan, so that you could distrust everybody else. Particularly with the press this was very effective; it was very important not to believe the press. We created our own myth or our own image. You didn't want to believe what you saw in the news; those of us who were there will never believe what we see in the news. We know the distance between the mass media and the truth. We had to have what we had together or we couldn't have had this attitude we had toward the press, toward what we were getting fed back from the general culture.

This was all going along and we were figuring out what to do, functioning in that mode, and we did the Mississippi Summer, and then after the summer we couldn't figure out what to do. The way I think of it is there were so many things going on that we couldn't weave anymore; there were so many threads in there that it was tangled up. There was so much happening, everything was knotted up.

We all presented these papers. Now, I don't remember doing this Waveland paper. I mean, I did it, but to tell you the truth, I don't remember it. I was really nervous about its reception. That I remember. The rest of it I don't really remember. I remember it was presented and that I was involved in it. I remember thinking it was not the right issue for that time. The issue at that time was what we were going to do next. We didn't know what to do next. We'd lost the convention challenge. We had all these new people down. The Atlanta office had incredibly ponderous problems to handle caused by the expansion. The cash flow was all chaotic. The issue to me was what are we going to do, because what I'd been doing was over. I had been working on the challenge for the MFDP. I didn't know what to do next. There was a big debate about what to talk about; should we talk about what to do or should we talk about how to structure ourselves to figure out what to do? The people who wanted to talk about what to do didn't want to talk about how to structure ourselves to figure out what to do. So nobody was talking except Forman, who was saying, "We got to figure out how to structure ourselves to figure out what to do." There was hostility. And all these papers. I'm telling this so you can see that between me and Mary, you history scholars, how difficult it is to discern historical truth. Those of us who were there can't get it straight. Don't ever believe what you read in the history books. At best it's a pale approximation.

I felt sorry for Forman and I tried to talk about how we should structure ourselves. I remember I was trying to talk about how we worked in Mississippi where we didn't have a hierarchy, to explain that what we had were work groups. We would have this group that would talk about this, and then that group would talk about this, and we would do it. I had this idea that we could send people to a coordinating group to tell each other what we were doing. Roughly, that was my idea of structure. I also thought that we shouldn't get money, the money should be sent to communities. The communities should fund the organizers. That failed, and was badly spoken of later, I hear.

It was said white people should work with white people and black people should work with black people, and if we could just get that straightened out and get some of these volunteers out of here and get structured, everything would be okay. So I thought, "Well, this is the new line." Off I went to Chicago to work with my people. I got to Chicago to organize a women's welfare recipients union with Appalachian women. It was an SDS project. I was on loan from SNCC to SDS to do this experimental work with white people in the summer of 1965. The group that I went to join was organizing street kids, white street kids, and I was organizing this welfare recipients union. Little did we know what the connection was between the street kids and the welfare recipient women, many of whom were involved with the street kids. It was very complicated.

By the end of the summer, I realized that I wasn't going to commit myself to the five or ten years it was going to take to make a dent, that we didn't have a clear strategy, and that I was burnt out. So I went to the West Coast and East Coast and traveled around for a few months and ended up in Virginia with Mary. And at that point it was clear that in this knottedness, we had lost our ability to be nurturing (what I consider radically feminine), the way we had learned to be to keep each other upheld. We'd lost it. Maybe we should have broken into small groups. It was very lonely. We didn't. Nobody knew what to do, and I certainly didn't know what to do. There were a lot of rumors. So I said we should write something. Now is the time to write.

That memorandum, which I do remember writing and which I will take responsibility for, and which I reread today—and it's a very good piece of writing and I feel good about it if I do say so myself—was really directed at the notion that it was important to talk about what was important. That it was important to find our issues and talk about them with each other. The sense that we needed to do more work with the women in our community before we tried to go out and organize white women was part of that. To some extent it was strategic, but there was also a sense that it was very important—and I think this is said in the memo—if we could find our own integrity, if we could speak to each other about truth and thereby establish our integrity, we could keep *working*, and that was the issue to me. It was, how are we going to keep working? What is to be done now? What can we do now? Really that was where I was coming from, more than organizing women, or raising the issue of women. It was a technique to keep the community intact.

I know this sounds off-beat and I'm not sure many people can follow it, but the SNCC people will follow what I'm saying, and that is what matters to me.

JEAN WHEELER SMITH: I don't usually get into setting the record straight; I usually don't worry about the record, but there is this one point on which I have some strong feeling and that is the common notion that women were oppressed in SNCC. I just was not oppressed in SNCC. I wasn't subordinate, I was high functioning. I did anything I was big enough to do and I got help from everybody around me for any project that I wanted to pursue. And I know we can put shadows to it and so on, but I wanted to strongly make this point and then maybe move to the shadows.

Stokely gave me my first ticket south. I think Stokely respected me. I think his comment about women, the position of women being prone, *was* humorous; he's a funny guy, and there was a lot of sex in SNCC. We were twenty years old. What do you expect? I think Stokely respected me and respected the women he was working with at that time. I think he might have wanted to be a successful male chauvinist, but I just don't think he could have gotten away with it.

I wanted to give you some examples of how I as a woman was very much enabled to function to my highest potential. I've heard several references to the death of Goodman, Chaney, and Schwerner in Mississippi, and I remember that when they were missing and we learned that they were probably dead, we all said, "Well, we have to go to Philadelphia [Mississippi], we can't let this go by, we can't appear to be afraid." And so I guess it was ten or twelve of us decided to go and people volunteered and I was one who volunteered, and nobody ever said, "You're a girl, you can't go." There was just no thought that I couldn't go at this very stressful time into this dangerous situation because I was a woman.

As I remember it, I did everything that everybody else in the project did there. I was scared all the time, but I think they were scared too. I remember that at the end of the time that I was in Philadelphia and the convention organizing had been accomplished, a bus came through. Bob Moses was on the bus and Bob wanted to know, did I want to come up to the convention, to the challenge, and I said, "No, I think my work here is more important than going to the convention." He said, "Fine," he got back on the bus, and I stayed in Philadelphia.

I just had so much freedom to decide how I was going to work and so much support for my decisions that I never ever felt this sense of limitation that people seem to be referring to. I think if we talked about it some more, it would probably fit into Casey's notion that at least before 1965, we were such an egalitarian group that there wasn't room for the limitations imposed by structure. People had titles, but the titles didn't matter. And especially they didn't matter when you were in Mississippi by yourself and there was some sheriff coming toward you with his gun drawn. The title of you or the guy next to you just had no significance.

I want to say something about the female role models that I had in SNCC. Again, I think that the examples before me were of strong black women functioning at their potential. And I want to disagree with Mary a little bit. It seemed like you were making a distinction between people like Mrs. Hamer and Mrs. Johnson and Miss Baker and us, and if you make that distinction then that pulls them away from the group. They really were a part of the group as far as I'm concerned. It didn't matter whether you got paid or not. I mean, you were making $9.64 anyway—some people made $27, I think, if they were married. The money didn't make any difference. The title, as I remember it, didn't make any difference. So I saw Mrs. Gray, Mrs. Hamer, Miss Baker as part of the group. And they were great role models for me. I still remember Miss Baker monitoring our activity, making sure we were thinking straight, making sure that we were looking at the economic side of things, making sure that this process of arriving at consensus was one that we were carefully sticking to and that everybody was participating in the decision making. She was so powerful that actually I really wasn't even that friendly with her, but she was definitely a woman who was functioning at her highest potential.

Mrs. Johnson—I remember in particular, June, that your father stayed home and took care of the children while she went to jail. I remember very clearly, I was staying in Mrs. Johnson's house, and I had a place on the bed and June's father was on the floor sleeping to accommodate us SNCC workers, and I just can't see that that was a male-dominated chauvinist situation there. I think that throughout our relationships and our working at least until 1965, that that just wasn't the case.

And I remember Martha Norman and I were working for Sherrod in Albany and he wanted to keep us and protect us, and we didn't want to stay there; we thought that Greenwood was a much more sexy place to be, much more exciting and dramatic and powerful, so we waited for Sherrod to go to jail, and as soon as he went to jail, we left at midnight to go and work where we wanted to work in Greenwood, which was much more powerful and dramatic.

I wanted to give some other examples of powerful younger women in the group. Ruby Doris Robinson everybody had incredible respect for. Ruby was executive secretary for a while, but she seemed to run the place as far as I know. My memory is that one day I was sitting around the office in Atlanta, I think I was drinking Cokes and flirting or something, and Ruby came over to me and said, "Get up and go get your license. If you want to go"—I wanted to go to some project—"you can't expect someone's going to drive you there," so it was Ruby who made me go get a license. I remember Annie Pearl Avery, she was a gun-toting cab driver, just completely independent, and functioning in what you would consider to be a typical male role, if you wanted to call it that.

I was thinking about what could be the reason for why this difference in opinion has developed. I don't claim to know much about the women's movement, so this is speculation, but I think one reason is it's a convenient difference; that is, as the time has gone by the history keeps getting rewritten and revised to the convenience of the people who are rewriting it. Maybe also there were some differences between the way the black women in the organization experienced their situation and the way the white women experienced it. I wouldn't say for sure, but it's something to think about. Casey and I seem to have had about the same experience, but it may be that that changed in later times and that after about 1965 people didn't feel as much a part of the organization and how things were being run.

My sense was that although admittedly the administrative structure on paper was men, the women had access to whatever resources and decision making that they needed to have or wanted to have, and I don't remember being impeded in this. I think another way to understand how we could have arrived at differences of opinion about this is that people had different views about what SNCC was. My view, as I look back on it as a psychiatrist, is it was a human potential movement and that what we were doing on a very large scale, had much in common with what I do in my therapy work on a small individual scale. We were creating a trusting and loving atmosphere and a supportive atmosphere; we transmitted the expectation that change was possible, people were going to get better. We let the person lead. We let the person we were trying to organize, lead. We let him express what was important to him and then we followed. And having let him lead, we then did two things: we'd point out the contradictions; that is, you say "You want this and this, they don't go together; could you look at this another way?" And then we would offer an alternative solution to the solution the person we were trying to organize had historically operated on. That is the way that I understood what I was doing when I was there. And if you look at it that way, then the hierarchical stuff just doesn't matter that much, and I don't think it mattered at least until 1965. I wanted to be pushy about that because I may not get this chance again in another ten years or something, and I do appreciate that there are a lot of grays and shadings to this.

JOYCE LADNER: If you ever saw a group of highly individualistic people, they were in SNCC. We had staff meetings that would last for days and days and you'd think you're going to arrive at a decision after all this dialectical stuff goes on, and then someone jumps up and says, "Well, who gave you the right to decide?" and then you start all over again. Ivanhoe Donaldson, God bless him, was one of the main ones, and Stokely Starmichael, and Courtland Cox, and the Howard University crew—we used to dub them that because they had studied with Bayard Rustin in New York and they were much more ideological than we locals. I was a local Mississippi person, and had a very strong local black southern identity. So there were all kinds of clashing identities based on how people perceived themselves and their roles and the purposes for being in SNCC.

I looked through Clay Carson's book on SNCC, *In Struggle*. Clay is a historian from Stanford who has written the definitive work on SNCC, and I've got a quote from it. What he writes is that "'assumptions of male superiority are as widespread and deep rooted and every much as crippling to the woman as the assumptions of white supremacy are to the Negro.' Not only did male staff members feel 'too threatened' to face the subject but many female members were 'as unaware and insensitive as men, just as there are many Negroes who don't understand they are not free or who want to be part of white America.'" It goes on to say that "SNCC should 'force the rest of the movement to stop the discrimination and start the slow process of changing values and ideas so that all of us gradually come to understand that this is no more a man's world than it is a white world.'" [pp. 147–148]. This is quoting the SNCC position paper on women.

I'm reminded of an incident that occurred with my dear sister, Dorie. When Dorie was about twelve years old and I was about eleven (she always says I'm the older), we went to the grocery store—Hudson's Grocery in Palmer's Crossing, four miles outside Hattiesburg, Mississippi—to buy some donuts. There was a white cashier, a man named Mr. Patton who had no fingers on his right hand. Dorie paid Mr. Patton for these donuts; he gave them to her in a brown bag. As she reached for them, he reached over and touched her breasts, which were just beginning to develop. She took the bag of donuts and beat him across the head. Now, why did I tell you that story? I stood there as the little sister watching this. We went home; we ran all the way home, we literally ran, and told my mother what happened. She said, "You should have killed him."

That story has a great deal of importance because we were just two little black poor girls, eleven-, twelve-year-old girls, growing up in Mississippi where you have all these stereotypes about how everyone's oppressed, how people don't even know that they're oppressed. We *knew* we were oppressed. We always knew. We also knew, however, that we came from a long line of people, of women, who were doers, strong black women who had historically never allowed anyone to place any limitations on them. Therefore my mother could say to us, "You should have killed him," and she meant it, because she would have killed him. She would have done precisely that.

Mother never heard of Harriet Tubman, Sojourner Truth; Mother was one of eleven children; Mother went through third grade. But Mother also inherited the tradition that a Sojourner Truth or a Harriet Tubman set before her. I'm not speaking autobiographically so much as I am trying to strike a responsive chord for a generation of young black women from the South who came into SNCC. Our mothers and fathers taught us that we are "as good as anyone." Never allow anyone to call you out of your name. Never allow anyone to abuse you or to misuse you. Always defend yourself. All of our parents had guns in the home. And they weren't only for hunting rabbits and squirrels, but for self-defense. The South has always been heavily armed, as you well know.

My mother was never involved in the civil rights movement. There were a lot of inherent contradictions in my mother and all the other mothers, because she was terrified of what might happen. When we became involved in the movement she was scared the Klan would come and burn down the house, but at the same time she was the same mother who allowed Vernon Dahmer, who was murdered by the Klan, and Clyde Kennard, who was killed by white racists in Mississippi, to take us as fourteen- and fifteen-year-old girls, to Jackson, ninety-four miles away, to the NAACP state mass meetings when Roy Wilkins came to town, when Gloster Current, the director of branches, came to town, when blacks from all over Mississippi would come to these meetings.

It was illegal to be a member of the NAACP in Forrest County, in Mississippi, in Hattiesburg, but people carried their cards very proudly, and we as children in the schools used to whisper and talk rather proud and say, "We heard that Mr. Clark, our math teacher, is a member of the NAACP," and we looked rather favorably on those people. That was the tradition that I come from. It was the tradition of my mentors, including Medgar Evers, who I met in early 1956, 1957, around then, when we used to go with these adults to meetings in Jackson. Medgar Evers came to Hattiesburg in 1959. We were in the eleventh grade, and he helped us to start an NAACP youth chapter. He never turned to us and said "You two Latin girls," as we were referred to, "should let the boys serve as heads of this local youth organization." No one ever told us anything about our limitations because of our gender.

When we went to college, 1960, we used to slip off campus. We spent our first year of college at Jackson State, and it was the single most oppressive experience I ever had in my life. I've had a lot of experiences, but never anything that oppressive. But we used to slip off campus and go two blocks up the street to Medgar Evers's office to talk to him, to keep in touch with what was going on. He told us that students at Tougaloo College were going to stage a sit-in. Sit-ins had occurred all over the South, but not in Mississippi. But the NAACP did not consider it in any way wise to stage a sit-in in a public accommodations facility. What they did decide to do was to challenge another kind of institution. They had Tougaloo students sit in at the public library. We asked him if we could participate. And a very strange thing, the one reason we couldn't was that we would have been expelled from Jackson State immediately on a technicality. If you can believe this, it was that we would have had to sign out— you had to sign out every place you went—to the public library and it was illegal to go there. So we didn't, but he told us, you can be very helpful, you can go back to your campus and you can tell people quietly, without attribution as to where this is coming from, that there is going to be an event taking place. So we did. We listened to the radio all day, waiting to hear the news about these students sitting in and being arrested. To make a long story short, we helped to organize a small core of people on campus. James Meredith was one of the people. We had to organize a prayer. The demonstration that evening in front of the library turned into a major altercation with the president of the college, who went absolutely crazy and knocked my roommate down and beat a lot of other people up. We marched downtown the next day and that became a protest against the school itself, and they told us not to come back. Tougaloo was the first time I really experienced true freedom.

Also in the spring of 1961, Medgar told us that there was a young man in his office and he said, "I'd like to introduce you to someone." You never asked questions back then; we were quiet. He said, "I want you to meet Tom Gaither, he's come here to help Negroes get their freedom." That's all he ever told us. As it turned out, Tom was the first organizer, he was a CORE field secretary who would come in to lay the groundwork for the Freedom Rides. I didn't know that. I never asked about it; I mean, what kind of freedom is he going to help us get?

It was soon after the Freedom Rides, in the early fall, that I began to meet some of the young women and men who were my kind of people. I began to meet people like Diane Nash, later Ruby Doris, and all the other people. And the most important thing was I began to meet local Mississippi people who had grown up feeling as stifled as I, who had grown up feeling that they had ideas they wanted to express and that they couldn't. To have things they wanted to do with their lives and to feel totally constrained is a horrible feeling. When I began to meet other people throughout the state who felt that, who were brought up the same way, it was like I'd died and gone to heaven, to meet people like Susan Ruffin who had lived on like $27—and Mrs. Hamer and all these other people, and to meet Guyot out at Tougaloo, was just an extraordinary experience.

None of these women I began to meet knew they were oppressed because of their gender; no one had ever told them that. They were like my mother, and they'd been reared in the tradition of my mother and my mother's five sisters. They had grown up in a culture where they had had the opportunity to use all of their skills and all of their talents to fight racial and class oppression, more racial than anything else. They took their sexuality for granted, for it was not as problematic to them as their race and their poverty. And perhaps they didn't know they were oppressed because of their gender, they were so busy trying to survive and to fight day to day. It would have been a luxury for my mother to focus on gender concerns. It would never have occurred to her; neither would it have occurred to me at that time because it was not a problem, it was never problematic.

We assumed we were equal. When we got into SNCC I would have been ready to fight some guy if he said, "You can't do this because you're a woman." I would have said, "What the hell are you talking about?" A lot of the women in SNCC were very, very tough and independent minded. In fact, the most independent-minded people you'll ever meet were in SNCC, men and women. They would argue with a signpost. If you were weak and didn't have really strong and firm beliefs about whatever it is you thought you believed in, you didn't survive. You couldn't survive. It was one of the most hostile cultures in which you were trying to operate, the external culture. You were trying to operate against a perceived common foe and that common foe was what kept us so tightly knit together, as Casey has so eloquently put it. Our enemy was always an external one. It was not internal, at least not through those early years, and I think we do have to make a division between pre-1964 and post-1964. There were very, very different kinds of ideas and ideologies and values and so on that operated then.

But for many of us, I think, SNCC gave us the first structured opportunity to use our skills in an egalitarian way without any kind of subjugation because of our race or our class or our gender. And also it's very, very important that we not be guilty here, or ever, of using retrospective analysis and imposing current feminist theory onto the realities of 1963. I think that's a critical fact. I read feminist theory, I teach it, some parts of it, I'm conversant with it, but we can't take those models and impose them onto a different historical era, a different time, a different place. The models that people have described here came out of the context of the times.

Sure there were no women who ever chaired SNCC, but I bet you ten to one Ruby Doris dominated SNCC. We'd have a little joke, is it Jim running SNCC or Ruby Doris? I mean, what was a chairman? Who cared? Nobody really even cared. People at SNCC were so antiauthoritarian that if they thought you were going to begin to emerge, they'd bring you back down, grab you and snatch you down. Some of the biggest jokes were made about Stokely, Stokely Starmichael, who does he think he is? But those same people, we still embrace him and love him very much. It was not a hostile, nasty comment at all, but it was just that we were very, very antiauthoritarian.

The point I'm trying to make is the context of time is very, very critical. And that for many of us, SNCC gave us the first structured opportunity to really use our potential, to use our abilities, and to express our views on the world, the state of the world. We assumed we were equal. We were treated that way.

Most people who came into SNCC were more independent-minded than most people in the rest of the country; most people on the outside. The fainthearted didn't last.

Our relationships were defined, like I said, first and foremost by the task at hand. Matters of life and death were abundant, especially in some of the tough times in Mississippi. I can remember February 1963, when Jimmy Travis got shot in Greenwood. I can remember any number of terrible events when you didn't focus on what we would have considered ridiculous concerns, but you focused rather on things at hand. I think to a great extent that is why we came here now and sang. It evoked certainly within me some of the same feelings, the texture of the same feelings I remember having felt thirty years ago. Those things fortified us against all of these other concerns out there; it fortified us against a hostile racist society. That was our common foe.

And it was within SNCC that this beloved community operated for a while, and it was within that context that I thought I was equal. I thought I was a full participant. Because all of us came with a stronger sense of our own identity, a stronger sense of purpose, I believe. Most of us did. It's not to suggest that everyone was tough and strong and so on. Some people really weren't, and we have a lot of casualties who aren't here today, and I think about that a lot. We discussed that, and but for the grace of God, any one of us could have been a casualty. It was a very tough time to be a young person growing up, but I think we were emboldened by those experiences.

It was not until a decade after leaving SNCC that I began to read some of the works on the movement, maybe even a little longer than a decade. Sara Evans's *Personal Politics* [1979] was totally rubbish. I mean, it's revisionist to the core. She didn't even interview the right people, the people she should have talked to who could have told her what really happened. Michelle Wallace, I would put at an even lower scale when she talks about *Black Macho and The Myth of the Superwoman* [1979]—I've waited for this chance for about ten years. And given the cheers I guess I speak on behalf of my sisters out there. At SNCC you never know. When I walked down here they all said, "Who gave you the right to speak?" But again, I think it is a real danger, people revising or trying to understand what happened without really taking the time and the effort to understand, to get the story right.

A final point I'll make here is that SNCC challenged authority of all kinds. It's not coincidental that people like Victoria Gray (who is my cousin) talked about having challenged authority as a child. I think all of us did. And what we used in SNCC were kind of shock trooper tactics. What I think that the analysts, the scholars, have gotten wrong, and other popular writers have gotten wrong, is that they say that feminism emerged because of dissension within the ranks. Rather, feminism is an outgrowth; it emerged because SNCC served as a model, a prototype of what could become a better kind of society. It gave rise to not only a feminist consciousness but other groups like gay people, the elderly, students, a whole range of people within the society who had also been oppressed. They began to use the SNCC model to pattern their own movements.

It was not dissension within the ranks. It's true a lot of people perceived themselves as having different kinds of experiences and different interests. It was normal, natural, it was to be expected. But I don't think that we were oppressed women who got angry because Stokely—and this is putting it overly simplistically, of course—because Stokely said that our position was prone. I would have said, "Stokely, what the hell do you mean? What are you talking about?" And he would have laughed and we would have just teased him and moved on. For a movement to use that as a rallying cry is very unfortunate; it's more pathetic than ridiculous. And again, the context was missing, the texture of the times was missing; it's missing so often by people today.

I can remember the men driving, and them pushing us to the floor when danger approached. I didn't want to sit in the front. For black people, black southern people, especially, we understood that as a kind of protectiveness, like a brother would protect. But someone else, if you were coming from the North, if you were white, if you had a different set of experiences, you might have perceived that to have been discrimination or whatever. Maybe you would have wanted to drive.

I wanted to make one last brief point. I've been thinking about organizing tactics that SNCC people would have used that would help us to begin to organize low-income black people. What kind of organizing would work, how could we stop kids from killing each other at twelve years old? I'm not content to sit here and talk about what *was*. I think the important thing is to address whether all these wonderful things we've just said about our glorious past, admittedly, the most important period of my life, whether we can extrapolate something from that period that could work today when we see black people and poor people of all races have sunk to new depths. How can we restore some of this, if not the beloved community, certainly some very basic commonsense organizing? How can we infuse the current generation of young people, young activists, with a sense of purpose and with some of our hope that we still maintain after two decades, to go out and to challenge some of the thorniest problems this society has ever faced?

P RATHIA HALL: I resonate with everything that was said, especially the outrage at the notion that any of us could have been oppressed because of gender in SNCC. Also, that kind of protectiveness, well, Sherrod tried it in southwest Georgia, a loving kind of protection, and it didn't work because the other thing is that when everybody was wounded, then whoever could get up first was the one who had to get up first and move, and that was just a reality.

However, something *did* happen in our community after 1965, something *did* happen as we moved to Black Power and as we moved to black nationalism and as the Black Muslims became very prominent in terms of their attitude toward women. I think that historically there's some kind of cycle here which I don't really understand yet, but I'm trying to, because things have happened generationally to us as black women in terms of where we stood with black men. After that, there was a sense of the whole matriarchy thing, and wanting our family to look like what we were told white families looked like, and so many younger black women at that point became very defensive about their strengths. And we have gone through a period of black women being extremely repressed, at least, in terms of ambivalence about strength, assuming a responsibility for the violation of black men.

And since work in the church where there is extraordinary baggage that is still alive, and operating against our being who we were in SNCC. So it is hard now for many male leaders. You're right, I am a strong black woman, and I could not have been that in SCLC, I've always known that. But there is a need, I think, for us to understand some of those dynamics in terms of some of the changes that we went through. Some of it is still a poison in the community. There's a whole lot of stuff going on between young brothers and young sisters—"you gonna be my woman, you gonna do what I say"—there's a sense of this, for instance, in the church, that in order to reclaim black men somehow black women have to step aside. In so doing, we assist our enemies in our oppression; we participate in the further dividing of us so that in what is referred to as the underclass, we have a hell over here in which black males exist, and a hell over there in which black women and children exist. Separate from each other: unable to inspire, to embrace, to strengthen, to renew, to support each other in the ways that we experienced in SNCC.

And there has been a movement to deny what the reality was that we so passionately affirm right now. I'm scared that what we experienced could be lost, in the naming and the blaming and the scapegoating, and I just know that black men and black women cannot stand that. We cannot survive it. So there's a need for us to move beyond this. Nobody could have pulled us down if they wanted to, but there were other ways in which subtly we were impacted. I see it happening among young brothers and sisters now, and if we don't name it, we won't be able to deal with it.

K<small>ATHIE</small> S<small>ARACHILD</small>: I had a different kind of experience. I was a volunteer in the summer of 1964, and I went back in the spring from March through June of 1965. I don't know if Mary remembers it, but I was recruited by her and Emmie Schrader to go back in March to work on the filmstrip project that they were organizing. I met them both on a New York street corner in late February and they talked me into quitting my job and going back down. And I subsequently became very involved in the early stages of the launching of the independent women's liberation movement. I had something to contribute later from what I learned as a volunteer; in that I agree. I agree very much that it was basically the positive experiences of SNCC rather than the problems of male chauvinism that were really the most significant in the stirring of the women's liberation movement and the mobilizing of it in this country.

Even though I did experience sexism as far back as 1964, in my case I was already aware or conscious of male chauvinism as a political problem. I had come from an Old Left family and people talked about male chauvinism and gossiped about who was a male chauvinist, and I had learned that there was discrimination against women in the society. So that running into it in SNCC was nothing really new or special about SNCC. It was rampant in the Old Left and the New Left. What was new in SNCC were these positive things. I'll get to that.

Anyway, in 1964 when I was down there in the summer, many of the classic things had happened. It's not just a question of being protected, although that was an issue that arose in the project I was working on. There were a lot of people registering to vote in Batesville, Mississippi; it was the only town in the state where there was a court injunction, and therefore you didn't have to read, cite, or write about the Mississippi constitution to register. Of course it was a risk: your name got put in the paper, you got fired from your job. But at least you could actually get registered if you were willing to take the risk. So there were all kinds of legal things that had to be done. You had to post a notice on the courthouse bulletin board, and there was a big discussion in the project about who should post the notice. There were both black women and white women in the project and black men and white men and all the men immediately decided that it should be a man who should go down and post the notice, whereas my first instinct had been it ought to be a woman because she would be less noticed. We just didn't take it, of course, we fought back. But we had to have a struggle over it and I think we actually won that struggle—through logic. That kind of thing was just interesting; it had been so illogical.

But there was the constant problem of sharing the housework and, once again, maybe it was because I expected men to share the housework and a lot of other people didn't. I expected especially radical men to, even though I knew it was hard to get them to do it. Still we would fight about the housework. I think Stokely Carmichael plays all kinds of roles in history about this too, because he was quite good on the basic issues, as I recall, like sharing the housework. In my project, I remember one time we had been struggling for a whole month to get the men to do the housework, and Stokely drove in as a roving organizer—helping all the projects—with his entourage. We were all sitting around in this farmhouse and he just gets up at the end of the meal and says, "Well, let's do the dishes," and proceeds to do them. So on the real nitty-gritty issues like housework he, in my experience, was good.

The other part that he played here, I think, was this line to the white people in SNCC that probably many people had, but I remember it mostly connected with him: it's time to fight your own oppressors. I remember he used that phrase; many other people did too. And even then I was thinking, "Fight your own oppressors," what would that mean? I knew there was a class problem, but I must say I began thinking about it in connection with women's liberation when I came back down in March. I almost thought it was my duty as a white organizer to start thinking about it. But I didn't think about women's liberation as a possible movement until I came back down in March. And I arrived back in Batesville, and another volunteer who had stayed all winter, Chris Williams, who later married Penny Patch, a SNCC staff person from way back, he came running up to me because he had been one of the few men on the project the summer before who had done the dishes and the housework. He came running up to me and he said, "Oh Kathie, you'll be so excited to know that there's something going on called 'women's liberation.'" And he mentioned something about how there had been a sit-in in the SNCC office and that Mary King and Casey Hayden had written a paper and Ruby Doris Robinson had read it to a workshop at the Waveland staff meeting.

Mary asks in her book where did this myth arise that Ruby Doris Robinson had written or read their paper. I don't know how it came about, maybe other people were trying to pin feminism on Ruby Doris Robinson, I don't know, but back then there was already a legend as early as 1965 in Batesville, Mississippi, that Ruby Doris Robinson had read this paper.

And somehow that was the connection—that a movement was starting on this issue, a movement like SNCC, like civil rights. I had always known the issue, but the positive thing of a movement on the issue, and a possibility of a grass-roots movement, such as had been spreading through the South but in this case of women, the white women who we were supposed to go organize—anyway, the point was this possibility of a *movement* on an issue that I don't think any of us had conceived of then. That it was possible to have a movement about it even though it was an old issue. And a movement like SNCC was what was so important and was another part of what was so important about SNCC.

JEAN WHEELER SMITH: It seems to me that your comments were just what you said you weren't going to do; that is, you said you thought that the more important thing was the positive modeling that the movement provided for, for women or for the development of the women's movement or other movements, and then you focused on the opposite. And I'm pointing it out because I think that's what happens when people write their histories.

KATHIE SARACHILD: Well, no, my point is that you can't leave that out, you need both, they're both true.

JEAN WHEELER SMITH: Yes, ma'am, I'm just saying I think you did what people do.

MARY KING: I would like to say something about that too. I think this is the same issue that I addressed myself to earlier, that what happens afterward is that all these people who see themselves as authorities write books or produce television programs which millions of people see and read and talk about, which then say X, Y and Z happened. And I think it's just like the rest of what happens in America where you can just barely, barely believe that there's a truth, a seed of truth in anything you see on television or appears in the media. Sure, you couldn't help noticing certain things that were happening if you were a man or a woman, and noticing certain patterns. But they were just what they were, patterns. They were like Jean says, gray areas. So you talked about it somewhat, then somebody else writes four books about it and says well it was this, that, and the other thing and completely distorts the reality and the emphasis. Just like the movement has been distorted in its reality and its emphasis and I think the same thing has happened here.

I think you have to learn to really read this stuff or listen to this stuff with only a very little bit of belief because most of it, just like most of the history of mankind on this planet, has been totally distorted by a group of so-called scholars.

MICHAEL THELWELL: With great trepidation, I speak. I just want to make two points. One is if one remembers the history of the organization and the founding president who gave form and spirit to it, it is Miss Ella Baker.

Miss Ella Baker had struggled with chauvinism all her life and particularly in SCLC, and she mourned it. And you know she wasn't going to create no organization that would recapitulate that.

And number two, it's with extraordinary pleasure and pride that I listened to my sisters in the movement. The only people who can say whether my perceptions of what that organization represented are right are my sisters, and I was very pleased and agreed with what they said. But the fact is, you don't have to take my word. I'll tell you what, you can solve it with just a simple application of intelligence. We were a very self-selecting organization. My recollection of the organization is that they were heroes, the women and the men. I'm a very irreverent person, I don't respect many people, but I had incredible respect for all those young people in that organization who were taking those kinds of risks and coming through. And the quality of support that they described is absolutely accurate in my recollection. But I ask you this simple question: no matter how brave and tough and firm the men in SNCC were, and I think they had to have been just to survive, but here you have Joyce Ladner and Mary King and Sister Jean, and this little fast one here, Prathia Hall—look at those women and tell me which man will oppress them.

CASEY HAYDEN: I just wanted to make two short comments. One is I worked for Ella Baker, she was my boss, in the Y job I had. Mary worked for her too, and I think a lot of the thinking that we did together really was inspired by her. And about cleaning and the issue of housework; as far as I remember, no one cleaned the Freedom Houses.

BERNICE JOHNSON REAGON: The Civil Rights Movement was the borning struggle for this time, and there's no progressive organizing that has come out of this society since that is not based on it, and that includes the women's movement. One always has the choice of looking for the strands of continuity and seeing that things have continued to move from one group to the other as they try to grapple with restructuring their space in society. Let us say that some aspect of the women's movement was generated in SNCC. The implication is still that it was not generated *by* SNCC, that there were these people who were in SNCC who created something that was not SNCC. The document in question critiquing the status of women within SNCC was authored by White members of the organization. That document moved through society as an aberration without any acknowledgment that this document is a SNCC document. SNCC, in fact, was an organization where you could say what you thought, if you found the courage.

I have a feeling that there was something racist working, that needed that statement, of women critiquing their experience in their organization, to not be a SNCC-generated memo or a SNCC-generated thrust. If it is a group, on retreat, that meets for four days inviting and hearing every possible proposal under the sun, then everything that comes up belongs to that gathering. And as far as I am concerned there isn't anything that's happened to Mary King or Casey Hayden that was not created in SNCC in terms of their being able to do whatever it was they did. I didn't do what they did, but SNCC is the place that gave me the opportunity to do what I did. We really have to watch racism, because if the group is integrated and an energy is created by some White people in the group, often when it is transmitted to the larger culture, and other people start to read into it, they will separate it out as if it was not created by the structure that made it possible for it to occur. And you can just look at the struggle in the women's movement around how White it is. I mean people really try to make stuff White, even if it ain't.

Black Power

The slogan "Black Power," first employed at a rally in 1966, was not so much a nationalist statement as an argument for empowerment. Nevertheless, in the racialized, often violent, always repressive society in which SNCC worked, the two goals became intertwined. In 1966 differences came to a head between those who continued to advocate the (by now) traditional strategies of interracialism and nonviolent civil disobedience and those who, given their experiences, considered liberalism a farce and white liberal supporters a hindrance to black self-determination. At that time the more militant and separatist faction took control of SNCC, and Stokely Carmichael was elected chairman. By then there were few whites left to alienate: antiwar and student protests and the feminist movement had siphoned off many; others had become increasingly uncomfortable with the separatism of some Black Power advocates, or had agreed with them enough to leave the organization of their own accord. Their more moderate white allies, similarly suspicious of both Black Power and SNCC's antiwar stance, had already pulled away. Nevertheless, the formal vote to become an explicitly all-black organization, taken at a meeting at the estate of entertainer "Peg Leg" Bates, is often cited as the beginning of the end for SNCC. Soon after, SNCC's organizing efforts dwindled. Factional fighting and FBI harassment (through a program the FBI named COINTELPRO) dominated the remainder of SNCC's short life.

MICHAEL THELWELL: I'll begin by focusing on what is clearly the most traumatic moment in the history of this organization, the moment of the "expulsion" of whites. I was not at that meeting. But I will say that I didn't think that that particular event needed to happen in the way it did, and I'll tell you why. It is not that it wasn't absolutely necessary historically and politically for SNCC to move into a very firm and clear nationalist posture. But if you listen carefully to the discussion thus far, you will see that we were that. We were nurtured by, informed by, and our programs reflected, whether we knew it or not, the culture and experience of black people in this country. It was a movement toward autonomy; it was a nationalist movement. It was a nationalist movement of black and white people. It was a black organization; that was the source of its militancy and its uncompromising nature. That was why it stuck so badly in the craw of the white establishment. And we had an earlier model and example that might have governed our decisions, and that was the question of red-baiting and McCarthyism. The organization took the position, a principled position, that we're not going to refuse to work with anybody or expel anybody for reasons of ideological conviction or past membership in any political group. Anybody can work with SNCC who respects and accepts the principles, the discipline, and the program of the organization. So it really doesn't matter if you're a Maoist, a Marxist, or a fundamentalist Christian; if you're in SNCC, you work in accordance with SNCC's policies and principles. And on that basis, I think it was possible theoretically for the organization to define itself in a firm, aggressive, militant, nationalist posture and say anybody who is in the organization will accept and work in that discipline.

. But there were forces and events and a context at work which made it not possible. But even as that vote was taken, I know that if many of the older staff who had soldiered through the struggles with Mendy Samstein, with Casey Hayden, with Bob and Dottie Zellner had been present at that meeting, the vote would have been different. In support of what I say, anybody who knows the organization knows that it wasn't an organization of people who lacked conviction, and the vote, I was told, was something like nineteen for expulsion, eighteen against, and twenty-four abstentions. There were never abstentions in SNCC. People supported stuff. So it was a traumatic decision. What were the elements of that?

All during the time I worked in SNCC, I never had the pleasure of organizing in the black community in the South; I organized, as it were, in the corridors of power. And what I ended up organizing was white folk—going to the AFL-CIO, going to this liberal organization, that liberal organization, going to the halls of Congress. What I was doing fundamentally was asking white people, out of the goodness of their hearts and their moral consciences, to support the black movement. Our allies, if that's the right word, were allies purely out of convenience. We brought very little power to the equation. We had no cards to play, so ultimately the movement for the liberation of black people had to go about its business in the absurd way of asking for support from people who could give it or not as their consciences or their convenience dictated it. It was clear that what we needed to do was to develop a base and a strength and a confidence and an organization and a cohesiveness in the black community so that we could enter into those discourses.

But it became very clear, once we had exhausted the agenda in the black South, once we had developed a movement built on the traditions and the co-hesiveness and the force and power of black culture and morality and its real history in the South, and had knocked on the doors of Jim Crow, that we had to come north. That the movement had now to set itself about the unfinished agenda of the black community. And the North is a different question, as Martin Luther King would discover in Chicago, than the black South. And at that time when we declared Black Power, I, alongside my comrade and brother and friend Stokely Carmichael, wrote a piece in 1966, from which I quote.

> The revolution in agricultural technology in the South is displacing the ru-ral Negro community into northern urban areas. Both Washington, D.C., and Newark, New Jersey, have Negro majorities. One-third of Philadelphia's popu-lation of 2 million people is black. "Inner city" in most major urban areas is already predominantly Negro, and, with the white rush to suburbia, Negroes will in the next three decades control the hearts of our great cities. These areas can become either concentration camps with a bitter and volatile popu-lation whose only power is the power to destroy, or organized and powerful communities able to make constructive contributions to the total society. Without the power to control their lives and their communities, without ef-fective political institutions through which to relate to the total society, these communities will exist in a constant state of insurrection. This is a choice that the country will have to make. ["Toward Black Liberation," reprinted in *Duties, Pleasures, and Conflicts,* p. 118.]

Well, Oral Roberts is not the only person who can prophesy. That was writ-ten in 1966, and you see the state of all urban centers today. What Black Power posited and projected, what I hoped for most profoundly, was that we would be able to move into these centers using many of the techniques that we had developed in the South and try to build some cohesion, some unity, some com-munity power and discipline so that those centers, which are very vital to this country and to the black community, could become positive entities. That that didn't happen is due to a number of factors which I do not have the time to go into. But it still remains the most pressing agenda for this nation and the most pressing agenda item for the black community. That is the area in which we are going to need to struggle, to fight, and to prevail not only for the future of the country but most precisely and most particularly for the future of the race. And that is the arena in which everything we have called on in regard to Black Power: cultural consciousness, self-pride, self-help, initiatives to enable us to empower and define our own lives, must move now and that, unfortunately, is the inheritance that we have to pass to the next generation of young black people.

CLEVELAND SELLERS: I think that I need to set Black Power into context. The reason for that is that Black Power has meant many things to many people. The other thing is that in the context of the civil rights movement in 1965–66, the repression and external forces working against SNCC were so massive that much of the information that was coming out of the organization was distorted. Subsequently many of those who reported on what was going on inside of the organization have a distorted point of view in terms of what was actually going on.

Let me begin by setting the tone. In 1965, America escalated the war in Vietnam with the bombing of North Vietnam. With that there began to come together the issue of Vietnam, the issue of fighting for democracy in Southeast Asia when, in fact, the right to vote in places like Mississippi and South Carolina, where I'm from, was not secured. It raised a major contradiction. As a matter of fact, if you follow the Vietnam scenario, what we find is that in 1966, after the murder of Sammy Younge, who was a SNCC worker in Tuskegee, Alabama, SNCC issued an anti-Vietnam statement and set the pace by which many of us, including myself, refused induction into the U.S. armed services. That was not a popular decision in this country. So that's one set of dynamics that we have to hold on to; it all comes together.

The next thing we look at is the urban areas. In 1964 you have urban rebellions in Harlem. In 1965 you have the Watts rebellion. The urban ghettos are thriving in terms of having a lot of agitation, a lot of energy that many of us are concerned may be misdirected and need some focus.

The third thing that we have to look at is after the Mississippi Freedom Summer of 1964, there was a delegation from SNCC that had an opportunity to travel to Africa, to Guinea and to Ghana, and through that trip began to see independent African nations and people running institutions and organizations that were never even heard of in America. But there was something else that was attached to that: that delegation, including Miss Fannie Lou Hamer and John Lewis, had an opportunity to come in contact with the person that many of us might have had an aversion to, and that was Malcolm X. So you begin to see the span in terms of our starting out with one man, one vote. We're beginning to expand our horizon, beginning to talk about the similarities between the struggle for independence in Africa and the struggle for the right to vote in Mississippi.

Then we look at the summer of 1964 and we examine the fact that the failed challenge to the national Democratic Party left in many of us a level of frustration and torment over the fact that we had presented the most persuasive argument of any group that I know of during that time of the plight of poor blacks in Mississippi to enter into the political process. Even with the documentation on the murders, bombings, the car of the three civil rights workers that was burned, and the bell from the church that was burned which got Schwerner, Goodman, and Chaney involved in Philadelphia on that particular occasion, we were rejected. Our moral concern and legitimacy and issues were turned down because of practical political considerations. So at that point in an organization like SNCC we are observing all these things that are happening around us. We're very conscious, we're very observant.

The other item that we have to look at is what happens inside the Student Nonviolent Coordinating Committee after the summer of 1964. Up to 1964, SNCC was primarily a small organization. The summer of 1964 there was a large influx of new people. There was a large influx of monies, the organization began to expand, we even operated a sojourner motor fleet with thirty automobiles. The dynamics of the organization began to change. And many of us have difficulties understanding that particular dynamic. But that dynamic affected how we saw things and how we began to move after that point. There was never at any particular time a consistent ideology in the organization; there were always competing ideologies inside the organization. There were always struggles around philosophy, around direction, around tactics, around strategy, continuously. It was a growth process. We're talking about a legitimate social movement that was legitimately concerned about bringing about social change.

At the end of 1964 with the change in the organization, we began to discover certain things inside of the organization. One was the question of the lack of an internal educational process so that we could keep our people informed and abreast of what was going on. There was also a certain fatigue. I don't know if you can imagine being in Mississippi for twelve months under constant, constant fear, oppression, not knowing whether or not you were going to live tomorrow, having to fend for yourself and fend off everything, not only the physical but the psychological and social. These things come together and what we do is we continue, we transcend the fear, we continue to try to have the discussions, the organization expands and we search and seek direction. And in that seeking direction, we do several things. One is that we know we have a legitimate target area while organizing, and that's in the South. We also know that with the rejection by the Democratic Party of our effort to create Freedom Democratic parties, that we had to talk about independent political organizing. So we moved to Alabama. And when we go into Alabama, our effort was to set up an independent political organization made up of people who we worked with in our organizing efforts in Mississippi and Alabama and Georgia and everywhere else, and that group was low-income peasant blacks. That's the reality.

Out of that we began to develop what we saw as a model, whereby we could begin to have an impact not only in Alabama but in other areas where you might be able to put together an independent political organization. When we began the process in Alabama, the press came in, saw the black panther, immediately went out and talked about the Black Panther Party and how anything all black was, in fact, negative. Anything that was not positive in terms of the Democratic Party was no good. That kind of propaganda was being disseminated all over the country. We made the effort to continue that process of creating independent political structures and what we needed was a springboard, because we didn't want to just talk about the political concept of black independent party building and organization but we wanted to talk about a development of a black consciousness. We wanted to talk about using that model in other places to begin to empower black people. That's where the whole empowerment concept comes from. No longer were we just seeking the moral transformation of America; we had began to change, to talk about the empowerment of black people.

Now, all this comes prior to the actual articulation of Black Power. Then, if we look at it in the political context, we begin to understand the political nature of Black Power. There is some concern about how Black Power was projected by the press and how people received it. Once we began to do the organizing in Alabama, we had to do something inside of SNCC too, and that was, unfortunately, we had to go and find out what SNCC actually had in terms of assets, resources, and we had to look around and make some kind of analysis. Stokely and I disagreed vigorously on this issue because he said that I had become a bureaucrat because we had thirty cars and I wanted to know where they were, and he was of the impression that everybody would take good care of them. We had that kind of conflict. But we did have to make that kind of assessment. The organization, or the nature of the organization, had changed.

So as we were going around to the different projects trying to determine what was going on in those projects, trying to make people aware of what was taking place in Alabama in terms of the independent political organizing, is the point where Meredith is shot, in June of 1966. Meredith is shot walking down the highway in Mississippi; Meredith was marching against fear in Mississippi. No better place for us to then use that as a leaping-off point to introduce Black Power. We had talked about "Freedom Now," we had talked about anti-Vietnam, we had had different issues along the way. So when we talked about Black Power it was in a political context of building political institutions and social institutions in the black community, where we worked.

I had no idea, and I'm being honest, that Black Power was going to take off the way it did. The only other incident that I can think of that took off like Black Power was the emergence of Malcolm X. And so I was thinking that how Black Power was picked up and rushed out across America was, in fact, an effort to make it negative and create the climate whereby it became easier for forces who were becoming threatened by SNCC's talking about empowerment of poor people and black people across the South to check those efforts, and that began to happen. That's when COINTELPRO becomes alive and alert.

Let me do a personal analysis of COINTELPRO. In February of 1968, while organizing in South Carolina, I was among students on the campus of South Carolina State College when forty-seven students were shot, three were killed— the "Orangeburg massacre." I was shot and imprisoned as a result of being involved in that incident. When I was taken to the state penitentiary in South Carolina, after I was arrested, I was placed on death row and remained there for three weeks while bond was set. After I got out of jail in 1968, shortly after that, I was brought to trial for refusing induction in Atlanta, Georgia. Shortly after I was found guilty, Martin Luther King was assassinated. I was called back after the assassination of Martin Luther King and ended up being denied a bond. I went to the Atlanta City Penitentiary; Fulton County Jail, Newman, Georgia; Rome, Georgia; Tallahassee Federal Penitentiary; Atlanta Federal Penitentiary; Lexington; Louisville; Nashville; and ended up in Terre Haute, Indiana. I stayed out of communication for the period of the entire summer of 1968 and was eventually granted a bond by Justice Hugo Black. Came back to Atlanta, Georgia, by way of Nashville, Louisville, and Lexington, Kentucky. Was arraigned, a bond was set, and as I was being unshackled, I turned around and was rearrested by the sheriff in Louisiana. Now, this is all happening in a period of a year, and that's not theoretical, that's what happened.

If you look at SNCC, these kinds of incidents were going on with people inside of SNCC the whole way. I was drafted out of turn because of my partici-pation in SNCC, and I was given the maximum sentence because I was in SNCC. The case was subsequently overturned. In the Orangeburg massacre one of the persons who was killed had my same resemblance and build. So the assumption is that I was a target. I was later tried for that. At first the charges were assault and intent to kill a police officer, breaking and entering. It was five charges. I was facing eighty-three years in the penitentiary. When I got to court there was absolutely no evidence. I was charged with being involved in a riot. The statute of the state of South Carolina says that in order for you to be charged with rioting, two people have to be involved. There was no other person involved. I was sentenced to a year in the penitentiary in South Carolina and did do that time in 1973.

So many of us were not outside of that; we were involved. And I think that might help put some perspective on what was happening. There was a conscious effort to undermine and destroy the black movement. I have been able to see a letter that was developed by the FBI to create an element of distrust between Stokely and Rap Brown. There was a conscientious effort on the part of the FBI to silence all black leaders. And I say that because I don't want to differentiate, it went all the way down to SCLC and all the way through RAM, the Revolutionary Action Movement.

So, back to Black Power. The other notion that I want to put forth is that after 1965, the Civil Rights Act of 1964 had already been passed, which dealt with public accommodations. The Voting Rights Act had already been passed, which dealt with voting, and so we were moving on, beyond that. We were grasping for where do we go and how do we assure that we bring about the kind of change that would in fact affect the destiny of those people who we were trying to organize.

One other point that I want to make, and I differ with my friend and colleague Brother Thelwell, is when the whole idea of Black Power emerged, it did not emerge around the idea of putting anybody out of anything. That's a process. And as SNCC grew, SNCC dealt with issues as best it could as an organization. That was not the thinking when we were talking about Black Power. Our concern was to get the organization moving again, to begin to establish programs and begin to have the same kind of impact on the communities that we were involved in as we had prior to that particular time.

The other thing I'd like to say is that in terms of the influences inside of the organization, we began to shift away from the mood and thought and existentialist thinking and we began to move toward Frantz Fanon and Malcolm X in terms of our thinking, our orientation. And I'm talking about a transition and people have to understand this transition. Because the way I read Black Power now is all of a sudden everybody got mad with all the white folk, put 'em out, and that constitutes Black Power. It's really important for us to put it in a political context.

The other thing is the question of tying in the urban areas to the southern areas, which was a mammoth kind of question. Our concern was that we had people in these urban areas that were just begging for somebody to come in and assist with the organizing of those people. And if we could use the southern model in the northern urban areas, we might have something. We were not successful. They were two different kinds of communities. That's a part of the reality.

One last thing. Young people from McComb, high school students, went to Harlem in 1964, had an audience with Malcolm X. I think it had an impact on him; it certainly had an impact on them. The fact is that that dialogue and communication continued over a long period of time. And it was SNCC people who in 1965 invited Malcolm X to Brown Chapel in Selma, Alabama. So there is a consistency here in terms of our growth and development. You take the assassination of Malcolm X, you take the Sammy Younge assassination, you take the persecution of people who said, "Hell no, I won't go," you take the COINTELPRO that disrupted many of our lives, distortions and lies, and you can begin to see the context in which Black Power emerged.

GLORIA HOUSE: I'm going to take up where Cleve left off. Generally, when you read about the southern movement there is a kind of one-dimensionality about the narrative, so that you don't get the full texture of what the lives of people were like, the lives of local people and the lives of young people who went south to work with those people. What I'm going to share with you will add to an understanding of just how complex and how rich the fabric of our lives were at that point.

I want to say something about the context of this organizing work that is left out in the history books. The people who joined in agreed to register to vote and to become a part of the Lowndes County Freedom Organization whose symbol was the black panther. Those people knew that they were taking extreme risks. Many of them were thrown off the land that they had farmed for whites for years and ended up in a tent city in the county. Lowndes County was one of the Black Belt counties in Alabama that SNCC had agreed to move into. These counties had for a hundred years since Reconstruction seen no participation of blacks in any electoral forum. Blacks had been denied all of the farm subsidies, all of the various programs that were supposedly theirs through the federal government. So this was bringing people who had been excluded for one hundred years back into this political process. This was a county where 95 percent of the land was in the ownership of a very, very tiny minority of whites. When sharecroppers agreed to be a part of this movement, they were also accepting that they were risking their lives and their livelihood. Many of those families ended up living in a tent city just on the corner of Highway 80, where whites would drive by at night and shoot at us. We learned very quickly to hit the ground and wait until the shooting stopped. This was the climate of violence in which organizing took place in Lowndes County, Alabama.

Now, while we were doing this work among the local folk, inside SNCC some very important things were happening toward Black Power, or what I would prefer to call the idea or the ideology of self-determination and independent politics. One, we were able, through much debate and hassle and fighting, to finally agree to take a public position against the Vietnam War in a statement I drafted to reflect the ideas of the staff. This position came out of our growing consciousness of ourselves as a people, as a nation oppressed, and understanding our identity with the Vietnamese and other third world nations also fighting for national liberation.

The other major political struggle within the organization was the one in which white field secretaries were asked to work in white communities or in the SNCC offices. There was *never* a vote to expel any field secretary. This point of history has been misrepresented repeatedly. There were no expulsions. The idea came out of the fact that we were talking about independent politics, we were talking about black consciousness, we were talking about pride in our own background, our own achievements. It seemed to us a major contradiction to ask white field secretaries to go among black sharecroppers and convince them of their power to be self-determining and independent. We simply said there's a great deal of work to be done in white communities, and white field secretaries can do it. But of course this position was projected in the media as SNCC racism, as separatism, and fund-raising in the North suffered from that. The $9.68 very, very rarely appeared after that.

Let me just make one more comment. I think it's very important for us to understand that what we were doing as students, young people in the South with local folk, was a part of a worldwide movement for national liberation. We were part of an upsurge that really took hold in the 1960s though it had begun as far back as the early 1900s in Africa and Asia and Latin America: people saying we want to determine our own way; we want a third way; we constitute a third world. If those people were fighting for national liberation, for national identity, so were we, and we were very much influenced by the independence of Egypt, of Ghana, of Tanzania, the struggle of the Portuguese colonies in Africa. We watched these things, and they had an impact on us. We did read Frantz Fanon, we did read Malcolm, we did talk about these things, and we internalized them and we were moving out of this consciousness toward what later was coined Black Power.

Finally, I want to add a few more details about COINTELPRO, the FBI and the CIA working together to destroy the black liberation movement in this country. For example, writing letters and signing the names of certain political workers and sending them to other political workers in order to undermine the movement. Between the West and the East Coast Black Panther chapters they did this; between the Panthers and the Republic of New Africa, they did this. They were responsible for calling Kwame Toure's mother and telling her that if she didn't encourage her son to leave the country, she'd find him dead. You know about the threats on Dr. King's life, about their meddling in his private affairs with his wife. This was an ongoing wide-scale program targeted at specific individuals but also at organizations. And I think the people who are activists now need to understand what you're up against on a day-to-day basis, because people are tracking you by telephone; they are watching you from cars.

COURTLAND COX: I'd like to talk a little bit about the reaction of the country to the slogan "Black Power" or to the issue of Black Power, and to give some thinking about the development of the Lowndes County Freedom Organization.

The issue of Black Power, when it came out of the Meredith march as enunciated by my good friends Mr. Toure and Willie Ricks, raised to this country that there was a major threat in the land. And to give an example to the people who were not around in 1965–66 of a similar circumstance that's happened more recently, on a small scale, is the reaction of the country after Jesse Jackson won his first caucuses in 1984. There was an alarm that went through this country that said the status quo is under attack. There was a call for politicians, for newspapers, and for everybody to denounce and attack Jesse Jackson. Those who did so were given a great deal of say and popularity, and those who didn't were not given the audience. That is the same thing that happened with a greater intensity and for a longer period of time during the question of Black Power.

The first thing that was called upon during that time in Black Power and at this point is the need to denounce. The second thing that usually happens in this situation, what happened to SNCC after the rise of the issue of Black Power, is they call on you to constantly answer questions. "What do you want?" "What do you mean?" "You cannot really mean that. Don't you mean this?" And I think as Cleve and others have talked about, the reason that the history books have a certain perspective is because history has to function within certain parameters, and the fact of the matter is that Black Power and things that are perceived as threats have to be exorcised and there is a process that goes on. It not only happened with Black Power, it happens every time there is a sense that there is a threat to the status quo.

The next thing that happens is they call on you to modify what you've said or they call on "responsible Negro leadership" to help you understand what is said, or they call on "responsible Negro leadership" to establish a different context for what is to be said. So that King, especially in the early days, gave a sense that what we were about was trying to be part of America. He was not saying we want to change America. And those things that picked up on that theme are given high visibility. Those things that do not pick up on that theme are given no visibility.

And, finally, once they see there's a crack in the discussion, they ask you to redefine and repudiate what it is you've initially stated, to make it less radical and more moderate. This process is almost automatic, not only in the issue of Black Power. When we issued the statement on the Vietnam War, when King gave his speech against the war in 1967 at Riverside Church in New York, there is a mechanism that goes automatically into play.

Now, on the one hand you have the reaction of the establishment to things they view as a threat to the status quo. In terms of Black Power, the black community came to the defense of SNCC and the chairman of the organization at that point, Kwame Toure. Because without saying it in any long letters to the op-ed, the black community believes that if the establishment is so adamantly against it, there must be something good in it. Because they understand in the final analysis through history and experience, that that is the same establishment that is responsible in many respects for their plight.

The other thing about the black community's response to the question of Black Power is that it delivered a positive message to them. It said, "You are beautiful, you must be strong, you have a proud history, and there's unity in strength." And people took the discussion into many arenas, into electoral politics, into the social arenas, into the economic arenas, and into the cultural arenas. While many people have given great emphasis to the cultural arenas, I think when you look at what has happened and what changes are made, the other two arenas have been just as profound.

I think the question of Black Power, while it was beaten about by the press, was very helpful to the black community. Because as they were alerting the white establishment community about a particular danger, they were also alerting the black community about an opportunity. I think that we could not have spread the word and the concept about Black Power and the thrust to give the black community a better definition of self, a greater sense of organization in terms of electoral politics, and a greater sense of economic organization through the various caucuses if it did not have the widespread currency that the press gave it.

So, in the final analysis, I think that the response of the press was predictably hostile; that there are certain mechanisms that they undertake when they feel the establishment is under attack; that while in some respects the issue of Black Power may have seemed to cause a great deal of confusion, I think as we look at it historically, there are a number of advances that occurred in the political, economic, and social arenas that can be directly attributable to that debate and discussion that occurred at that particular time.

I think that in the discussion of Black Power, Lowndes County was a logical reaction to trying to deal with people's concrete realities. It was, in fact, when you look at it, the only way to deal with their concrete realities. I think for the SNCC organizers, what it began to say to us is that we must find ways to stop asking those who oppress us to deal with the nature of our oppression. And, secondly, that in limited areas such as Lowndes County where we could exercise power and control, that we should. So I think that as we look at the discussion of Black Power, that we can say that there's been a distortion of the concepts, there's been a distortion of the reality, but while that has operated and has triumphed at one level in terms of the media and the press, when I sit down and have a conversation with John Jackson and find out what is going on in Lowndes County, when he is talking to me about putting in economic development activities in Lowndes County, when he's talking about joining with whites in the county to stop a toxic waste plant in the county, when he talks about what ideas he has both in terms of the political and the economic, I know that the logic of Lowndes County Freedom Organization has triumphed in the end.

KWAME TOURE: All philosophers, whether materialist or idealist, admit of change. Discussions and disagreement only arise when the question is posed: how does change come about? Certainly, if we are to speak about the development of Black Power and what it meant, we must look at how the changes evolved to this point. Change comes only through one process: it is the dialectical process, which has many aspects, but the aspect we'd like to deal with now is that the dialectical process says that everything has inside of it its own contradictions, and it is a struggle of these contradictions for a position of dominance that allows for the fluidity of change. We must understand that this possibility of change is instinctive to many of us. For example, every human understands that it is incorrect to cheat or to lie. And thanks to the wonderful mechanism of the human body, when one lies, one's body acts abnormally, one's palms can sweat or one can shiver. Of course, the human body can get accustomed to anything and after a while you can lie so your palms do not sweat. But it is clear that there is this constant struggle that exists between us: either one cheats and so the negative is dominant, or one does not cheat, a positive characteristic. But one must dominate, either one cheats or one does not, there is no in-between. And, of course, if one does not cheat, the possibility of cheating is always there. Consequently, even when the positive is dominant, there's a need for constant struggle, for increased struggle so that it remains that way. The constancy of the struggle is clear.

In order to understand Black Power we must look at some of the contradictions inside SNCC. Obviously, in a limited time, we cannot touch them all. Consequently, I have picked just two and picked some of the examples of these two within SNCC to show the weaknesses and the contradictions that allowed for the development of Black Power. The major contradiction in SNCC was between revolution and reform. Here we must be careful. When we speak of revolution, we mean here a change of values of the society. When we speak of reform, we speak of a change of the structure of the society. Thus we can see here that revolution is fundamental, affecting the very values of the society. Reform is not fundamental and only touches the superficial aspects of the society. There was a constant struggle inside of SNCC between those who were revolutionary and those who were reform. This, of course, demonstrated itself in the political arena by those who were anticapitalist and those who were procapitalist. It demonstrated itself in practical activity. Those who were anticapitalist understood that in order for Africans in this country to be free, the American capitalist system must be totally and completely destroyed. Those who were reform felt that some aspects of the capitalist system were unjust, for example, its racist aspects, and perhaps if we knocked out the racism and allowed some Africans to join the bourgeoisie, then the problem itself would be solved. This contradiction must be properly understood. At no time was the revolutionary aspect of SNCC dominant; at all times the reform aspect of SNCC was dominant, and certainly we can see that today from the activities of those who are no longer in SNCC. But they've produced some sterling revolutionaries, of course.

Its second contradiction was African nationalism versus American nationalism. The word "African" here is to replace the incorrect word of "black" nationalism. This constant conflict between the allegiance of Africans in this country totally to Africa or to America is one that has plagued us since we first came here. This contradiction, of course, was found uppermost in SNCC.

These are the two contradictions, then, that we wish to touch on. We want to say one thing about some of the problems that existed inside of SNCC that affected these contradictions. The first was a lack of a clear ideology inside of SNCC. We must understand here that every society has an ideology. Every organization has an ideology, whether that ideology is spelled out or whether it is not spelled out, whether it is overt or covert. Each individual in every part of the world is dominated by an ideology whether they are conscious of it or unconscious of it. SNCC's ideology was not clearly spelled out. In fact, SNCC's ideology was a capitalist ideology.

SNCC had no clear ideology simply because an ideology is not just something negative. In America we hear people say they're against this, they're against that, but they never tell us what they're for. In order to be a revolutionary, to have a clear ideology, it's not just that you're against something. More important is, what are you for. And while in SNCC all of us were against the brutal exploitation of the oppressed masses in this country, we never came to decide exactly what it was we were fighting for. Thus our coming together in SNCC was really coming together in opposition against that which we were fighting, for different reasons and for different objectives. This can be seen clearly, for example, in the struggle that occurred in Angola. The three liberation movements, the MPLA, the Movement for the Popular Liberation of Angola; UNITA, the National Union for the Total Independence of Angola; and the FLNA, the Front for the National Liberation of Angola, fought seriously against Portuguese colonialism in Africa, each of them inflicting great damage upon the Portuguese colonialists, but they did not have the same idea of what they were fighting for. It was only the MPLA that had a clear analysis of a socialist society, a society in which all aspects of exploitation must be totally uprooted. UNITA and FLNA did not have this idea. They wanted to put the colonialists out so they could take their place and continue to dominate the suffering masses. This is a clear example of what occurred inside the Student Nonviolent Coordinating Committee.

The second contradiction: the Student Nonviolent Coordinating Committee saw the necessity for organization in order to make clear their protest and to make it more effective. This was in clear contradiction to that of Martin Luther King and the spontaneous movement that everywhere followed. Indeed, Brother Mants explained the spontaneous nature that existed inside the movement. But SNCC itself recognized the necessity to fight against this spontaneous nature and to become more organized. Unfortunately, relying again on the contradictions between revolution and reform, revolution sees the necessity for eternal struggle; reform sees the necessity for temporary struggle.

Indeed, if one only wants to get rid of racism under the capitalist system, it is clear that once this is done, we can easily melt into the capitalist system and live happily ever after. If one takes a position against capitalism, one sees the necessity for constant struggle to uproot the entire system. Because of this, SNCC saw organization only as temporary in terms of its being effective as a protest movement and did not see the necessity of eternal political organization to guard the vigilance of every human being. This is an error. Racism is part and parcel of capitalism. In order for capitalism to continue to exploit the people, it must divide them, whether it be on race, class, or sex. So consequently, until capitalism itself is destroyed, these divisions will continue. Those who took the reform line have not solved the problem even if they occupy elected official positions. This error, then, was completely reflected when Black Power in fact did come and SNCC no longer was able to carry out the struggle, because of the temporary nature.

SNCC did not see the necessity for a political party. SNCC helped to create two political parties, the Mississippi Freedom Democratic Party and the Lowndes County Freedom Organization. Yet SNCC itself, because of its lack of clear ideology, had some sort of stupid and anarchistic trend which made it appear as if things by itself would pop up and go along and we have no reason to worry about it. This struggle, of course, was clearly seen and most dominant in the figures of James Forman and Bob Moses Parris. That's where the struggle was; if you missed it, I didn't.

The role of the intelligentsia in SNCC was crucial. SNCC shows clearly the truth of the statement of Karl Marx that ideas when taken over by the masses become material reality. Certainly, this is what SNCC was able to do with students. They sent students to the South, peasants, sharecroppers, and it was this combination that gave to the world Black Power. One must not misunderstand it the other way around. Some think that Black Power came out of the northern ghettos; it did not. It came from a combination of the work with the intelligentsia, the African intelligentsia in this country, and African peasants in the South.

The other shortcoming of SNCC, and Cleve touched upon this, is that it was a southern organization; it was not a national organization, and thus when called to respond nationally to events, it carried a southern mentality with it. This really was its greatest problem.

Now we want to see the development of Black Power within this context. Black Power arises after the Mississippi Freedom Democratic Party is refused seating at the Atlantic City convention of the Democratic Party. One must come to understand this properly; it's swept under the rug quickly by many who have made their compromises with the Democratic Party. The Democratic Party is a racist party; of that there isn't the slightest question. The Democratic Party is a corrupt party; of that there isn't the slightest question. We think even if Jesus Christ went into the Democratic Party, he would come out corrupted.

Once the Democratic Party gave its racist response to the Mississippi Freedom Democratic Party, those in SNCC who were reformists, those in SNCC who assured us that we could easily melt into the Democratic Party, had no program for SNCC at all. It was the revolutionary and the nationalist element that was able to come forward and give a program to SNCC. Courtland Cox is absolutely correct: because of the floundering of the liberals and the reformist elements in SNCC having nowhere to go, Lowndes County became their only program. It was Lowndes County that became their program because Lowndes County spelled out clearly no relationships with the Democratic Party at all. Independent political party. The struggle in Lowndes County is a crucial one and shows SNCC clearly where its path was to go; it was this struggle that will in fact define Black Power, its strategy, and its tactics for SNCC. I will just put here in passing that Dr. Martin Luther King himself came into Lowndes County to urge the people of Lowndes County to vote in the Democratic Party and not to follow the line of SNCC. We might also add in passing that the SNCC chairman at that time himself went into Alabama and preached the same thing against the very workings of his organization.

The contradictions then in SNCC were boiling clearly to a point whether or not the Democratic Party was or was not our savior, whether or not, as Courtland Cox eloquently said, we will continue to speak to our oppressors to stop oppressing us or whether we will speak to the masses of the people, organize them, and let their strength turn against the wrath of the enemy, hit him without pity and without mercy until he's knocked down. This is precisely what Black Power represented. We said Karl Marx says that ideas become material reality when the masses take hold of them, and the masses took hold of Black Power. Of that there isn't the slightest question.

Mike Thelwell is absolutely correct. Black Power has not been achieved and cannot be achieved. Certainly, we cannot consider African elected officials as Black Power. This is indeed an insult. The Africans in this country have more elected officials than any other ethnic group in the country. They have over three hundred mayors; they have congresspeople; they have thousands of county and local elected officials, the overwhelming majority of whom belong to the Democratic Party, and Africans have less political power than any other ethnic group in this country and less power inside the Democratic Party than any other ethnic group in the country. It is clear then that Black Power, which emphasizes depending upon no one except the oppressed masses of the people, is still the correct line for the liberation of our people not only in this country but throughout the world. In no way must you think the struggle is not continuing. It is continuing everywhere.

Black Power came to transform the struggle. It came down in the first place, as Cleve clearly pointed out, to knock out this idea of morality as if morality will decide our relationship to capitalism. It is only power that will decide this relationship. And, indeed, it is the power that we have that will be able to show us how to transform the Democratic Party, how to transform the bourgeois electoral politics in which we say that we must take part. It certainly is a trag-edy that Africans in this country in order to become mayors had to shed their blood, and when our people become mayors they act just like a white man who had to play corrupt politics to become a mayor. Thus the logic of Mayor Wilson Goode bombing MOVE in Philadelphia in 1985 becomes even more tragic when he took the position from Frank Rizzo who, in fact, oppressed and bru-talized Africans everywhere.

Black Power came to put clearly in line the tactics and the means of struggle. Dr. King's error had everywhere come to affect the struggle: the error of mak-ing nonviolence a principle in a violent world. Nonviolence can only be a tactic, and Black Power came to show properly the tactic of nonviolence: if it works, use it; if it doesn't, toss hand grenades. Let's be free. That's the only issue on the floor.

Now, King's error was that he tried to take nonviolence and make it a prin-ciple in a violent world. Because of King's honesty, the error was compounded. King, being an honest man, understood that there is no gray area in principles. Either one is honest or one is not. Either one believes in God or one does not. Either one is for the people or one is against them. There is no middle ground. Consequently, once you take hold of a principle and you're an honest man, you must under all conditions at all times adhere to this principle. Since King took nonviolence as a principle, it meant that at all times, under all conditions, he must use nonviolence.

Just an aside, King himself came into contradiction with this principle. We are reminded of when his house was bombed in Montgomery, Alabama, on January 30, 1956. While King himself took out guns from his house he did not stop the bodyguards who had guns from staying on the lawn of his house. Of course, we understand that the Montgomery Improvement Association, the organization in which he worked, insisted upon it. But later on King himself came to publicly and politically understand this compromise when on the Meredith march he allowed the Deacons for Defense to march behind us and to provide armed protection for the marchers. This, of course, was a result of Meredith's being killed and people saying that we have to take reality into our hands.

So King's error was this: you cannot make a nonviolent principle in a vio-lent world. Let me be clear. All of us admired King. All of us loved King. All of us want what King wants—that all problems between all human beings, indi-vidual or groups, be worked out nonviolently. But King's error was that he was working with capitalism, and if you read nonviolence, even according to King, in order for nonviolence to work, the opponent must have a conscience. Capi-talism has no conscience at all. All of us know that we are oppressed through force, and the oppressor maintains oppression through force. Consequently, it is only through revolutionary force that we will break this hold on the oppressor. So if nonviolence doesn't get to the conscience, toss some hand grenades at the pig and walk on and be free.

The destruction of the capitalist system depends on two words, Black Power. The job of the capitalist system, of course, is at all places at all times to derail the people's just movement for their just liberation. Thus everywhere the Black Power movement has been derailed. We are told that it represents voting strength. We are told it represents this and that. We are clear here—it is only the organized masses that will free us; thus our energies must be directed only toward this area. Anytime we direct our energies anywhere else, we're serving the interest of the enemy. Certainly all the improved, quantitatively speaking, number of elected officials we have clearly demonstrates we are still a powerless people. We are still the victims of racist attack not only in Mississippi but in New York City. These will not end through getting us a President; they will only end when our people become firmly and properly organized, determined to smash capitalism in every aspect, who will be followed by those who truly love justice. Then will we arrive at our total liberation.

Of course if you are a worker of any color, you are exploited. What the Black Power movement says to the white workers is that you are more exploited than we are because you're exploited and don't think you are. Thus what you must do as a white worker is to help wake up the white working class, which is the fundamental class in this country, to make revolution and not leave it on the shoulders of the African masses.

We must look at violence in this context. The riots in 1968—let me ask you a question. Would you rather have a lot of property or would you rather be free? Would you rather be rich or free? I'm sorry, there is a misconception here of the struggle for freedom. In 1803 when the slaves began to fight in Haiti for their liberation, to make the most democratic country that the world had at that time, do you know what the first act was that the slaves engaged in? They burned all the crops and all the houses on the island of Haiti and then they told the French, "Come, let us fight to the death. We are talking about freedom and you're talking about a house being burned." I don't see how anyone can expect to get freedom without shedding blood. No one can demonstrate to me any social movement in the world, starting with the great movements of religion, which have not shed blood to advance their cause. Consequently, pointing to the shedding of blood or the burning of buildings as a means to stop giving support to a just cause shows that one has no understanding of the struggle for justice. You cannot get freedom unless you are willing to shed your blood.

Black Power, we said, has not been achieved. It's clear. Kwame Nkrumah told us Black Power can never be achieved until Pan-Africanism is achieved. And Pan-Africanism is nothing other than the total liberation and unification of Africa under scientific socialism. It is only when Africa is free, unified, and socialist that Africans all over the world will be free. This solution is tied to the contradiction of African nationalism versus American nationalism—a struggle that still continues in this country within the African masses, but one that African nationalism will win without a doubt. Its tenacity, its determination, and its hold on the African masses has not lessened at all; it is only the American system, its press system, which tries to confuse us.

Let me first show you one of the problems with the contradiction of the African nations or Africans in America versus the American nation. This country is populated mainly with aliens, and we want to remind everyone that if you are not an American Indian, you are an alien in this country. So that means most of these aliens in the past came from two continents, Europe and Africa. Those who came from Europe came looking and expecting a better life, whether or not they left as adventurers, or indentured servants, or whether they came fleeing religious or economic persecution in Europe. All of them, including the indentured servants, were expecting a better life out of America and had a choice whether or not they would go to America or not. Europeans coming to America came with a different outlook and different relationship to America than the Africans. No African came here voluntarily. No African was fleeing anything in Africa, not religious persecution, not economic oppression. All Africans who came here came against their will and were put into slavery. Thus if we understand historical reality, if we look at material reality, the relationship that the Africans in America would have to America and the relationships that the Europeans have to America must be different. They expected a better life and got it. The Africans got hell and still live in hell.

Now it is clear that the job of the American capitalist system is to confuse the Africans. Let them think that they are part and parcel of the American nation. But this yields some contradictions that are really bizarre. You will have to agree with me that more Africans in this country die fighting in wars that America waged than any other ethnic group, out of proportion to their numbers. At the same time, more Africans are killed in this country by terrorist groups such as the police and the Ku Klux Klan than any other ethnic group in the country. The contradictions are clear. These contradictions have to be spoken to. And unless we speak to these contradictions, we're not touching the essence of the problem of oppression. This problem can only be resolved when the Africans in America come to have a healthy attitude toward their past. This healthy attitude toward their past has been denied them by the American capitalist system. Which, as Malcolm X precisely pointed out, is such a tragic system that it turns a man against himself. Thus the Africans in America hate Africa, have no relationship to Africa, and if they have no relationship to Africa, certainly they cannot understand the present position in which they find themselves in America. Once Africans begin to understand the true history of Africa, they will be attracted to Africa with an enthusiasm that will shock the world.

America today is more ripe for revolution than it was in the 1960s. This is clear for all those who truly love justice and who have continued to work for the people. Those who have abrogated working for the people are lost in bourgeois hallucinations and cannot see clearly. They become confused by the press which informs them that the people in America don't like politics. This is nothing but another lie by the American capitalist system. Every segment of America today, every social class, every national minority is more conscious today of their oppression than they were in the 1960s. No one can tell me that women today are less conscious of their oppression from men than they were in the 1960s. No one can tell me today that Africans who have produced more than three hundred mayors are less politically aware than they were in the sixties. No one can tell me that the right in this country is less politically active than it was in the sixties. On the contrary, the right today is involved in activities which they considered communistic in the sixties. That's a fact. Every segment of this society is more politically conscious, even the handicapped are more politically conscious. It is a fact that the conditions are worse today than ever before. We didn't have nine million homeless people to discuss when talking about problems facing this country in the 1960s. Today, anyone discussing problems in this country, and not discussing nine million homeless, has lost all touch with reality. The conditions are worse today than they were in the 1960s.

In addition to this, throughout the world wherever American imperialism has been strong, it is being knocked down everywhere. In South Korea, the gallant students there, followed by the masses, have come to turn out a military dictator. We have seen since 1979 the Shah of Iran fall; we've seen the Nicaraguan dictator Somoza fall, Marcos in the Philippines, everywhere, we've seen the puppets that America put forth. American imperialism is so weak today; everywhere it's on its final stand.

American imperialism will be destroyed; of that there isn't the slightest question because of the instinctive love of justice of the masses of people everywhere. American imperialism, we say, is weaker today than it's ever been. The people, we say, today are more conscious than ever before. All that is lacking is revolutionary organization. The All African Peoples Revolutionary Party continues to make its contribution to humanity by playing its humble role in organizing the masses of our people for a unified socialist Africa, which will ensure the destruction of American imperialism. This is Black Power. Ready for the revolution.

MICHAEL THELWELL: Kwame, I do not share, sir, your disdain for the Afro-American community. I'm certain that the Afro-American community's attitudes toward Africa have clarified themselves in the past twenty years, are evolving in a very healthy manner and direction, and that the struggle in this country is neither simple nor superficial. It cannot be solved by slogans, and it cannot be solved by wishing. The capitalist system in this country is entrenched and is intransigent. If the liberation of black people—and the contradictions to which you point are absolutely clear and we all know them—if they admitted to so simple a solution, the Afro-American community would have liberated itself a damn long time ago. What has to be made very clear is that the organization that we've been discussing was at its most effective when it anchored itself in the legitimate aspirations and possibilities of the people, when it was respectful of evidence, and when it creatively engaged problems which are massive and very difficult indeed. The only reason why we're talking about this organization is because it engaged some very massive and formidable problems, some very dangerous problems and some violence, and engaged them to a measure of success. What we need to do is look at how it was able to do that.

Now we need to look very carefully at the late sixties, when because of the pressure of the Vietnam War, when because of the disaffiliation of white youth, when because of the rhetorical excesses of the so-called New Left, people who had no base, who had no organization in the masses of the people, who couldn't put fifty people in the street if their life depended on it, were talking on television about revolution, world revolution even, and adopting a set of slogans which had no basis in reality. When that developed, it became possible for the system to introduce itself into that movement, to subvert that movement with all the COINTELPRO practices that we have seen. There was a quality almost of hysteria in this country, with black people firing on black people in the name of ideology. It did not advance the struggle a half inch, it didn't liberate anybody; it created a hell of a lot of confusion which I see us in danger of recapitulating right here.

What people have got to understand and understand very clearly is that wishing for liberation or wishing the capitalist system would disappear ain't going to make it so. That struggle is going to have to be creative, it is going to have to take many different forms in many different communities, and we're going to have to struggle to articulate a practical, workable set of strategies which can *involve* people. SNCC never accomplished anything in Mississippi or in Alabama, to be very precise. It is local people like Hollis who came forward because we presented them with an opportunity in which they could come forward and work in a creative way. That has to be done and it ain't simple. It isn't simple at all. The history of the Afro-American community has been a history of incredible struggle against the forces of capitalism and of racism which have entrenched themselves in a very serious way.

Now we're going to have to look at the painstaking process of translating the black vote for which we struggled in the sixties into some kind of a force in the legislative apparatus of this country. The Congressional Black Caucus at whom you sneer and the black elected officials at whom you sneer have played a positive role in every progressive piece of legislation and development. I believe that the transformation of American society is going to have to depend on leadership, inspiration, and an energy which is going to have to come from black people, but we're going to have to approach it intelligently and maturely and cut this bullshit.

KWAME TOURE: Bourgeois fantasy.

MICHAEL THELWELL: Kwame, there is an African proverb, my brother, two of them. One says: Truth is like a goatskin bag, each man carries his own. But there are certain truths, my brother, which people who experienced them can agree on and know to be the case. The other one that I want you to ponder, my brother, is an Ashanti proverb which says: A log can lie in the river for ten years but it will never become a crocodile.

GLORIA HOUSE: I agree that the question of whether or not you struggle for revolution in this country has to do with whether or not you want to see the end of capitalism and the structuring of a new society. Where I disagree with Kwame is to hold those of us who were students in the sixties, in our twenties, trying to do what we knew how to do at that moment, responsible for what we could have learned only as we matured. Struggle goes on, the commitment to struggle goes on, and you learn each time and you consider new strategies and new ideological references as you move and as you develop as someone committed to struggle.

And of course many people who were student organizers didn't end their work as political workers, as makers of change, when they left SNCC. Black Power as an ideological reference found expression in many other organizations: in the urban centers up north, in the Black Panther Party, in the Republic of New Africa, in community organizing where people demanded community control of their schools or demanded decent housing or spoke out against the inhumanity of prisons. So people go on struggling around things that are clear and immediate to them and they develop in that way. And at some point they say, "Look, it doesn't matter how many reforms we're able to make, this whole thing has got to come down." But it seems to me that we have to admit that that is a process and that people go through that developmental process, and no one can say that if a certain organization stops at a certain point, it has failed. It served a certain purpose up to a certain point and other organizations, other forces, other directions, other individuals pick up or even some of the same individuals continue as Kwame has, into a more radical or revolutionary posture.

I also want to look at the question of nationalism in different terms. I think it's a very important question. It's important for whites and it's important for people of color in this country. Again, I'm disagreeing with Kwame on this issue of African consciousness. It seems to me that we have had since the sixties a very strong rise in consciousness of the motherland on the part of Africans here. And even before the sixties we had sediments of this consciousness from the Garvey days and from the Universal Association of Ethiopian Women days. I think that we're going to go on growing in this embracing of the motherland. That's become less of a problem than what happens after the embracing of the motherland, because we have many so-called cultural nationalists among us who embrace the motherland for some very interesting reasons, not necessarily having anything to do with struggle or making revolution or improving the quality of lives for people in the society.

Now I'm going to share with you my own vision of how the change can take place in this country over the long haul. It seems to me that we have to go on developing a national consciousness among Africans in this country that moves toward national liberation. I am a nationalist, after all; I am also, I think, an internationalist, but it seems to me that the first order of organizing and development has to begin among one's own people, responding to the needs of one's own people. Clearly, there are other people of color in this country, Asians, Native Americans, Chicanos, Puerto Ricans, who have begun to move their struggles forward. It seems to me that coalitions will be essential in moving us to a new level of struggle. I think it's very important for whites to come to grips with where will *they* be in all of this. And are they capable of defining and developing a new American identity and consciousness that allows them to work at a progressive, radical level with these other organizations that are engaged in struggle. That's, I think, a challenge for progressive radical whites— are you capable of doing that? Over the last twenty years or so we in nationalist organizations have had to withdraw from any efforts to work with whites. Because of their persistent racism, because of their insistence on their superiority, because of their cultural chauvinism, it's been impossible to move together to make revolution in this country. So I think the question is very, very important: what are whites going to do about this? Can you define a new American nationalism that is progressive? That understands the need to struggle and to be in alliance with people who are truly about overturning capitalism here? Can you do it?

Tom Hayden: Black Power, I think, had everything to do with the historical context. The moment when the concept of integration had power was closely related to the fact that we had a new President and there was a somewhat more hopeful context. As that soured, particularly after Kennedy's death, the context became much more bleak even though people didn't recognize it overnight. It soon became clear that there wasn't going to be a country coming to the aid of the black South unless triggered by confrontation and massive pressure, and that meant that the idea of a human community or politics based on morality started to decline and was replaced by politics based on power. In other words, not expecting the federal government to move out of conscience but expecting the federal government to move out of necessity. And once you arrive at that conclusion that it's power versus power, it's a short step to whose power, whose interest, and then it becomes Black Power. So there's kind of an evolutionary logic to it. It might not have happened in that way if the national context had not changed and if Kennedy had remained President and had become more responsive to the movement. All of those questions became academic in November 1963.

Hollis Watkins: I'm still one of the local people from Mississippi. I'd like to try to bring things back down to earth a little bit. I think when we look at things properly, we have to make sure that we look at them in terms of context and levels. Granted, as we all say, the revolution in this country has not taken place, but there are many, many small revolutions that have taken place and continue to take place. To me we have a small revolution up in Belzoni, Mississippi, where blacks had not taken the political seat of power in that city or had any part of anything since 1874 and now they are the decision-making bodies of that. To me, that's a small revolution.

SNCC and the
Practice of History

The historiography of the civil rights movement, or how the events of the past have been understood and presented by those studying them, has proved controversial. The trouble lies both in getting the facts right and in the accuracy and fairness of the interpretation. As the conference itself demonstrated, even participants do not always agree on what happened. For scholars, usually conducting their investigations after the fact, pinning down what took place becomes still more difficult. Even when the facts are agreed upon, the analysis of those facts and the relative importance of particular events or individuals rarely are. The literally hundreds of books and articles on the civil rights movement have each described the roles and contributions of the various organizations very differently, and SNCC members have often felt slighted. The widespread focus on Martin Luther King, Jr, as leader of the movement has frustrated many who believe that ordinary people, local people, contributed more to civil rights triumphs than any single individual. Further complicating matters is the relationship between the writer and the time in which he or she is writing: contemporary politics, contemporary concerns, necessarily inform one's perspective, whether one was a participant in the event or is a scholar of it—or both.

MARTHA PRESCOD NORMAN: I'm going to talk about historiography. I've worked with it a little bit over the past ten years as I've been teaching and trying to think how to present the movement to my students, as I've been a perennial graduate student and tried to keep up with some of the literature on the movement. I want to talk about some of the problems and oversights that I see in the work that's been done. I hope this approach will provide a discussional framework for reading and learning and teaching about the movement.

Before I go any further, I want to stress that my connection with this history is, obviously, deeply personal. I was sixteen when I first became involved in movement support activities in the North. I was twenty-one when I left Selma to return to Detroit. During those years movement activities either of a supportive nature or working in the South took up most of my time. Like other people here, I can't think of any job or any activity that I've been involved with before or since that has played such an important role in shaping my life, both politically and personally. I grew up in the movement, it shaped my views, I married in the movement, and now twenty-five years later, many of the people that I still feel closest to are movement people. This is a group of people that I know that when I've asked anybody for anything, a room, a place to stay, a meal, support, comfort—that I've always gotten back what I asked for and much more. And I have always found it difficult to put into words the bond of comradely love that I feel here. Beyond this, I feel another kind of personal interest in how this history is written; I have three children. And I have read interpretations that have made me cry, to think that my boys would be left with such ridiculous explanations of what it was that their mother and their father were doing in those days, and why it was that their parents decided to put their lives on the line in the early sixties.

That said, I'd like to title my presentation "How They Stood," or, "Not Seeing the Forest for Being Too Close Up on the Trees." "How they stood" is a quote from Amzie Moore, a tough, longtime Mississippi activist who stopped his work with the NAACP to support SNCC's first efforts in Mississippi. When he was asked by Howell Raines to explain what it was about SNCC when compared with the other civil rights organizations that led him to make such a decision, Mr. Moore mentioned a number of things about SNCC people. He suggested that they were just regular everyday kind of folk. To quote him from *My Soul Is Rested* [1977]: "[These] kids wore blue jeans, and I used to have sleeping in my house six and eight and ten, twelve who had come. I bought lots of cheese and always we'd eat cheese and peaches, and sometimes would get spaghetti . . . and make a huge tub of meatballs and spaghetti to fill everybody up. And this is how we were . . . They'd eat that without complaining." Similarly, when it came to meeting, "It wasn't a matter of meeting in the Masonic Order or office or at a church to do this. They met anywhere at any time." Mr. Moore further complimented us by describing us as a group of "strong, intelligent young people" who "always had a smile" [pp. 236, 237].

Another characteristic that he referred to a number of times was an orientation toward action. "They were moving," he noted, "always ready to try to do something, . . . and certainly did not hesitate to get about the business for which they came" [pp. 236, 237]. Also Moore remarked that SNCC brought a notion of leadership as something broad-based and nonelitist. Quoting him again, "One great thing I think was introduced in the South with reference to SNCC's tactics was the business of organizing leadership. If eleven people went to jail this evening who the power structure considered leaders, tomorrow morning you had eleven more out there. And the next morning eleven more" [p. 236].

The thing that impressed Moore the most was the courage of these young people. Several times in his short recollection he pointed out how we seemed to have no fear of death. This is how he put it: "I found that SNCC was for business, live or die, sink or swim, survive or perish" [p. 236]

In an effort to further emphasize this quality, Moore brought up the following image. "But when an individual stood at a courthouse like the courthouse in Greenwood and in Greenville, and watched tiny [SNCC] figures standing against a huge column, . . . [against white] triggermen, and drivers and lookout men riding in automobiles with automatic guns. . . ." At this point he stopped and exclaimed, "How they stood . . . how gladly they got in the front of that line . . . and went to jail! It didn't seem to bother them" [p. 237]. In this short description Amzie Moore went right to the heart of SNCC, capturing our spirit and our substance. His final quote is the essence of writing SNCC history; that is, describing how we stood at the front of the line or on the front lines during the civil rights struggle.

Unfortunately, we don't have much scholarship that does that with anything near the accuracy that Amzie Moore did some ten years ago. In fact, the current history, in spite of its tremendous good points, tends to distort and obscure our role. Why? Let me suggest a number of reasons that center around assumptions about the movement as a whole and youth in particular. To begin with, public discussion of this period has become dominated by the figure of Dr. Martin Luther King, Jr. He is presented as the creator, builder, and shaper of the civil rights movement to the extent that we could easily believe it was the force of his presence that brought the movement into being and his spirit that propelled it along. King and the civil rights movement have become so interchangeable that many of the students who come into my classes have no idea that there was a black student movement in the 1960s. And if they are interested, once they learn this and probe further, they will find a literature that either neglects or minimizes the role of young people in the southern civil rights movement.

The scholarly work reflects a public view, and focuses on King, and leaves students almost completely out of the picture. For example, David Garrow's book *Protest at Selma* [1978] is aptly subtitled "Martin Luther King, Jr., and the Voting Rights Act of 1965." In this book, the continuous activism of the Selma students which Silas referred to earlier, as well as the ongoing programs of SNCC, are relegated to an occasional mention of this particular activity or that specific arrest. Similarly, when Aldon Morris discussed the origins of the civil rights movement in *The Origins of the Civil Rights Movement* [1984], he assumed, in his words, that SCLC was, and I quote, "the organizational center of the movement" [p. xiii] and suggests that the charisma of King and his fellow SCLC ministers was indeed the major factor in mobilizing the southern black community [pp. 91–93]. In his introduction he does acknowledge that SNCC represented what he calls "another source of power," but then is quick to mention that SNCC's presence fostered interorganizational tensions in Albany and Birmingham [p. xiii]. Morris's further minimal treatment of SNCC in the book remains quite disparaging. SNCC was handicapped, he suggests, by its own ambivalence of having "adopted an antileadership and an antistructure ideology at the outset" while at the same time feeling the need for leadership and coordination [p. 231]. He further derides what he believes to be SNCC's concept of leadership. He quotes James Bevel, saying that for the SNCC activist the slogan "Let the people decide" really meant "his people, that agree with him" [p. 231]. Morris then goes on to suggest that the interorganizational conflict which he believes SNCC injected into the Albany Movement was the primary factor in the defeat of the Albany Movement [p. 246]. There's a biography of King by David Lewis, *King: A Critical Biography* [1970], that has that same kind of interpretation of events in Albany.

I think Morris strikes his most serious blow at student activism with his analysis of the sit-ins in seventy cities in the two months following the February 1, 1960, Greensboro, North Carolina, sit-in. Finding that the news of these sit-ins was spread through established civil rights networks and that many of these sit-in groups met in SCLC churches or bore some connection to CORE organizers or the NAACP Youth Council, he suggests that Howard Zinn's notion that the sit-ins represented independent collegiate actions has to be abandoned [p. 209]. While it's really good that he stresses the tradition of activism in the black community previous to the sixties, Morris goes a little bit further than saying that the students received tactical advice and support and bond money from adults. He suggests that really it was the adults who organized the students and put them into action. "In many instances," he states, "it was the adult leaders of the movement centers who organized the student protesters." And on this basis he concludes that SCLC was essential to the rise of the

1960 sit-in movement; not helpful, but *essential* [p. 197]. Because there were adults present, Morris just assumes that the adults were in charge and so the students ceased to be the prime movers in their own social protests.

There's also another way in which some of the history minimizes the role of SNCC— through an emphasis on discussions of SNCC that dwell on the notion that a kind of undisciplined, middle-class, youthful rebellion against authority played a significant role in the motivation of SNCC workers. The problem is that this can be focused on to the extent that it seems to become the major characteristic of the organization, and you'll have histories that put together some expressions that just seem ridiculous given the context.

Also in the discussion of the question of growing consciousness within the movement, somehow our early vision becomes extraordinarily limited as does our decision to support a nationalist position with Black Power. All this adds up to a notion of students ceasing to be serious actors on the historical stage and instead becoming some kind of nearsighted, bumbling, stand-ins in history's eyes.

Looking at all these works, I think there are two basic problems in their interpretation. The first is that the wrong standards are being used to judge the success or failure of movement activities. The second is a kind of confusion about what people were fighting for. In both cases, the difficulty stems from applying a narrow and superficial vision to a broad and deep social terrain. In the first instance Dr. King's weight is, again, disproportionately felt. He judged the success or failure of any given activity by the fairly simple standard of whether or not he was able to get a negotiated agreement from the city officials and leaders. Hence Birmingham was a huge success; Albany, Georgia, a dismal failure. As we have already seen, a significant number of movement scholars have adopted this view. Others use the passage of legislation as the same kind of standard. The March on Washington was followed by the Civil Rights Act of 1964; the Selma to Montgomery march by the Voting Rights Act of 1965; therefore, they're both successes and events of great historical importance. But what is the sense here? What is the context? A movement for social change ought not to be judged by some unenforced local agreement or even by the passage of an almost equally unenforced piece of national legislation, but by the degree and amount of social change that is accomplished and by the actions that bring about the change.

What made change in the South was not the Birmingham agreement of 1963 or the Civil Rights Act of 1964. What made these agreements get made and got this legislation passed and ultimately ended segregation in the South, clipped the wings of white southern terrorism, and brought the franchise to many areas where black people had not voted since Reconstruction was the consistent, widespread, relentless activism of southern black communities. Communities who refused to stop struggling in the face of all kinds of harass- ment, physical and economic, arrests, convictions, beatings, dogs, fire hoses, bombs, and bullets. When these communities went into motion and stayed in motion, everyone understood that the South had to make significant changes. If we understand that continuous activism and a serious level of commitment on the parts of hundreds of thousands of black people across the South are what made change, then, in that context, we can understand the role of stu- dents in helping to make that change. We did serve in a vanguard role, set- ting the pace and then supporting continuous activism.

From 1953 to 1960, there was a bus boycott here and there and a number of national demonstrations. From February 1, 1960, onward, after the Greens- boro sit-in, there was activity all the time, every day, everywhere. When the Freedom Rides seemed finished after two weeks and Diane Nash and the Nash- ville students stepped in, the students carried on the rides for three months. Through SNCC workers finding the courage to support a number of programs during this period, we supported the continuous activism that maintained and strengthened the civil rights movement. We don't have a book that even be- gins to describe the length and breadth of SNCC activities, but there were a lot of them. In this conference you've heard of many of our activities. I want to look at those and more you haven't heard about: There were beachhead projects in Albany, Georgia, and Selma, Alabama, and Pine Bluff, Arkansas, that spread out into surrounding counties all during this period; an almost com- pletely statewide program in Mississippi. There were sit-ins, marches, voter registration activities, union organizing, co-op organizing, Freedom Schools, Free Southern Theaters, the Mississippi Freedom Democratic Party, the Lowndes County Black Panther Party, and on and on and on—an assortment of creative and continuous activities. All these carried out by a couple of hun- dred students who really brought nothing more, as Sherrod has said, but our bodies and souls as our main resources to make social change. When I read these accounts I wondered how it was that we managed to maintain all these programs if we were so undisciplined and "floating" all over the place. To me, as Spock says, it does not compute.

Let me bring this down to a personal level, and the whole issue of disci- pline. I know it took a lot of discipline for me just to be there, just to stay in Mississippi. To be there and then to go out and canvass and teach—that was a plus, that was in addition. My stint with the movement was nowhere near as exciting as all these wonderful stories we've heard, and I know other people have said just the opposite, but I was scared, I *was* scared. When I arrived in Mississippi there were white men riding by the office with guns hanging out the window. It took every bit of internal discipline I had not to bolt and run home. Then in addition to making the decision to stay, I remember thinking, "Well, maybe if I leave the office, go out and canvass, it'd be a little better." I joined George Greene and Stokely Carmichael going out to canvass plantations around Greenwood. I thought since we were going on these places, technically where we would be trespassing—people could feel free to shoot you on sight—that we were going to quietly sneak into the plantations, stay near the car, and talk to people and move off. No, no, we got out of the car, walked far away, and George and Stokely were singing freedom songs at the top of their lungs. I did this for a couple of days and I went back to Bob Moses and asked, "Couldn't I please stay in the office with those people riding by?"

Also, some of the methods of operation that SNCC people and historians have criticized in SNCC were the things that I liked the most. I mean, the long discussions where people figured out fifteen different ways to approach something and then looked at twenty-five possible significances to place on each approach. I've been to school a lot and I have never been in an environment that was as intellectually stimulating as SNCC. This fluidity and creativity along with the sense of trusting each other's judgment is exactly what made us strong as young people and able to do so many things. For example, someone from the Atlanta office called me up when I was an inexperienced nineteen-year-old and said, "You all have to canvass the Democratic Party in Michigan for support of the Mississippi Freedom Democratic Party." That's all they said, there weren't any instructions. We had never done this before. We had never done anything like this, yet it made sense to us and we *did* it.

In addition to supporting and generating continuous activism, students in the sixties set the pace in terms of commitment. We've heard that participation in the struggle was to be based on a willingness to go to jail and a willingness to risk life and limb. SNCC students did so in the sit-ins, again in the Freedom Rides, and again when we entered the rural southern communities of McComb, Mississippi and Albany, Georgia. You could search the history of civil rights activism in the previous fifty-year period and you cannot find a national organization making struggle on this level a requirement for participation, a matter of national organizational policy. This is a big deal.

SNCC workers also, I think, heightened the struggle with their sense of immediacy, that now was the time to fight. We demonstrated this by the simple action of leaving school, leaving promising careers, stopping all other activities to work full time in the struggle. We didn't go back every other Sunday to keep up with the church in another city, or to take a part-time course to somehow continue our education. I remember one of McDew's frequently used lines that was that we were going to make more changes in the next five years than had been seen in the last fifty. I think it was that, just believing that and taking that as a reality, that made a significant difference in the nature of the civil rights movement.

We also changed the focus and direction of struggle by moving into the Black Belt. Again, this represented a change, a significant change in civil rights strategy which to that point had been to emphasize the border and urban areas to win over the moderates and isolate the hard-core South. Jim Forman refers to this strategy in *The Making of Black Revolutionaries* when he talks about the difference between what the Taconic Foundation thought of voter registration and what SNCC did with it. In this context, when King entered Albany or SCLC developed a program for Selma, it represented that organization following SNCC, not just in organizational terms, but following SNCC's strategic lead. Our move into the Black Belt heightened struggle by tapping the strength of these communities; first in the obvious sense that on the basis of numbers these areas had the greatest potential for political and organizational power. Then, there was also a broader sense that these communities, by virtue of their level of oppression, were composed of some fairly tough struggle-oriented people whose courage and determination, whose willingness to risk everything they had, whose refusal to quit, is in fact what propelled the civil rights movement along—much more so than someone's charisma or some specific organization's presence in an area. As Kwame Toure says, "The people struggled and struggled and struggled." This is what made the civil rights movement. These Black Belt communities were where we found families like the Harris family in Albany, Georgia, the Jackson family in Lowndes County, Alabama, people like Miss Hamer and Hartman Turnbow in the Mississippi Delta.

This link between SNCC and Black Belt communities needs to be examined from a number of angles, but before we do that, we're going to have to drop this notion, this myth, of the black community's awakening in the fifties or sixties. You see that word in a lot of presentations, "awakening." The problem is that term suggests that before this point there was a totally quiescent, slumbering, and passive black South. Common sense ought to tell us that the way that we saw these people struggle—and you've seen it now too, in the documentary "Eyes on the Prize" [1986]—facing dogs, bullets, bombs—you know that struggle was not some new skill that these people learned in a two-hour workshop on nonviolent direct action.

When you see these mass meetings and demonstrations, voter registration efforts, remember nobody *had* to come. What we cannot do is tell or understand this history without recognizing that southern black folk played an activist role in initiating and carrying out the civil rights struggle. Again, neither charisma nor "outside agitators" were key in creating this movement. I'm not saying that these factors didn't heighten the struggle. What disturbs me is if we posit a passive community then the prime movers in the struggle do become King or the group of activist civil rights organizations, SNCC, CORE, and SCLC. Presently, that's essentially the way histories of the struggle are being written. Then we miss all the local activism that preceded our efforts, and a lot of that was youth-based; and we also miss all the activities that took place in the hundreds of communities that were not initiated by civil rights organizations.

For example, the efforts of sharecroppers in Fayette and Haywood counties, Tennessee, to register in 1959 aren't mentioned anymore in the sequence of events from 1954 to 1960. Similarly, Danville, Virginia, and Cambridge, Maryland, also tend to be left out of later histories. As a result, we really can't even understand the March on Washington. Why was it that far more people showed up than the organizers anticipated? So many people came because they were part of hundreds, thousands of communities in action all across the country. If we successively narrow movement history down to the history of civil rights organizations, that's only part of the story. With such a narrow view, we can't even understand what it was the national organizations were doing.

If there is any one thing for which SNCC ought to be remembered it is that we had the good sense as college students to realize that we ought not to struggle just on our campuses but in our communities. And given the variety of communities that we could have entered, we chose to join with those hardest hit by racist oppression. And that we approached these communities in a manner appropriate to their experience with hard struggle. It's in this context that our nonelitist notions of organization, of leadership, of democracy make sense. If you're preparing to join with a community that's ready to struggle on the highest level—and that's what we're talking about, people lose their jobs, get shot, their homes get burned and so forth, risk everything they have—*of course* you have to let the people decide what it is they're going to struggle for. This is not some confused, ambivalent, rebellious idealism but a commonsense approach to organizing for serious struggle.

I think that nobody here would have gone up to Miss Fannie Lou Hamer in Louisville, Mississippi or Mr. John Jackson in Lowndes County or Amzie Moore in Cleveland, Mississippi, with some other approach, and if they had, I don't think there would have been a lot of response. We did just what we should have done when we met these people: we sat down and listened. And when we think on this level, we know it was not some sense of emotional bravado that led us into these communities but a rational understanding, conscious or unconscious, that these communities had what it took to wage a difficult and hard struggle. Sharecroppers in Fayette and Haywood had already demonstrated this. They were ready to do a lot more than boycott and sing. And it's to our credit that we created a focus and an approach that gave us the opportunity to struggle alongside such courageous and determined people, and in doing so support these communities' methods of hard struggle: the solid foundation of the civil rights movement.

Now I think we should see the specific historical victory in Albany, Georgia. Here it was that a Black Belt community showed the level at which it was going to struggle for civil rights. When Albany, Georgia, citizens marched to the courthouse by the hundreds in 1961, they said, "We're going for broke. We're not worried about arrests. We're not worried about our jobs, and we really aren't worried about our lives." They were the first Black Belt community to launch a citywide protest in the sixties. They were the model. They created the mold on which the rest of the civil rights movement was based. Their numbers and their seriousness served notice that the South could no longer maintain its system of racial oppression, because that's all there was to uphold it, the threat of arrest, of beatings, of economic reprisals and loss of life.

When Albany, Georgia, citizens went to the courthouse, they announced that these threats weren't going to work anymore, and I can't see that as anything but a victory. And as an aside, I hope when we later rest the interpretation of Albany as a defeat, we'll also get rid of the other notions of Chief Pritchett as a nonviolent person and, worse, as a smart man. I mean, there is something wrong with a history that makes Charles Sherrod's actions in Albany so difficult to understand that he has to constantly explain them and at the same time glorified Laurie Pritchett's actions as being not just reasonable, but smart and precocious.

So all I'm saying here is historians can get very confused when they get all caught up in the details of things and don't see the forest for the trees. All that was a talk about getting the proper perspective from which to view the success and failure of a movement. Now I want to briefly address what I think is a confusion over what it was people were fighting for.

One could easily leave the history with the impression that SNCC activists were motivated primarily by a kind of youthful emotionalism, an acting out, a rebelliousness against authority, and somehow they garnered a sense of pride from their activism, but at all times reflected a certain stubborn middle-class individualism. Again, it's here that the context is lost. How can that be? How can you tell my children and everybody else's children that when their parents put everything they had on the line for their community's welfare, that they were acting out of individualism? There's no sense here. If we wanted to act out some kind of youthful problems with authority and flaunt rebelliousness, we didn't have to go to Mississippi. Whether we were white or black or rich or poor, we could have stayed on our college campuses and smoked dope and worn flowers in our hair, which some people did do. When I read these kinds of interpretations, I want to borrow an expression from my kids and say, "Get real."

Second, there is this matter of goals. In describing SNCC's changing perspective from the liberal inside the system to the radical, maybe there's something fundamentally wrong with the system. There is this sense of at first struggling for very limited goals such as having a cup of coffee sitting down, and then the notion that these goals broadened into a fight for political rights, and then there was this glimpse of economic concern. Now, as I said, in a certain sense this may seem obviously true, but the problem is we can concentrate on the notion of ideological growth and miss the overall sense of the movement. From the beginning of the sixties' student activism there was a consistency and a depth to our goals which is the only thing that explains the consistently serious level on which we struggled from beginning to end. And to miss this is indeed to take the heart and soul out of the civil rights movement. I've heard a number of SNCC veterans after reading certain histories commenting that somehow the most exciting period of their life has been made dull and prosaic in these works. And I think this is why; these histories do take the life out of the movement.

From the onset we acted with deeper goals in mind than having a cup of coffee sitting down. When the students formed the sit-in committees, they didn't call themselves Students Tired of Standing at Lunch Counters; they didn't even call themselves Students United to Build a Truly Integrated Society. The Greensboro A&T students called themselves the Student Executive Committee for *Justice*. The Atlanta students called themselves the Atlanta Committee on Appeal for *Human Rights*. And when we focused on political rights, we didn't form groups called Black Mississippians United for the Vote or even Black Alabamians Fighting for Full Citizenship. No, we formed the Mississippi *Freedom* Democratic Party. And when we moved outside we didn't call it the Black Independent Political Party, we called it the Lowndes County *Freedom* Organization. And in so doing we didn't limit our sights to full citizenship or full political rights.

I've heard one SNCC veteran comment that when you see the image in "Eyes on the Prize" where the marching feet turn into the American flag, it's a little disturbing because this image suggests, as does a good deal of the literature, that the end goal of all that struggle was to be complete Americans. People don't put their lives on the line for a cup of coffee or even to get the right to vote. You know you didn't see all those women suffragettes constantly facing dogs, bullets, bombs. This level of commitment suggests that people were moving out of the most fundamental desires for freedom, justice, and equality, that is what we talked about, that is what we sang about from 1960 right on through 1968. Maybe we were singing "Freedom's Coming and It Won't Be Long" in 1960 and by 1965 we were singing "They Say That Freedom Is a Constant Struggle," but we were singing about freedom from start to finish, from beginning to end, and this was a fight for justice and freedom and we cannot understand it if we overlook this fact. It was something with great height and great depth.

We must keep a clear and broad perspective of the movement as a whole, its nature, its overall significance and its major components. That's the only way that we can write an accurate history of those days. When we do that, obviously, SNCC and student activism will have to have a prominent role in that history. For the truth is no matter what we did before, no matter what we've done since, and really no matter whatever else we happened to be doing at the time, when the call came for people to stand at the front of the line in the fight for freedom, we answered. When a history is written that reflects our activities in that true light, our children will be moved like Amzie Moore to remark "How they stood." Then our children can understand why we chose to sing songs like "We Are Soldiers in the Army."

When all is said and done, it shouldn't be left to history to give our children a sense of us, because we're still here. And given our past, we have every reason to keep struggling to make a more just and humane world. I hope all of us will be able to continue to testify with the verse from that song—"I'm so glad I'm a soldier and I have my hand on the freedom plow. One day I'll get old and can't fight anymore, but I'll stand here and fight on anyhow." Brothers and sisters, fight on anyhow! Thank you.

MARY KING: The past twenty years have seen the most extraordinary historical revisionism or rewriting or distortion of history. The movement was an enormous phenomenon that swept particularly the South in the 1960s, but it was not simply Dr. Martin Luther King. What I am so concerned about is that young people today who are interested in the movement see it revolving around the focus of Dr. King. I believe that he is the last person who would have wanted it that way and that he was actually one of the few people in the other civil rights organizations who was willing to acknowledge what an extraordinary entity SNCC was.

The current notion that the movement was made up of the followers of Dr. King is such a grotesque distortion of the reality that those of us who were involved almost don't know how to respond, because it was so much the antithesis of the truth. The fact of the matter is that, yes, Dr. King was an extraordinary figure and orator, and his impact through television helped people to overcome their fear. We must remember that many people were dreadfully afraid. They stood to lose everything, not only their jobs, not only their homes but also their lives for any deviation from the protocols of segregation, and Dr. King helped isolated people through his messages, through his speaking, through the television. That communication helped people to overcome their fear, but he did not organize them. He *could* not organize them from a television tube. Who were the organizers in the Black Belt counties of the South? They were people that are here at this conference. And who were the leaders of those communities that were thrust up? They were people who had been living there. That was based on our philosophy that leadership was inherent in everyone. And from that we took the belief that our job was to identify individuals with that potential and to elicit that which is already there from them. And, in fact, there were thousands of people who demonstrated leadership. Many of them will never be noted in the history books, but as Guyot and many others can say, the leadership was there and it was abundant. The courage was extraordinary. People born into the most debilitating circumstances, the most extreme oppression that this society has been capable of, were able to show the most unbelievable leadership qualities. This is the true story of the movement and were Dr. King here with us right now, he would agree.

CHARLES MCDEW: Dr. King got a lot of the credit for the movement because he was the only person that could be identified. The people at SCLC that we admired most, like C. T. Vivian and Fred Shuttlesworth, most of those guys folks have never heard of. I think that once the movement started to dissipate, there was a feeling among most of us that this was not going to be a lifelong occupation, or an organization that was going to continue to live. It became easier for the historians to identify the progress of that period with one person, and that was Dr. King. I don't think it was a deliberate attempt to subvert—yes, it was. It was a deliberate attempt to subvert history. One of the things that we were always criticized for was that we would not turn away the Young People's Socialist League, we would not turn away members of the Communist Party, we were a mixed bag of people. We were uncontrollable, too demanding, too radical, and ultimately, unacceptable. And we were unacceptable in the history of this country. That's why people haven't heard about us.

DIANE NASH: I think it's deliberate, too, to a certain extent. I think that if young people, especially today, knew that it was kids, just like them, then when they look around today and see things that need to be changed, instead of saying, "I wish we had a leader today, like Martin Luther King was," they would ask themselves, "What can I do?" Or "What can my roommate and I do?" I think it subverts present and future efforts toward liberation.

I think it's complicated further because of our religion. There's the idea of the charismatic leader, starting with Jesus Christ; we have to go through Jesus to get to God, being Christians. Then there's the paternalistic family where children are raised to obey father or obey mother or obey an external rather than obey their own connection with God, morality, and their conscience. So people tend to be afraid to take on responsibility for their own lives. Many people seek a father or a leader to tell them what to do. There's a cold feeling when you finally face the fact that there is nobody out there to lead my life but me. That is a considerable amount of responsibility. I think that kind of mentality sometimes finds a benevolent figure or positive figure like a Martin Luther King, but that same kind of place in the psyche will allow a Hitler to emerge. A charismatic figure that seems to have the answers and that people can follow instead of being their own leaders.

Robert Zellner: That's what I'm concerned about. People don't know about our history. But we have watched the sainting of Martin Luther King. Martin Luther King has been made a saint of the movement, the way Booker T. Washington was the saint before. The great black leader. Now, when they sanctify someone—"they," the power structure, the ruling class, whatever you want to call it—when they choose the leader of the black people, the leader of the oppressed people, whoever, and they sanctify that leader, they don't even sanctify the whole leader. Did you ever hear them talk about Martin's economic program? Did you ever hear them talk about Martin taking a position against the war in Vietnam? What we did at that time, was we felt that we were an ox and we were dragging Martin Luther King along. People can't imagine that kids dragged Martin Luther King along. And sometimes we felt that we had him by the nape of the neck.

Listen, let's get history straight. In private, we called him "De Lawd." Right? We were very irreverent. We were not reverent with that reverend. We weren't reverent with any reverend. We were bodacious to the maximum. We were kids and we changed this country. We were kids and we changed America. I remember in 1964, going to the White House to visit "Ears Johnson"—that's LBJ. When we had lost three comrades in Mississippi, and I went with Rita Schwerner and Jim Forman and so forth to the White House, Mr. Johnson came in from one side of the room and came over and shook hands with everybody and said, "I'm so glad to meet you, Mrs. Schwerner." And she said, "I'm sorry, Mr. President, this is not a social call. We've come to talk about three missing people in Mississippi. We've come to talk about a search that we don't think is being done seriously. We've come to talk about what we think are the shortcomings in the federal government in terms of protecting civil rights workers in Mississippi." And the President of the United States said, "I'm sorry you feel that way, Miss," and turned on his heel and walked away. And then we got a lecture from the press secretary, Pierre Salinger, that you don't talk to the President of the United States that way. And Rita Schwerner said, "We do." It wasn't a social call. He wanted to make a social call out of it. We were here on something serious. So we were bodacious. We dragged Martin Luther King along. We dragged LBJ along. They sanctified LBJ. Look at the pictures. There's LBJ. There's Robert Kennedy, and there's Martin Luther King. And SNCC dragged all of them around, kicking and screaming. Not Martin, so much, because sometimes Martin was willing to do what he had to do. And we don't take anything away from Martin Luther King. And we don't take anything away from JFK either. But those people were not saints. We had tremendous problems with those people. Read the history of the March on Washington in 1963. Read about John Lewis having to change his speech. We were bodacious and they were afraid of us, because we were making great changes in this country. But when they sanctify somebody, they leave out all of that person. They don't even talk about Martin's economic program. Martin was coming around on the war in Vietnam. He was coming around on the need for economic struggle. We had ended segregation in public places. And now people needed the money to buy the hamburger.

Jack Chatfield: Mr. Toure believes in the dialectic and so do I. But my dialectic is somewhat different than that of Mr. Toure. Rather than feeling that one force is always in the ascendant and one always in the subordinate position, I see many societies, not least American democracy, I see many cultures, I see many personalities as characterized by an ongoing dialectical tension in which no force is for long in the ascendant or at least not permanently in the ascendant. Since there was so much that has been said by Mr. Toure and in some cases by others with which I graciously disagree, it gives me great pleasure to say that we at least agree about the centrality of the dialectic in human affairs. Ironically, I still see myself as an early 1960s liberal, albeit with a profound sense of the limitations of liberalism; I see myself as a capitalist, albeit a pinched capitalist, with a profound sense of the limitations of capitalism; a pluralist, albeit with the sense of the limitations of pluralism. I would be less than candid if I did not say that I was unsettled by some of the events of the late 1960s, and perhaps I have not yet recovered. I'm a former member of SNCC but I am a historian as well, and for all of the tension this may create, I do feel a devotion to the intellectual life. Larry Guyot, a man whom I profoundly admire and respect, told me in Jackson, Mississippi, in 1969, after a very tense exchange which made me feel more uneasy than I did when I faced Laurie Pritchett in Albany, Georgia, "You're just one more typical northern white intellectual floating through the South, disconnected, rootless, a peripatetic intellectual." I have never forgotten those words and I will not deny now the force of that statement.

Historians have come under attack at this conference, a partial vindication, I hope, of our democracy. As a historian I should say that I am keenly aware of the limitations of the craft of history. But I would say this: that writing history is an extremely difficult task, perhaps only slightly less complex than witnessing it and recording it faithfully. Indeed, one of the striking things about this gathering was the degree of disagreement about the latter history of SNCC and perhaps even to a degree about the early days. When we hear one of the most distinguished members of SNCC say that Allen Dulles was at a meeting held at Greenville and then we hear the irrepressible Guyot correct Jim Forman and locate the meeting in Washington, we understand the difficulties of reconstructing the past. They are nearly boundless. In Mary King's book she quotes a seminal staff meeting in the spring of 1964 on the eve of Freedom Summer, and then quotes a remark that could only have been made in 1963 before the assassination of Medgar Evers. For those who think that historians have it easy and that they are traitors to the truth, bear these things in mind. Indeed, Mr. Toure spoke eloquently in defense of socialism; let it be recorded that in the late sixties he said, and this is a paraphrase, "Socialism is not for black people. Communism is not for black people. Marxism is not for black people." Views change, interpretations of the past change. It is infinitely difficult to reconstruct what went on. The past is full of pain, it is full of tension, it is, I think, full of ambiguity. Thus I would not be faithful to my mission as a historian, albeit with an affection for SNCC that practically paralyzes me, if I did not say that I remain a foe of ideological systems, suspicious of rhetoric, and I think this is an indispensable condition to the writing and recording of history.

ALLEN MATUSOW: The conference seems to have many purposes, but above all the purpose is historical. It is a conference conceived by a historian and it is a conference which has relied on the memory of participants to set the record straight and to tell the story. We have heard a series of very moving testimonials by people in the movement about how the movement transformed their lives even as they as members of SNCC were transforming America. And in the speeches we've heard and the songs that we've listened to, we have seen re-created here that community that SNCC created twenty-five years ago in the Deep South. I think we were privileged here to get a glimpse of the interior reality of what SNCC was and to understand something of the historical truth that SNCC was. And so the question becomes, why this topic? Because it's obvious that the veterans of this movement have clearly identified two enemies: sheriffs and historians. I'm guilty. I'm an outsider. I wasn't there. I'm a historian, and I'm a historian who has presumed to write about these events and to tell something about the history of SNCC.

I was very appreciative of the critique of history that has been offered here. I remember in particular the remarks of Bernice Reagon. When women spoke about their experiences within SNCC, the accounts were all different. In fact, they were contradictory. Ms. Reagon said that that shouldn't be surprising; that for every woman in SNCC there was a different experience and a different perspective and a different history and it would be a mistake to try to generalize about that, to make a comprehensive statement; that the generalizations you would make would be in the nature of distortions, and she was right.

And I remember this remarkable exchange between Mary King and Casey Hayden. Mary King explained how she and Casey had co-authored the paper that raised the issue of women in SNCC. And then Casey Hayden remarked that she doesn't remember writing the paper. And she turned to Mary King and she said something like, "If you and I were there, and don't know what happened, pity the poor historian that's going to have to write about it years later because they'll miss the truth," and Casey Hayden was right.

All that said, that's not all that needs to be said. The other part is that history by participants is no less distorted than history by the absent professionals. Because it will not surprise anybody here that memory fades, that memory is flawed, that memory evades, that memory resists bringing forward the material that was repressed, that what we heard here was an exercise in collective and individual autobiography and that all autobiography is to some extent self-justifying. That's not surprising. So what we heard ultimately was a kind of history that in its own way is just as limited and just as distorting as academic history. My point is, there's still a lot to learn.

What I would like to do is to raise some of the questions and some of the issues which I would like to see addressed the next time SNCC has a reunion. The first issue I would really like to see SNCC people talk about as participants is what became known as participatory democracy; that is, democracy within the movement. It's clear when you hear the people who were there that the community that they created changed lives. It was a community without hierarchy, without bureaucracy, without leaders. It was a community in which every individual was entitled to equal respect and the same hearing and in which decisions were all made collectively. And it was not an easy community to create. It was hard. And when it was finally done, there was something special there. Casey Hayden said that when she and her Freedom House were busy creating her community, what she envisioned was that this community would move outward until it took over the whole world. Only that didn't happen, it never got out of the house. And what I'd like to hear discussed is the limiting aspects of this beloved community; that is, whether in fact it did not impose limits in its attempt to create internal democracy. There are some reports of people who went to Mississippi in 1964, for instance, who felt that they would never be accepted by those who went through this process, that they would always be excluded. They hadn't gone through what the others had gone through. They had not participated. They didn't belong. And that might be one of the underlying reasons for the ultimate failure of the organization. At the end of her wonderful presentation, Casey Hayden said that she didn't know whether what she said made any sense to anybody, but she thought that it would make sense to other SNCC people. I wonder if given the kind of movement SNCC was, whether that's enough.

Another issue that I would like to see explored is the relation of SNCC to the liberal tradition. It's clear that the people who went to Mississippi and southwest Georgia in 1961 went to testify for traditional American democracy. They thought they were going there with the encouragement and the promise of protection by the Kennedy administration. What they learned when they got there was that they couldn't trust liberals. Liberals in Washington wouldn't protect them. FBI agents stood around taking notes while they got beat up; people in the Albany Movement got arrested for allegedly obstructing justice while the people who shot at them went free, and in 1964, there was a tremendous disillusionment resulting from the failure of the challenge at the Democratic National Convention by the Mississippi Freedom Democratic Party. And at the end of that, there occurred in SNCC a kind of collective nervous breakdown which in some way relates to the failure of the liberals to redeem their promise, to the destruction of the beliefs on which the organization was founded.

What I'd like to hear SNCC people talk about is whether they hadn't given up on liberalism too soon, because at the moment of the breakdown the Civil Rights Act of 1964 was already on the books, the Voting Rights Act of 1965 was already on the books, and those acts vindicated, however hesitantly, the promise of the liberals to do something about the problems of black people in the South. In Lowndes County in 1966, the Black Panther Party got as far as it did because the Johnson administration sent registrars or examiners into the state to register black voters under the 1965 Voting Rights Act. Mary King says in her book that she wishes she had known then how important the rule of law is and was. I'd like to hear what SNCC people who went through this experience think about it. When you hear these people sing, they are singing about a triumph, and why they feel triumphant is that they did, in fact, change things in the South. They helped destroy the segregation system, and they did that with the help of liberals.

I'd like to see the issue of interracial sex addressed. It's been addressed, and it's been addressed by participant observers, it's been addressed by Alvin Poussaint who treated people in the movement. What Poussaint says is that white women who went to the South in 1964 got bombarded by black men and reacted in neurotic fashion and that at the heart of SNCC, at the heart of the racial breakdown in SNCC in 1964 and 1965, was a problem of interracial sex.

I've got one last issue I'd like to see raised and that is the development within SNCC of revolutionary nationalism. What happened was that there began to develop within SNCC an identification with colonial peoples in Africa, and there began to develop a seductive analogy between black people in the United States and black people in Africa, that Africans in both continents were the victims of white racist colonial oppression. And when Frantz Fanon's book *The Wretched of the Earth* [1961] was translated, we have accounts here, confirmed elsewhere, about the way that the movement consumed that book, how it assumed a kind of biblical status. What that book does in part is talk about the therapy of violence. It was a short step from that, the analogy and Fanon, to conclude that black people in the United States should assume a revolutionary and violent posture toward their colonial oppressors in the United States. And that became the line that SNCC offered black people through its spokesmen, Stokely Carmichael and then H. Rap Brown in 1967, when black people were in the process of burning down their own ghettos.

I've got a quote from Stokely just to show you that the man is consistent. He went to Havana in August of 1967 and he said there, "Comrades of the Third World of Asia, Africa and Latin America, I want you to know that Afro-North Americans within the United States are fighting for their liberation. We have no alternative but to take up arms and struggle for total liberation and total revolution." H. Rap Brown less ideologically was making the same point. Stokely can face that. I'd like to hear other people in the movement respond. A lot of the people here had gone by then; what happened split those who were left, but many went the whole way with Stokely. I'd like to hear about that.

I've been interested in this movement since 1961 when Charles McDew came to Boston and talked to a bunch of us about it. I belonged to Friends of SNCC, picketed Woolworth's, and helped organize a Belafonte concert to raise money for SNCC. Then the Freedom Rides came and people got assaulted in Montgomery and other people started to go down there and I said to myself, maybe I should go. I said, I was a little busy, I'd go some other time. And then 1964 came and I could go and I knew that if I didn't go then I probably would never go. And I said to myself, was I ready to go down there and get killed, because I knew something about it, and I tried to imagine what it would look like if I looked into the barrel of a gun and what would happen if I got beat over the head and I knew it wasn't in me, that I couldn't go there. I'm not ashamed to tell you that, because a lot of people thought about going and hardly anybody went. I was normal. But these people went and that's why they're the authentic heroes of the 1960s and why they deserve a full and complete history, not a history that's going to romanticize, not a history that's going to ignore the warts, but a history of a great organization that's a full and complete history, and maybe sometime the participants and the historians working together can produce that history.

CLAYBORNE CARSON: I think if I have one good quality as a historian it's that I listen a lot and try to take in what I hear and then try to come to terms with aspects of it and try to make some sense of it. I think that one of the things that I would certainly agree with in some of the defenses of the craft of history is that the kind of truth we arrive at is not the truth with a capital T. I think the kind of truth we arrive at is something that is personal to us, it's very limited in terms of time and, most of all, it's limited in terms of the kinds of materials that we had to work with.

I'd like to just start by saying a bit about an experience that's now thirty years old. Kwame Toure might remember the first time we met. It was the summer of 1963. I was a freshman in college and just beginning to get involved. I went to a National Student Association conference, I think with the idea that I would meet a lot of these people who had been active. I had met some of the people from SDS. And I saw not only the man who was then Stokely Carmichael, but Bob Moses I saw also within that same period. That to me was the start of becoming a historian.

I'm a product of the movement; my work is a product of the movement. I wouldn't be teaching at a university if it were not for the movement. They didn't have black professors at Stanford University twenty-five years ago. There wouldn't have been a Black Studies program. None of my ability to do my work would have existed without the movement that I had my first contact with then.

One of the reasons why Kwame was there was that he was trying to get the National Student Association to do a very radical thing. You know what that radical thing was? It was to support the March on Washington. It was a very interesting experience to watch an organizer at work and to begin to understand something about an experience that was quite different from the one I had grown up with.

When I had gotten out of high school my ambition as the first person who had a possibility of going to college in my family was I had the chance of going to the Air Force Academy. I thought that was the top of the world. A few years later, as a result of meeting people like Kwame and Bob Moses, I was a draft resister. I think that that transition was very rapid and one of the things that I think becomes clear, is something else that has come up as a general theme in this conference—that experience that people had of meeting the movement and being changed by it in very dramatic ways. Most of the people we have been talking about are people who were changed in a way that brought them into SNCC. But there were many thousands of people out there like myself who were changed in just as fundamental ways, became part of the movement, who didn't join SNCC, who didn't become a field secretary in the South, but who considered ourselves part of that movement. So that when I went to school and became a historian, it would have never occurred to me to make a distinction between being an activist and being a historian. My activism was writing *In Struggle*. Now that is not to say that that is to make it any better or any worse than any other kind of work. It is simply one of the activities that I chose in addition to other kinds of political activities that I chose to engage in.

One of the things that I think that I saw as a result of looking at SNCC is that the story was multifaceted and the process by which the book got written I think tells a lot about the historian's craft. SNCC didn't have an archive, at least when I did my work. When I began to do my work on SNCC it came from interviewing the people in it, meeting them individually. I remember sitting down with Kwame a number of times at different locations. I remember sitting with Cleve Sellers. I typically went where these people were. Some I didn't reach. I really tried to reach everyone. One of the things that people do not understand, I think, who have not done this kind of history, is how difficult it is sometimes to have this sense that you've got to reach these people who have the story. Everyone was telling me, for example, Willie Ricks is going to be this really hard interview. Some of you who know Willie Ricks probably told me that. And yet what I found is that the people I did reach wanted to tell the story. They invited me into their homes. Many of you put me up overnight and introduced me to your attics. Sometimes you had boxes of material up there—and those were the SNCC archives. That's what had to be brought together. Sometimes the message that you delivered to me that was very, very important was not so much what you said but where you were and what you were doing while you were saying it. That was very important to me, to see people who were still in Mississippi. I visited Maria Varela in a small town up in northern New Mexico, still doing organizing, still in the community. And that delivered a message.

I'd like to end by talking about what I would see as the main theme throughout this conference. That is that SNCC was most of all organizers. We hear a lot about political leadership, we hear a lot about demonstrating, and most of what is delivered about the sixties is this notion of protest and rallies and these big marches, the March on Washington and so on, and yet the story that I got was a very different one. I remember when I told Kwame that I wanted to go to the March on Washington and he said that was a middle-class picnic. I thought that was the most radical thing that I had ever thought of doing in my life, going to that march, because it was the first protest for me. But he was talking about Albany, Georgia, he was talking about Mississippi, he was talking about this other reality out there of people organizing communities. And that was something that was very central and remains very central in terms of understanding SNCC. I think that if we have a message, it is the importance of community organizing and how to do that. I think that we've gotten not only some lessons about the centrality of that but also some very important lessons on how that is to be done. One of the things that historians can do is to begin to understand that organizing experience, begin to write about it in very creative ways, and that means that they have to begin to get into that experience.

I think that there is some unfinished business. Where do we go from here?—that question Martin Luther King addressed in 1968 in his last book. One of the ways in which I would like to address that is to recall something that Bob Moses once said. I think it was on the seventy-fifth birthday of Ella Baker, and he said one of the questions implicit in that is who are "we"? We have to still deal with that question of who is the relevant "we" as well as where are "we" going. I think as we can see from this discussion, that is still an important and unresolved question.

But I would add that historians, like everyone else who looks at SNCC or any other subject, have certain kinds of obligations. I guess the easiest way of expressing it is, why are you asking? What purpose is being served? I think that there is a real distinction to be made in the writing of history about radical movements, about whether or not the purpose of it is in some way to move the struggle forward. I think that I write critical history, so a lot of people in this room have brought to my attention things they basically disagree with in my book. But I don't think very many of them have any doubt that my purpose in writing it was to criticize in order to move something forward, and I think that that is critically important when we talk about the academic profession where the purpose of writing history is to move one's self forward in terms of career advancement. You get career advancement in this country by being cynical. They call it irony, but it's cynicism.

There's a larger question about mythology and history. That's an interesting question because as a historian you would expect me to come down on the side of history as opposed to myth. But I think both are very, very important and I'd like to explain that just a little. Because they both deal with the past. History re-creates the past for the benefit of the intellect, and it's an intellectual exercise. Myth also re-creates the past, and I would argue that myth plays the same role with respect to culture as history does for intellectual life. And that culture ultimately is the medium that carries on as the basis of any struggle. I think that when you look at what Bernice Reagon did you understand the importance of the cultural medium that allowed the struggle to take place and how that can be not only a basis, a foundation, for struggle, but that culture itself has to be transformed.

The reason why I mention myth is that right now I'm in another project, the Martin Luther King Papers. I think most of you recognize that there is already in the process of being created, perhaps already in place, a series of myths about the sixties and there's also what I particularly call the King myth. It's been referred to before. It's a myth, and I'm not saying this pejoratively. I'm saying it is very necessary that there should be a King myth and what King represented just as there should be an American white culture. We have a George Washington myth and an Abraham Lincoln myth and we have a variety of myths; well, we have a King myth. And the importance of myth is that it is that aspect of history that can provide lessons, cultural lessons that enable us to get into a future, enable us to survive, thrive, move forward.

Now, what I'm saying is that in addition to that King myth there has to be another kind of myth, a myth that is based on a different kind of struggle that also took place during the sixties. I think in a way that King myth is only an aspect of a story and SNCC is another aspect of that story. And in addition to that analytical history that I think historians like to have—those mind games where we sit around and we talk about interpretations of history and analysis of history and somehow we wonder why we don't get a wide readership and why no one even listens to what we're talking about, and why we are so irrelevant to what is a political process that we would like to have impact on—I think part of that is that we don't play that other process of doing cultural work, of creating stories about the past that help people get to a future. And those stories, I think, have to be created because that is what really survives. Anything we can do we should begin to do right now as part of our process of perhaps celebrating the King holiday. A basic aspect of myth is ritual. That is how we pass on stories to a new generation, stories about heroes, stories about people who did tremendous things on behalf of their people. Those stories have to be told and they have to be told well. That's not to say that we can't engage in analysis and all these other kinds of things, but that has to be a central part of our activity also.

Reflecting Back

Despite their frustration with the efforts of historians to render a true and fair account of the movement, SNCC activists themselves struggled to make sense of it all. Here they take on questions of SNCC's historical trajectory, its contributions, legacy, and meaning for today.

MICHAEL THELWELL: With your indulgence, I rise on a point of personal privilege. I want to make certain acknowledgments. When one thinks of the movement, in retrospect, after these years, one tends to think that one's recollections are colored by nostalgia and sentimentality. The people could not have been as heroic and as sharp and as clear as you remember them; it just wasn't possible. And then you come to a meeting like this and you see the old SNCC folk come out and you listen to them and you say, "By God, they really were as you remember them; they really were that impressive." I remember the first SNCC staff meeting that I was in. I thought I had fallen in among felons, because this very earnest young man dressed in SNCC blue was talking about decadence. He said, "This money that we have gotten has corrupted the movement; now that people are being paid, they no longer work, they hang out in the cafés and drink beer all day," and he was deeply distressed. He was talking about the $9.68 a week. That was Mendy Samstein. Extraordinary people made extraordinary contributions in many different ways. We talk about our great leaders—I never talked about Annie or Victoria; to me they will always be Mrs. Gray, Miss Hamer, Mrs. Devine, our leaders. Miss Ella Baker will always be transcendent in my memory and my recollections for the contributions, for the spirit, for the inspiration, for the direction she gave us.

But there are other people who in their own ways made contributions. I remember one person who long before I ever met her was always referred to as SNCC's angel. What the hell is an angel in that context? It's a person to whom when six or seven people doing what they should not have done ended up in jail and you need them somewhere else, and the bond is $10,000, they would say, "Call Lucy Montgomery." If the Freedom Democratic Party needed to bring a bus full of people from Mississippi to lobby Congress, "Call Lucy Montgomery." And she was always there, more than just a checkbook, more than just a rich white woman with a conscience. She soldiered through that with us. She ran workshops in Bolivar and Sunflower counties on how to run for public office. Amzie Moore asked her to do it. Now, how did she know that, this wealthy white lady from Chicago? Because she had funded and supported every black candidate who had ever challenged the Daley machine from time immemorial. I want us to recognize that very shy and honest human, Miss Lucy Montgomery.

And having made those encomiums to SNCC's brilliance, I remember one case when we were not so brilliant. A good friend of SNCC who happened to be a banker was so impressed with the organization that he arranged to have a SNCC speaker come to address a convention of American bankers, thinking that we would enlarge the coffers of the organization thereby. So they sent a speaker whose name I remember but I won't mention it. He went there and gave an impassioned and very stern lecture on the redistribution of wealth. I won't tell you what the contribution looked like from the bank.

All right. Now, SNCC was an extraordinary experience for a large number of people, both the small group of organizers who constituted a staff and the large number of people that it put in motion. I think that the historians and the media of this country have failed to properly interpret and demonstrate the change and effect that that little organization had, not only on the way black people live and are defined by this country today, but on a subsequent wave of social activity, the extent to which it gave form and language and a posture to any number of political movements which have since come out. But it can be demonstrated, I say, without resorting to a kind of parochial self-serving analysis. The work that SNCC did was perhaps the most profoundly effective work both in the kinds of legislation which came down to affect the conditions of life for black people and in the institutions that it left behind. It was also, however, the formative experience for almost a generation, certainly for the people who were involved, of young Americans, black and white. And that experience proceeded with a certain logic. And if I can just jump ahead to 1966–67 and the ultimate demise of the organization, one really has to understand that that roller-coaster ride of political activity, a very dangerous, very intense, very heightened experience in the South, left people profoundly emotionally exhausted. It doesn't matter how young and how fit you were, that would have sapped your physical, psychic, and emotional energies anyway. So there is a period of time, it seems to me, when also the political events of the nation had escalated and careened almost out of control largely as a consequence of the disillusion of a whole generation of American youth in the myths and in the principles and in the values that we had imagined that this country held. They were all dissolved in the violence, bloodshed, and class injustice and racial injustice of the Vietnam War.

And in that period, that really chaotic, almost hysterical period, this band of brothers and sisters, this circle of trust, having soldiered their way through and begun that process, were caught in a wave of forces that even today we're only beginning to understand. The logic of the movement was very, very clear. I want to talk about that logic and I want to talk about its character.

It began in the American South and it began with students protesting non-violently against the overt symbols of humiliation and discrimination in public accommodations. The point I want to make here is that the movement proceeded in a creative, pragmatic, problem-solving way, addressing real problems; and theory and ideology, to the extent that they existed, were always disciplines in service to very concrete material problems and how to affect those. Strategies and tactics evolved, some of them extraordinarily creative and intelligent in response to the pressing need of how do you organize people, how do you put people in motion, how do you analyze the system to find where the chinks are, to find where the weak spots are, to find the vulnerable points and then how do you best exploit them. And it is that creative process of pragmatic analysis and the willingness, not only to risk lives, not only to jeopardize your existence, and to risk torture, which sometimes is worse than just assassination, but also the willingness to work. I have a letter from Casey where she talks about the drudgery, the tedium of it. It wasn't always excitement, but there was a willingness to do the back-breaking, slow, unglamorous, serious work of working with and organizing people.

The movement, the resistance to the indignities of public discrimination, soon ran upon the very hard fact of political power in the country. And it became clear that the political parties of the country were of no help—that this system was prepared to coexist with, live with, and countenance the systematic disfranchisement of millions of black people in the South which robbed them of any political representation and left them the victims of legal discrimination, left them the victims of violence, left them absolutely powerless.

When we talk about victories and failures, you must cast your imagination back to what it was like for a black person to live in Mississippi in 1960. The cops didn't have to respect you. I remember in Canton, Mississippi, when the sheriff would go in and deputize all the drunkards in the bar on Saturday night and give them sticks and guns—the garbage men, rednecks, drunks—it's 12 o'clock and they're deputizing them, giving them badges, sticks, and guns and sending them out to cope with black people. Where the murder of somebody black wasn't a crime. Trying to impanel a jury to try the murderer of Medgar Evers who was being feted up and down Highway 49 in every bar he went. People would buy him drinks as he told them how he had assassinated Medgar Evers. Trying to impanel the jury; the federal prosecutor asked the prospective jurors, all of whom were white since they are taken from the voters list, "Do you think it's a crime for a white man to kill a Negro?" And a lot of people were excused from duty because they didn't think so. One old white farmer gave the most honest in terms of Mississippi answers; he said, "Well, that depends on what the nigger done done." Now, these are very real conditions. And they don't exist in quite the same way anymore. But what I want you to envision is the sense of absolute and total vulnerability that American citizens had who happened to be black, knowing that none of the institutions of society existed on their behalf or would protect them. That was changed.

But, now, the movement moved into the question of voter registration, the most profound decision it could have made, and we are still seeing the consequences of that. It isn't finished yet. I do not believe my brother, Stokely, that the Democratic Party is going to save us or that the vote will liberate us. But I do believe very profoundly that to the extent that the black vote in this country is organized into a precise instrument of pressure, one of many that we will need, is the extent to which the political institutions of this country will take black people's needs and demands much more seriously than they have traditionally done. And it is our responsibility to advance that process in every way as we look for those other processes and those other strategies which will help us to hasten the liberation which we all seek.

Now, when people went into the rural South, a remarkable thing happened. A remarkable thing happened for those black organizers from the North who went and for those white organizers from the North who went, and I'll tell you what that remarkable thing is. What we encountered was a massive dignity and power and principle and evocativeness and the force of traditional black southern culture. And that discipline then instructed us, because it's a culture not only with the theatrical expressiveness, the great artistic beauty and power that is our African heritage, but it is a culture winnowed by oppression and infused with a clear moral vision, a certain principle. When we talk of the local people with the reverence that we do, it is because we went down there, many of us, expecting to find the most oppressed people in the country, the most psychologically beaten down people in the country, people deprived of much formal education. In some counties in Mississippi they didn't have schools for black people until the Supreme Court decision to integrate schools. People deprived of education and economic opportunity. We're talking the wretched of the earth.

When we got down there what we discovered was a dignified, proud, principled, decent people in a culture which had sustained them, ironically enough, because of segregation. Where they had developed institutions and practices, one of which, of course, was the black church, an institution widely misunderstood in this country. They developed institutions and practices and values before which we were humbled and instructed.

We also discovered another thing. We discovered the youth there, and the power and the effect of SNCC is due to the Dorie and Joyce Ladners, and the Lawrence Guyots, and the Hollis Watkinses, and a host of other young local black Mississippians and Alabamians and Georgians without whom there would have been no movement. And my respect for those young people was and is profound because they knew better than anybody else what the consequences of resistance to American racism were. I remember a case of one guy who refused to drive a car into some town and people got to him, saying you're undisciplined and you're not working, why won't you go there? Well, it turns out he had almost been lynched in that town. And a member of his family had indeed been lynched in that town. And those young people came forward and made the movement work.

It didn't work because of the Howard intellectuals, it didn't work because of Jewish liberals and radicals who came, though they contributed. It didn't work because of the Anglo-Saxon liberals who came down to work. It worked because of the power of traditional black culture and the courage and bravery of the local people.

And the other thing that we discovered that was very instructive about these oppressed and depressed and psychologically worn down people who had been converted by slavery into Sambos—we heard all of that—when we got there, what did we discover? That simply by constructing the institutions through which they could struggle, we were in the presence of some of the most creative, resourceful, ingenious people and that all of that suppressed by the system of racism flowered in an incredible way. And it is that period, the so-called heroic days of SNCC, that we talk about and we glorify in our imaginations when we remember the development of the organization.

But the point here is a little more profound than that. Because what I'm saying, without saying it, is that the character and spirit and strategy of SNCC was in fact an expression, therefore, of Afro-American culture. Sure white liberalism helped to color it, Camus, Sartre, certain intellectuals helped to color it, but it was fundamentally an expression of Afro-American culture, Afro-American southern culture, in its principles and its values and its character.

And this didn't only affect the black northerners who went down there, it affected the white people in the organization as well. When we talk about, for example, the radical nationalist strategy of the Lowndes County Freedom Organization, the Black Panther Party, the person who discovered the legal basis to protect it was Jack Minnis, who was white. There was a certain pressure that was going to move us inevitably into a certain nationalism, and I want to discuss that. And the effect of liberalism on the organization, the alliance with liberalism, we should look at that. SNCC was not only democratic, it was not only courageous, it was not only egalitarian, but it was profoundly principled. There was nothing cynical about it. What it says it was doing, is what it did. What it says it was about, is what it did. And it took very principled and honest positions and continued to do so.

When we decided on the strategy of the Mississippi Freedom Democratic Party, that was because black people couldn't vote in Mississippi. So what kind of political activity is possible? It wasn't ideology that led us to this, it was strategy and a very creative strategy. Since we can't vote and we can't participate in the Democratic Party, since the Democratic Party in Mississippi is the state and it's racist, then let us stick it into the wider arena of the country and let us summon the forces of national liberalism and let them decide the case. And of course we know what the result of that was at Atlantic City. But the fact of the matter is that what is also not said about Atlantic City is that if President Johnson had ever permitted a vote on the floor of that convention, the party would have rejected his leadership, given the forcible arguments, the tragedy of that summer, and the massive organization effort that we launched on them. Had that happened, the political history—at least the electoral history—of this country might have been very, very different. When we came back with another challenge, it was Arthur Kinoy who found the statute saying that when Mississippi was admitted to the Union it was admitted on the basis that it would not discriminate against people or else it wouldn't have seats in Congress, and we launched that challenge.

We also came very damn close to succeeding. The political institutions of this country, turning their backs on the very constitutional principles out of which their own power derived, rejected that challenge. And it was at that point that people saw very clearly that traditional liberal morality and political practice were not dependable; that the interests of black people could only be advanced when there was a base of strength, political strength, from which to advance it. And that started the thinking in the direction of black folk. It wasn't simply a response to some ideological insight on the part of somebody; it came out of the concrete material experiences of people in that struggle.

We also began to see that we perhaps could get civil rights laws knocking out the visible symbols of discrimination and oppression but that there were problems, and these are problems which are still with us: economic problems and social problems, problems having to do with the status of and the place of the black community in this country which are anchored in three hundred years of racism and discrimination, and that to get to those problems there would have to be profound changes in the way the black community defined itself. That's another thing that led to Black Power.

What is not generally talked about very much, and I was in Washington, D.C., so I saw it, is the extent to which once our liberal allies were not able to determine the agenda—once we didn't simply follow whatever they handed to us, once we began to say, look, this is basically and fundamentally not in the interests of black people, this is not what we are about, we want to do something else, when the black people of Mississippi didn't accept two seats at-large in the Democratic Party—the vituperation, the anger, the attempt to exile us from the political community, the attempt to make pariahs of us, the attempts to red-bait us, was a whole revelation about the limits of and the viciousness of so-called American liberalism. And another thing that proved interesting for the Marxists was that the labor movement, the organizations of the white working class in this country, was the worst.

And as I say this, I have to say there were certain figures who were splendid: the late Reverend Robert Spike of the National Council of Churches behaved with uncommon principle and courage. And the churches and the religious organizations, which in my experience I tended to think of as wishy-washy Christian do-gooders, took positions which were really very progressive and fundamentally politically effective, and they would be important allies to have if you are going to attempt to make any changes legislatively and politically in this country.

So those were failures in liberalism. Also there was a very real and growing perception of the dangers of integration which we are now experiencing: I think that as we've begun to articulate the necessities for Black Power pointing to the limitations of integration, that those statements were prophetic, because what we saw was—and this is the irony—in a segregated situation the culture could flourish, institutions could flourish. The solution to the oppression that black people were undergoing was projected as this mythical integration. People failed to understand that like the working class, who according to Karl Marx wanted to abolish itself, the logic of integration was that the black race wanted to abolish itself and its culture. And so the call to Black Power was absolutely necessary and again coming out of concrete and material experience.

Let's examine this thing now. Here is an organization inspirited by and implemented by and fashioned by and strengthened by traditional black culture that is working for a solution which will lead to the obliteration of that culture and of that reality. And recall very well when we started talking about Black Power, people said we were going to segregate ourselves again, that we were calling for a reinstitution of segregation. In a certain sense. In a certain sense, not in the sense they intended it. And in the ironic sense it was certainly true. We had to begin the process of creating within the black communities responsible political institutions whether these be for electoral politics or any other kind of politics. Responsible cultural institutions. We had to, as we used to say, take over, which we have not succeeded in doing, the education of our young, because as Kwame used to say, no people ever freed themselves by allowing their oppressor to educate their children. And that's part of the unfinished agenda.

It is that consideration that led me, if I may speak personally for a minute, into Black Studies as a professional vocation. So that as we engaged and improved conditions for black people, as we engaged and opened up the more obvious expressions of racism and oppression in the country, we began to see the profundity of the problem and the problems beneath that which are being exposed. And as we opened those problems up we saw the problems beneath them. And now I believe we are at the place where we're facing the crucial and fundamental problem: how are the inner cities to be organized? How are we to take control of what are in effect—and this is not rhetoric, and I'll join my brother Kwame on this one—colonial enclaves, where land is owned by people who don't live there, the laws are enforced by people who don't live there, the institutions are run by people who don't live there, and the people who are the victims of these institutions have absolutely no power or control over them? What are the techniques we are going to use to develop those?

Also exposed were the limitations of political power. I confidently expected in 1965 that as the black populations in the inner cities grew, we would take control of them politically. That has happened. I did not anticipate that corporate America would move the taxpayers to the suburbs, that they would abandon those cities. That Marion Barry would become mayor of Washington, D.C. and discover that he doesn't have the economic base or the leverage or access to the kind of financing to put into place the programs that he wanted to put into place when he first sought that office: the very real constraints on elective office to change and affect fundamental situations in a society.

So that, clearly, a whole bunch of other problems have been exposed, not so much by the failures of the movement but by its victories. The problems -that we now have to engage that this generation inherits are fundamental and profound. It's going to require an incredible amount not only of commitment, but of creativity. Now that the Afro-American community's vote is beginning to express itself in the national arena with something of the force and the power that it should have commanded all along, I see that as the fruition of the struggle, but I see it also as the starting point for talking now about realistic coalitions. We've got some cards to play. And we will see and we will be instructed and we will learn by how well those cards are played.

The seeds that were planted bear fruit in many and profound ways. I remember a few years ago going to Tchula, Mississippi, meeting a young black man, Jesse Banks, who introduced himself as mayor. I was overwhelmed. We got into a conversation and I said, "How did you get into politics, where did you get the notion that you could be mayor?" He said, "My first introduction to politics was in the Freedom Schools in 1964 in Mississippi."

The other thing about SNCC is that when that small group of organizers moved in the American South to engage the problem there, they didn't set out to build themselves into a permanent organization. They didn't recruit members, they didn't sell membership cards. They encouraged the people to address their problems by their own independent organizations. That was a departure from any practice in the ongoing struggle for civil rights by any previously existing civil rights organization. And though SNCC may not be on the scene, when you go down and look, for example, at the local elections, you find that many of those organizations are still in place; that those people are working and developing and that the character, the political character of the South is being changed by organizations that a ragtag group of students helped to bring to life in the early sixties.

Not being in the business of prophecy, I don't want to make any predictions for the future, but I have to say that I have an incredible sense that there's more of a feeling of confidence, more of a feeling of effectiveness, more of a feeling in the black community nationally that we're beginning to pull into ourselves those collective resources, both the people and the material, that will enable us, the black community, to really make a much more effective drive on power and on wealth in this country. I also think that the black community is getting poised to be in the vanguard—I hate to use that word because of certain resonances—to be in the vanguard of a progressive movement in this country. And white progressives are going to have to learn that there ain't no harm being members of an alliance, members of a movement with a black leadership. Our white members learned that and it didn't bother them, because that is what SNCC was, that's what SNCC always was. Those people operated in the national spirit, operated in terms of the needs and necessities as it grew and as we understood the problems and as we developed strategies to engage them. When they left the organization, described by one person to me as the worst thing in her entire life, not one of those comrades went to the press that was really looking for sticks to beat SNCC with. Not one of them went to the press and said a mumbling word. That was the kind of principle and devotion of all those white folk. I call them that because they don't make white folk like that no more as far as I can see.

DANNY LYON: SNCC changed in the time that I was there, and it continued to change. I think historically that has to be clear; this was an organization that was growing like a person and changing and growing in size, and things that might have been accurate, six months or eighteen months later weren't accurate anymore.

My own feeling was that the antiwar movement took the wind out of the sails of the civil rights movement. To put it another way—one of the many victims of Vietnam was the southern civil rights movement, if only because the country's attention was turned away from the South and the movement to a war. I also think a fundamental difference between the movement and the antiwar movement was something that Tom Paine calls "sunshine soldiers and summer patriots." Had the involvement of those tremendous numbers of people, students, many white students, in the antiwar movement been as total as I think many people in the other movements had been, I think you would have seen a much greater revolution in this country. There were many people in the antiwar movement who were as committed and who were as changed forever as anybody in SNCC. But I don't think that was true of these tremendous masses of people who came out for rallies and then went home.

I'm not putting down going out for rallies, but I say look to yourself, you must change yourself. We are the problem. I'm the problem. I have never stopped believing that. I come from a middle-class background. I can eat anywhere. I can eat anything I want. I changed myself. I keep trying to change myself. I change my children. I think if you change yourself, everybody changes themselves—ain't gonna be no more problems. Of course, the world doesn't work that simply. I try to do it through the media; I think there has to be a revolution in the media. James talked about changing the values of the people of this country. I think in one sense that was a goal of SNCC that you can struggle toward through two more generations, and you should.

JOANNE GRANT: When I'm asked what SNCC's greatest achievement was, I find it's hard to say. I suppose just the creation of it as an entity was its single greatest achievement because of the way it functioned. It was so innovative, so imaginative, so creative, and basically so democratic; its own being was its greatest achievement, I think.

HOWARD ZINN: I'm thinking about the problem of historical perspective. I'm thinking of the fact that we are talking about SNCC, an organization which was founded about thirty-five years ago and a quarter of a century ago was carrying on its activities. This is a good thing to do, because if there's anything we need today, it is the kind of historical perspective which takes us away from the 6 o'clock news and the 11 o'clock news and the daily newspapers, and all the attempts to crush our hopes by giving us the most limited possible picture of present-day reality. And it takes some going back and it takes some looking at the kind of changes that have occurred over the years in order to build up our sense of what it is possible for people to do.

And for that reason I agree with Joanne that SNCC's existence was its greatest achievement. Maybe it's because all of us who were involved with SNCC had the same feeling about it. There wasn't a specific accomplishment, it wasn't putting pressure on the government to get this law passed or these signs removed or getting the Voting Rights Act finally passed, it was a remarkable and unique example of how social change can be achieved, of how people who are being blocked by the channels that be, who have been rebuffed and ignored by the Supreme Court, the President, the Congress—by all the organs of American society that they tell us in elementary school are going to solve our problems for us—how very ordinary people, seeing their neglect, banded together, organized, sacrificed, put their energy and their lives on the line, and created a model for what social movements can do and for how social movements should be.

And another thing. The most qualified people were the people running the country when we got into Vietnam and we stayed in Vietnam. They had terrific qualifications. They had all the degrees. They had all the experience. They were Phi Beta Kappa, Sigma Chi Nu, everything. It seems to me one of the great lessons we can learn from history is this business of qualifications and how the criteria that they give us to determine who is qualified are things that we should immediately discard and start using our own.

LAWRENCE GUYOT: One additional point. The Mississippi Freedom Democratic Party in 1964 was told it was unqualified, that it should stick to civil rights and leave politics to those who know how to do it. And when the

Freedom Democratic Party took a position against Vietnam, we were told you shouldn't be involved in foreign policy.

MENDY SAMSTEIN: It's a strange feeling speaking about a piece of history of which you were a part as though it's something in the past. You're able to comment on something that occurred a long time ago, but what occurred then is amazingly still alive. And it's been alive in me all this time. And every time I get together with people from SNCC I find how much it's still alive. We've changed. We've gone through a lot. We're older. I'd like to think, however, that it's not only that this experience is alive, but the people who were part of it are alive; that is, that we're still in there, we're still capable of doing things, and that we *are* going to do things. That there is a period of history still to be made. And some of what we went through and some of what we experienced is immensely valuable for what has to come now.

ROBERT ZELLNER: It's amazing how things have changed. It's very difficult to get across to ordinary people now, especially young people, what it was like to be in the South in the fifties and the sixties. Some meetings where I say that I lived under the system of apartheid in the South, some people get mad. They say, "What do you mean? You're in the United States." And I say, "Exactly." That's the only way that some people now can understand the system that was in the South just thirty years ago. It's sort of strange that our dialogue here, about what happened to us only thirty years ago in our own country, has to be explained in terms of somewhere else.

One of the most important contributions I think that SNCC made and one of the most important things that SNCC did was to give us in this country, in terms of political struggle, the concept of the mass struggle or community struggle. It was brought home to me a few years after the height of the SNCC years when I was involved with other political organizations and I would hear about somebody having a mass march. And I'd say, "How many do you have?" They'd say, "We had forty people." And then I would remember what a mass march was *really* like, when SNCC went and mobilized entire communities from the wino on the street and the cab driver, right on up through all the preachers and the teachers and the funeral home directors. I mean, when we had a movement in a city or in a town it involved everybody from the bottom to the top.

Another thing that we used to always do in SNCC meetings and Southern Conference Educational Fund meetings in the South, we'd want to know what was going on in the local community. What can we do if we get a bunch of people ready to march somewhere? We got up this morning to go speak to a high school. And we must have had a couple of thousand students at the high school and Julian and James Bond and June and I went out there, and it wasn't long before we had them on their feet and we were singing, "This Little Light of Mine," and we were talking the talk and walking the walk. And Julian said, "I think we can march them out of here." And I said, "Right, where are we going to go?" So that's what I want to talk about. Remember how we used to say, "What did so and so get arrested for?" "He was tending to liberate himself." One of the things that SNCC gave us was a life-long commitment to political action, to struggle. And each one of us is doing that in our own way.

People talk about how there's apathy now, no sense of urgency. Well, I think that you create a sense of urgency that grows out of an understanding of what's happening around you. I'm distressed and have a sense of urgency. I see people starving in the streets now; you didn't see that twenty-five years ago. You didn't see people sleeping on the ground. The infant mortality rate of black youngsters is rising. You gain a sense of urgency by understanding the systems that we all have to deal with, the misallocation of funds to armaments and war, and health-care suffering is the result of it. The tremendous costs of education, and how many people are going to suffer. The muzzling of academic freedom and what you can say. You create a sense of urgency out of analysis of what is going on around you.

TOM HAYDEN: I'm asked all the time about why SDS changed the way it did, and I think you can extend the question to SNCC as well. I think these were clearly temporary organizations that were suited to a specific historical purpose, to give expression to something that needed expression, but they were not bureaucracies; they were communities of martyrs. There were always people saying we have to build for the long haul and they were respected, but nobody knew what they meant—because if you don't believe you have a future, how can you build for the long haul? And it's hard to believe you have a future if you're facing death and destruction every day. So organizational structure follows the temperament of the people who are being served by the organization, and this was, as I've said before, a time of apocalypse, and apocalypse inevitably contains no future. And so the organization was only designed for the apocalypse. And that's fine. I don't think it could have been otherwise; that's just the way it was.

See, other organizations don't rise out of an apocalypse. Somebody says, "I want to build an organization around an agenda." An agenda is a more sterile concept by far. You can build a long time around an agenda because inevitably to achieve an agenda, it takes a long time. But you hear these people, they're still talking in their 1960 mode; they're saying you did what you had to do when you had to do it. Zellner is ready to march out of here if he can find a target.

Well, that's what I mean by an apocalyptic, spontaneous attitude. He'll stay around a long time but you can't organize an organization; it'd be like trying to turn a volcano into a skyscraper. The structure doesn't fit the purpose, the volcano is erupting and that's why it's a volcano.

In my view, SNCC's evolution had to do as much with the killing of Kennedy, the escalation of the war in Vietnam, and the neglect of the domestic issues as it did with things internal to SNCC. As far as SDS was concerned, the organization was so voluntary and so idealistic and so spontaneous that its structure was never stable. So if a little group wanted to penetrate and take it over, it was fairly easy. All you had to do was stay longer at meetings. And the Progressive Labor Party folks did that. But form follows function. Their only purpose was to take over SDS. They had no larger purpose. It's like a fungus on a dying body: they took it over but as they took it over, it died. So then they disappeared. There was nothing further to do, so they perished into smaller and smaller subgroups. It's hard to take over something that's just unorganized.

And the times—when Robert Kennedy died, in June of 1968, I was in New York. We went over to the church and we went in. They were just building the platforms for the funeral and we discovered that the coffin had just come in. There were a few of us there and we stood an honor guard, and I cried. The bullet killed hope, it didn't just kill a person. And I think you can only take so much of that, and so much of the sixties was seeing your best potential leaders shot. I think I was twenty-seven, which meant I was twenty-two when John Kennedy was killed, twenty-seven when King and Robert Kennedy were killed—it meant for me that the best political possibilities of our lifetimes were already behind us and we were not yet thirty. And that's an awful prospect to face—to be twenty-one, twenty-two, twenty-three years old and feel that for sure you've already seen your best possibilities come and go. And that experience, I think, was pervasive in our generation.

International issues were important too, but they cut both ways. The Vietnam War obviously galvanized a whole generation one way or another. But I think there was a tendency to overinvolvement in the foreign revolutions in the sixties that detached many of us from ordinary Americans and got us off track as well. Remember, it wasn't remote internationalism that moved people in the sixties, it was the fact that they were seeing death and destruction and the burning of villages on television and young men were being drafted. It was very "at home."

And although those students were on the outside politically, they were much on the inside in terms of being brought into the system with the draft. The draft was very significant. Those who want to reduce the protest to the drafts are wrong, though. There are some people who want to rewrite the history of the antiwar movement and say that all that those people were trying to do was save their asses from being drafted and that accounts for the apathy today because students are not being drafted, but it wasn't so. Before, during, and after the coming and going of the draft there were all sorts of antiwar explosions. But it was a factor. And in terms of galvanizing the moral energy, the draft did make it real. Even for people who weren't being drafted, it was something that the system could really do to you. You couldn't vote, but you could be drafted into an army and get killed in Vietnam. That did get your attention.

As for the question of apathy, my experience was in the early sixties. Remember, I'm an old guy—I went to Ann Arbor in 1957 through 1961, not during the time when everybody was a hippie and everybody was a radical. So we felt that we were alone and different, and that we were a 1 percent of the campus that had to wake up the 99 percent, and we went through the same strange looks and abuse that people are talking about today. What was bizarre, as I look back on it, and I'm proud of it, but it was bizarre, was despite the fact that we were 1 to 10 percent of the campus, we were convinced that in a very short while we would change the whole world.

J UNE JOHNSON: In 1833, at the founding convention of the American Anti-Slavery Society, William Lloyd Garrison demanded that the abolitionists' purpose be to secure the colored population all the rights and privileges that belonged to them as men and as Americans. But by the spring of 1865, after the Emancipation Proclamation, it was also Garrison who proposed that the society should be disbanded because as he saw it, its work was already done. Slavery had been legally abolished and even though the freedmen were far from enjoying the rights and privileges that belonged to them as men and Americans, Garrison came to believe that blacks no longer needed any special help to secure those rights. Garrison's position was opposed by black abolitionists, especially Frederick Douglass, who staunchly opposed the self-destruction of the best-known abolitionist organization. Obviously, Douglass knew what many blacks and whites today are still discovering: breaking down legal barriers is only the first step in struggling for freedom.

The newer abolitionists today are those men and women who are persevering in that struggle, who continue to strive for the inclusion of black Americans into the mainstream of our society politically, socially, and economically. They are those who realize, as did Dr. Martin Luther King and Malcolm X, that it made no difference that I had the right to eat at any lunch counter if I could not afford to buy the food.

It seems the South of today is a vastly different region than it was thirty years ago. Then we were murdered and beaten, fighting for the right to vote.

I will never forget being with the late Fannie Lou Hamer on June 9, 1963, in the Winona jail after being brutally beaten for trying to eat at a Trailways bus terminal lunch counter. Amazingly, in 1988, the Reverend Jesse Jackson finished first in the race for the Democratic presidential nomination in Louisiana, Mississippi, Georgia, Alabama, and Virginia. The significance of that accomplishment cannot be overstated, for it shows the modern abolitionist movement is still alive and well. Blacks can now sit at any lunch counter, but the vast majority are still too poor to buy food. On the one hand, blacks who could not vote thirty-five years ago now have elected mayors in Atlanta, Birmingham, and other segregated cities. There is even a black congressman from Mississippi, Michael Espy, the first in over a hundred years, but on the other hand blacks are forced to migrate into too many big large ghettos seeking to escape grinding rural poverty.

Progress alongside extreme stagnation: Atlanta with its prosperous black middle class, its well-known black government officials, had a higher poverty rate than any major American city except Newark, New Jersey, from 1970 to 1980. The portion of Atlanta's population that lived in poverty rose from 20.4 percent to 27.5 percent. And yet people still migrate to southern cities in today's South because life in rural areas is harder still. Even where blacks by sheer force of numbers and court orders have attained a measure of political power, the lack of economic power has left the rural South an isolated place where thousands of descendants of slaves are no longer needed to work on the plantation. Even where blacks have control of municipal and county government, the white men who own the banks, the farms, and the businesses are still in control.

In Mississippi, with over 35 percent of its population black, there are hundreds of black elected officials, but most are mayors and officials in small towns with very few resources available to improve the life of the population. At the same time, at-large elections, second primaries, and other schemes to dilute voting strength remain. These are falling, but slowly, as the same lawsuits are heard in courts throughout the southern region. Thus while the number of black elected officials represents a great improvement over twenty years ago, it remains minor compared to the black proportion of the population. In Mississippi blacks are still a tiny fraction of all elected officials, and no black has been elected to a statewide office since Reconstruction. Nearly 40 percent of all blacks in the state live in poverty. So, in many ways, the new South is different from the old but there are still far too many similarities.

Today abolitionists are still fighting for economic and political power to make the southern transformation complete, and even though the movement today is not always in the national headlines and takes different forms from years ago, it is still pressing forward. For example, in Mississippi alone there have been boycotts in Indianola, Senatobia, Natchez, Brookhaven, and Raymond from the northern to the southern end of the state. In most cases local blacks have come together to protest the injustices in the local school system, where black majority school districts are still controlled by white administrators, or the separate and unequal system of justice, which still prevails and makes it less of a crime, or no crime at all, to attack a black person.

Modern abolitionists are using the court system to knock down discriminatory election laws which still curtail black voting power. In a case which had national implications, a federal judge ruled in 1987 that Mississippi's system of electing circuit and chancery court judges discriminates against blacks. Victories are still being won, but there is still a long way to go. In reality, the destiny of the South is intertwined with that of the rest of the nation. Today's abolitionists are not just fighting a problem confined to one region. Too many people, black and white, are unable to eat; they are at the table but the struggle today is to insure that everyone at the table gets food.

ROBERT MANTS: I think, as I look back over my movement experience and my involvement in SNCC, I would classify the periods of SNCC into four parts. The early part in 1960 to right around 1962 was what I would call the beloved or redemptive community. It was a period in which nonviolence was not only a philosophy for some of those people in the early days, but also was an attempt to establish nonviolence as a way of life. The other period, and some of these overlap, was a period of desegregation, where there was more direct action, especially as a test of the 1964 Civil Rights Act. There was another period right after that, what I would call the Black Power era, that came right on the heels of the Voting Rights Act of 1965. Right before that, too, was also a period of what was called the Great Society program or the antipoverty program. That period—and some of these periods again, overlap—was about 1965 to 1967 or 1968. The fourth period I want to mention, because I think it's imperative that people understand, is the period that I call "after the storm." That period after the storm is defined by me as the period after the SNCC workers left the South and those of us like John Jackson, C. J. Jones, and Cleve Sellers have a different story to tell. I say that we got the chicken shit between our toes, and we have a different perspective and a different story to tell.

THERESA DEL POZZO: I worked in SNCC in Mississippi. Several things that have been discussed all tie together. This question about what happens to communities and why Martin Luther King is seen as the only leader. How people don't look beyond the surface, and the surface to a large extent is what is portrayed over the mass media. How people hear about Martin Luther King and not about all the people along the way who have made those things possible, all the people in those caucuses in Mississippi who made the Freedom Democratic Party, who came to meetings, night after night and week after week, who made that movement strong. Cumulatively we end up feeling that in the end the movement died. We hear there is apathy on campus. Meanwhile, there are all these other things happening in this country that were not happening thirty years ago. There's an environmental movement, protest movements—over every issue you can think of, people will pick up a placard and go out and demonstrate. And that is the result of the movement. You know it doesn't have to be that SNCC went on ad infinitum. The fact that SNCC as an organization no longer existed after a certain point does not matter. What mattered was that protest and opposition became a way of life and a way of thinking in this country. And everybody who opposes polluted water, nuclear power plants, a highway coming through your land, farm closings, plant closings, unemployment, housing—every one of those people is continuing the struggle. It's not true that all of a sudden there was this big movement and now all of a sudden it's not there. One day they are going to say, "Oh, it happened again." And everybody is supposed to turn around and say, "Where did it come from?" It's always been there.

We grew up hearing about the House Un-American Activities Committee in the fifties, the muzzling of all those people, and we didn't hear about the people who didn't hide, who refused to answer those questions about being communist. The Carl and Anne Bradens who took their books and put them in their front hallway so the first thing you saw when you walked in their door was those books. We all grew up in the fifties thinking all these people went underneath their beds. Well, that wasn't true, and it isn't true that SNCC just died and all those feelings died. All the things that happened since are related to what has happened in the past and what's happening now.

VICTORIA GRAY ADAMS: The attitude in this particular moment is the body of hope. Hope for this country and possibly hope for this globe. And when I say that, I say that in all sincerity. Some of us are the heart of this body, some of us are the eyes of this body, some of us are the ears of this body, but we are all a part of this body. And as a part of this body, we all are the seeds that are going to determine the ultimate product. I'd like to have us end by sharing with you what I call a send-out. Some people call it a benediction and that's okay, but I'm saying it's a send-out for each and every one of us, and the title is "A Seed." I feel we are at the threshold of a new age, and that we need now more than anything else a new approach to human relationships and to social organization. We need a planetary approach. We need a synthetic approach. We need something in which the individual learns his own function in the world, because if you are to have a global world, the individual has to be so well established in his own identity that he can afford to cooperate with other people all over the world independent of their culture, their race, their traditions, and so on.

It is very important, therefore, that one should learn how to establish one's self and one's own identity. We need a new type of human being. We need something which is based no longer so much on conflict but on a full acceptance of the total human being, body, mind, soul, feelings, everything, an aesthetic approach versus an ethical approach. So that you can see the relationship in which everything stands inside of the whole. So you can look at the whole and become identified with the wholeness of that whole, rather than with any particular part.

Now this is, of course, a very difficult situation. We're certainly in a difficult time. And what is ahead of us today I do not know. I'm rather pessimistic as far as the immediate future is concerned, considering the way the world and our nation is moving at the present time, but you must realize that crises are sometimes necessary to accomplish what is to be accomplished. The only problem, however, is this: something must be ready before the great crisis comes, when the new cycle begins. For it will have to begin on the foundation of those seeds which have been sown before the crisis. If you have a winter followed by a spring but there was no harvest in the fall, no seed will germinate during the spring.

That's why I stressed so much all my life the idea I call the seed person, the person who is willing and able to gather within him- or herself the past of humanity, as it were—particularly of the Western world, of course, but also of other cultures, because what we want to emerge from the future after whatever crisis will come is a global world. We therefore need persons of great vision, persons who are not specialists, generalists as they are sometimes called today. Persons who have the vision and courage to wait and to in some way, through their lives, through their example, and through whatever they leave after their deaths, to become the seeds of the future world.

That's the choice, the great choice we all will have to make, and we all can make it. We can follow the mass vibration and decay like all the leaves of the world in the fall. However beautiful the golden leaves may be, they will have to decay and to become manure for the future of civilization. But it is only the seed persons that really count. And it is those you should look for, if yourself do not feel yet to the point of being ready to become a seed person, because that is the only insurance for the future rebirth of humanity.

I think today it is no use to try to look to the immediate future, because it looks very dark, but to look, to prepare for the possibility that a new world may arise, if not tomorrow, the day after tomorrow. I think it is the only thing which gives value to our sacrifice, all our courage, decisions, and choices today. It is to become seeds for the development of the future world.

So I hope every one of you, each one, in your life, in your own way, can someday very soon, if you have not done so already, make the choice and become seed persons, seed men and seed women.

Hollis Watkins: Miss Gray's words compel me to ask a question. And the question I want to ask is (sings):

> Do you want your freedom?
> Certainly Lord, certainly Lord, certainly Lord
> Certainly, certainly, certainly Lord.
>
> Will you fight for your rights?
> Certainly Lord, certainly Lord, certainly Lord
> Certainly, certainly, certainly Lord.
>
> Will you go to jail?
> Certainly Lord, certainly Lord, certainly Lord
> Certainly, certainly, certainly Lord.
>
> Will you fight for justice?
> Certainly Lord, certainly Lord, certainly Lord
> Certainly, certainly, certainly Lord.
>
> Do you want to be free?
> Certainly Lord, certainly Lord, certainly Lord
> Certainly, certainly, certainly Lord. (Adaptation of a traditional song)

Glossary of Names and Terms

Abernathy, Ralph, Sr.: An organizer of the Montgomery bus boycott and a Baptist minister, Abernathy was a founder of the SCLC and became its secretary/treasurer in 1961. He was a close advisor to Martin Luther King, Jr., and became head of the SCLC after King's death. His autobiography, *And the Walls Came Tumbling Down*, was published in 1989.

Aelony, Zev: A CORE worker charged with inciting insurrection in Americus, Georgia, in August of 1963 for protesting against the arrests of civil rights activists.

Alinsky, Saul (1909–1972): Chicago activist who pioneered crucial techniques for community-based organizing. His writings include *Reveille for Radicals* (1946) and *Rules for Radicals* (1971).

All African Peoples Revolutionary Party: Organization promoting socialist Pan-Africanism, led by Kwame Toure (formerly Stokely Carmichael).

Ashmore, Harry: The executive editor of the Little Rock *Arkansas Gazette,* Ashmore editorially opposed Governor Orval Faubus in the 1957–58 desegregation crisis. In 1958 he won a Pulitzer Prize for editorial writing, and the *Gazette* won one for meritorious public service. He has written *The Other Side of Jordan* (1960) and *Hearts and Minds: The Anatomy of Racism from Roosevelt to Reagan* (1982).

Assembly of Unrepresented Peoples: Led by Bob Moses, an assembly of poor people, intellectuals, and students who gathered in silent vigil at the White House in 1965 to protest the Vietnam War.

Atlanta Committee on Appeal for Human Rights: Activist civil rights group formed by Atlanta college students, including Julian Bond, Lonnie King, Marian Wright (Edelman), and Bernard Lafayette, Jr., who had participated in the 1960 sit-ins. They presented an appeal for human rights, asking area merchants to desegregate, and led demonstrations and protests.

Attorney general meeting: The meeting regarding Justice Department involvement in providing sufficient protection for blacks registering to vote and in reversing the convictions of eight SNCC leaders.

Baker, Ella (1903–1986): A civil rights activist throughout her life, Baker traveled south to work with the SCLC and Martin Luther King, Jr. In 1960 Baker called a conference at Shaw University in Raleigh, North Carolina, for students involved in the sit-ins. Nearly 150 students representing nine states attended the conference. It was here that SNCC was born. Baker insisted that SNCC remain autonomous from SCLC and served as one of its senior advisors for many years.

Barbee, William: A participant in the Freedom Rides and John Lewis's colleague at American Baptist Theological Seminary in Nashville, Tennessee.

Barnett, Ross (1898–1988): Governor of Mississippi (1960–1964) who campaigned on a white supremacy platform. In September 1962 he barred James Meredith from registering at the University of Mississippi. When Meredith arrived a riot ensued, requiring both the National Guard and the army to restore order.

Barry, Marion: In April 1960 Barry was chosen as the first chairman of SNCC, a position he left within a few months to return to graduate school. In 1964 he again became a full-time civil rights activist, at first planning demonstrations and boycotts, then opening a SNCC office in New York City, and finally becoming Washington director of SNCC. He is currently mayor of Washington, D.C., a position he previously held from 1979 to 1991.

Baton Rouge (Louisiana) bus boycott: Organized by the Reverend T. J. Jemison and others in 1953 to protest segregated and inferior treatment on buses. It ended with a compromise that increased the number of seats available to black riders. A definitive court ruling against segregation came in 1962.

Belafonte, Harry: A singer and actor, Belafonte was also an active civil rights participant. He served on the board of directors of the SCLC and the Dr. Martin Luther King Foundation. In addition, he participated in many civil rights marches and helped raise money for SNCC.

Belfrage, Sally: A Freedom Summer volunteer in Mississippi, where she helped register blacks to vote and taught in Freedom Schools. She is the author of *Freedom Summer* (1965) and *Un-American Activities: A Memoir of the Fifties* (1994).

Bevel, James: A black Baptist minister, Bevel was a member of SNCC and SCLC. During the early 1960s he helped to organize protest movements throughout the South.

Bingham, Stephen: Nephew of Congressman Jonathan Bingham, he was a Yale University participant in the Freedom Vote. He later became a lawyer and worked in the prison movement.

Black panther: This symbol was chosen for the Lowndes County Freedom Organization (also known as the Black Panther Party) because the panther would not back up if attacked.

Black Panther Party for Self-Defense: A party inspired by the Lowndes County Freedom Organization formed in October of 1966. The Oakland chapter was organized by Bobby Seale and Huey P. Newton and based on a Ten Point Program of self-defense and community improvement inspired by Algerian freedom fighter Frantz Fanon. Members defended themselves by openly bearing arms, which was legal in California.

Black Power: Slogan first used as a mobilizing tool by Willie Ricks and Stokely Carmichael in June of 1966 in Mississippi. It was a call for blacks to unite, lead their own organizations, and reject the racist institutions of American society. Often caricatured or exaggerated by the mainstream media, Black Power split the civil rights movement; the NAACP and SCLC rejected it as racist while many young people rallied around it as a cry for more aggressive action.

Block, Sam: Amzie Moore convinced Block to work full time for SNCC in

1962; he became field secretary in Adams County, Mississippi, focusing on voter registration.

Bloody Sunday: On the March 7, 1965, on their way to Montgomery, marchers were brutally attacked by state troopers on Selma's Edmund Pettus Bridge. As a result of this violence SNCC workers came to Selma to join a protest march. In that march, on March 10, Martin Luther King directed marchers to turn back, leading to much SNCC disillusionment with King. A third march occurred on March 21 under federal protection.

Borinski, Ernst: A sociologist at Tougaloo University. He was an opponent of segregation and helped develop the idea of parallel institutionalism embodied by the Mississippi Freedom Democratic Party.

Bowie, Reverend Harry: An African-American Episcopal priest from New Jersey who participated in Freedom Summer and was a leader in the Delta Ministry in McComb, Mississippi.

Boynton (Robinson), Amelia: An African-American woman who ran a small insurance office and was a central member of the Dallas County Voters League. She kept a list of all those who had attempted to vote, and John Doar of the Justice Department used this to file voting suits in Selma. Her home and business served as headquarters for local voting rights efforts.

Boynton, Samuel William: A local activist who, like his wife, played an important role in involving SNCC and the SCLC in the Selma voter registration project. He died in 1963.

***Boynton v. Virginia* (1960):** A case in which the Supreme Court ruled against segregation in terminals serving interstate transportation. This case followed the Motor Carrier Act and *Morgan v. Virginia* (1946), which prohibited segregation on interstate travel. Nevertheless blacks who tried to exercise these rights were often arrested or ejected. CORE tested *Boynton v. Virginia* with the Freedom Rides.

Braden, Anne and Carl: White leftist members of the Southern Conference Educational Fund (SCEF) who developed close ties with SNCC leaders as early as the fall of 1960. In 1961 Anne convinced SCEF to provide SNCC with a $5,000 yearly grant to hire a white field secretary. Both Anne and Carl stressed the importance of white involvement in SNCC and the civil rights movement as a whole.

Brown, Benjamin: Student activist and sit-in veteran from Clark College in Atlanta.

Brown, Hubert "Rap": Director of the Nonviolent Action Group, a SNCC affiliate, in 1964 as a student at Southern University in Baton Rouge, Louisiana. In 1966 he became SNCC project director in Alabama, and in 1967 he replaced Kwame Toure as SNCC chairman. Brown proved controversial as a result of his involvement in the northern urban black rebellions and his book *Die Nigger Die* (1969), which alienated many white liberals. He was arrested in 1973 for robbery. He converted to Islam in 1976, following his parole, and changed his name to Jamil Abdullah Al-Amin.

Burgland High School: The predominantly black high school in southwest Mississippi attended by many students who joined civil rights protests in McComb. Most of the students to whom Marion Barry and Charles Sherrod taught nonviolent practices attended Burgland. Brenda Travis, a Burgland student, was arrested in 1961 for protesting and sentenced to a year in a juvenile state school. After her arrest, 130 students protested and were expelled for participating in this and other SNCC-sponsored demonstrations. School officials agreed to reinstate students provided that they sign a pledge agreeing that they would be expelled for participating in further sit-ins. Most students refused to sign, and SNCC therefore established the first Freedom School, "Nonviolent High," in October of 1961.

Chaney, James: A native of Mississippi and a CORE staffer. In 1964 he and two northern college students (Michael Schwerner and Andrew Goodman) were arrested in Philadelphia, Mississippi, on their way to visit a Longdale, Mississippi, church that had been burned by the Ku Klux Klan. Upon their release they were killed by white supremacists. Their bodies were uncovered in a dam after a massive FBI search.

Chestnut, J. L.: Civil rights activist and attorney in Selma, Alabama.

Churchville, John: An Atlanta staff member who quickly became disenchanted with the civil rights movement and embraced black nationalism.

Civil Rights Act of 1957: The first civil rights law passed by Congress since

Reconstruction. It upgraded the Justice Department's Civil Rights section into a division and gave federal prosecutors the right to obtain court injunctions against interference with the right to vote. Additionally, the act established a federal Civil Rights Commission and provided it with the authority to investigate discriminatory conditions and to recommend corrective measures.

Civil Rights Act of 1964: A landmark piece of comprehensive legislation banning discrimination by businesses offering food, lodging, gasoline, or entertainment to the public. It also forbade discrimination by employers or labor unions when hiring or dismissing. It authorized the attorney general to file suit to force the desegregation of schools, playgrounds, libraries, and pools. The act declared that any person with a sixth-grade education was literate for the purpose of voting in federal elections. After it was passed, the desegregation of public facilities occurred on a wide scale.

Clark, Jim: Sheriff of Dallas County, Alabama, from 1955 to 1967. A militant segregationist, Clark used force against protesters taking part in the SCLC-sponsored demonstrations in Selma in 1965. On March 7 ("Bloody Sunday"), state troopers and Clark's men used tear gas, nightsticks, and whips to block the Edmund Pettus Bridge from an attempted march from Selma to Montgomery.

Cobb, Charles: SNCC communications director and field secretary in Mississippi, and a poet, who was instrumental in the formation of the Freedom Schools.

COINTELPRO: An FBI counterintelligence and disinformation program against civil rights activists and organizations. This effort helped cause internal splits in the Black Panthers and SNCC and damaged other civil rights groups and leaders as well. Agents infiltrated protest groups in a deliberate effort to disrupt their activities and prevent the creation of a unified black militant movement.

Congress of Racial Equality (CORE): Organization founded in 1942 by George Houser and others affiliated with the left-leaning pacifist group the Fellowship of Reconciliation. CORE members pursued nonviolent resistance to segregation. With the help of James Farmer and Bayard Rustin, CORE became a national organization. In 1962 the group began to focus on voter registration. Working with the Council of Federated Organizations, it helped organize Freedom Summer. CORE also organized communities in the North. In the late 1960s CORE was decimated by factional and philosophical disputes.

Congressional Black Caucus: Established in 1971 by Congressman Charles C. Diggs of Michigan. The caucus is an affiliation of black Congress members, generally Democratic, created to advance the social, economic, and political interests of African Americans.

Connor, Eugene "Bull": Police commissioner of Birmingham, Alabama, whose men attacked civil rights demonstrators in 1963 with batons, dogs, and fire hoses, helping create widespread support and sympathy for the demonstrators.

Council of Federated Organizations (COFO): Founded by Bob Moses of SNCC and David Dennis of CORE in 1962 as a statewide coalition of civil rights organizations in Mississippi to prevent conflict between groups over Voter Education Project funds. The NAACP's Aaron Henry was president and SNCC workers made up most of the organization's membership. In 1962–63 COFO conducted a voter registration campaign, but because of white opposition, few blacks were actually registered. In 1963 COFO mobilized approximately one thousand black voters to cast protest ballots in the August Democratic primary, and then orchestrated the Freedom Vote campaign. Aaron Henry was selected as gubernatorial candidate. White northern college students came to help with the campaign, which helped lead to the conception of Freedom Summer.

Cox, Reverend Elton: Traveling field secretary for CORE; imprisoned repeatedly in Baton Rouge, Louisiana, in 1962 and 1963.

Current, Gloster: NAACP director of branches from 1946 until 1977. He later became a writer, orator, and musician, and served as pastor of the Westchester United Methodist Church, New York.

Curry, Connie: A member of SNCC's Executive Committee and a member of the National Student Association (NSA). Because of SNCC's limited resources, she allowed SNCC the use of NSA equipment and facilities in Atlanta. More recently she worked for former mayor Andrew Young in Atlanta, Georgia.

Dahmer, Vernon: A long-time Hattiesburg, Mississippi, activist who died from respiratory failure after two carloads of Klansmen firebombed his house in 1966.

Daniels, Carolyn: A beautician in Dawson, Georgia, Daniels provided housing for Terrell County SNCC workers doing voter registration. In retaliation her home was shot into and bombed.

Daniels, Jonathan: Ministerial student from Cambridge, Massachusetts, who worked in Selma, Alabama. He was killed in August 1965 in an ambush after being released from jail in Hayneville.

Deacons for Defense: Organization of African Americans who armed themselves to protect civil rights workers and demonstrators in the face of white supremacist violence. At the invitation of SNCC and CORE, armed Deacons patrolled the highways before the 1966 James Meredith march.

Delegation to Africa: In 1964 Harry Belafonte extended an invitation for SNCC members to visit Africa on behalf of the government of Guinea. The trip ran from September 11 to October 4. The delegation included Julian Bond, James Forman, Prathia Hall, Fannie Lou Hamer, Bill Hansen, Donald Harris, Matthew Jones, John Lewis, Bob Moses, Dona Richards, and Ruby Doris Robinson. Here they saw entire governments run solely by black people. John Lewis and Don Harris extended their tour of Africa for another month and as a result of their meetings with African leaders and African-American expatriates, concluded it was necessary for SNCC to establish permanent ties with Africa.

Delta Ministry: Established by the National Council of Churches as an offshoot of its Oxford, Ohio, training sessions for ministers and volunteers during Freedom Summer. The Delta Ministry centered on community development in the Mississippi Delta region, with the main office in Greenville. Its goals were to improve economic, health, and social conditions for African Americans and to bring together local black and white communities. It established community centers and created literacy and vocational training programs. The Delta Ministry also supported striking plantation workers and picketed companies guilty of job discrimination.

Dennis, David: A CORE member and Freedom Rider, Dennis along with Aaron Henry, James Forman, and Bob Moses founded the Council of Federated Organizations. He organized demonstrations and helped launch the Mississippi Freedom Democratic Party's challenge to the Democratic Party. In 1964 he became program director for CORE's Southern Regional Office.

Devine, Annie: Raised in the rural segregated town of Canton, Mississippi, Devine dedicated herself to the civil rights struggle at age fifty. In 1964 she helped to organize the Mississippi Freedom Democratic Party along with Fannie Lou Hamer and Victoria Gray. She was among the sixty-eight elected representatives who challenged the seating of the all-white state delegation to the Democratic National Convention in 1964.

Diamond, Dion: A Freedom Rider who left Howard University to participate in SNCC. Diamond helped to organize students at Southern University in Baton Rouge, Louisiana, and was arrested along with Bob Zellner and Chuck McDew in 1962 and charged with criminal anarchy.

Diggs, Charles C.: African-American congressional representative from Michigan. A Democrat, he founded the Congressional Black Caucus in 1971.

Doar, John: Deputy director of the Civil Rights Division of the Department of Justice. Closely involved with the civil rights movement, he was instrumental in helping the Voting Rights Act pass.

Donaldson, Ivanhoe: Black student from Michigan State University who organized the provision of food and supplies to needy black Mississippians after the state legislature cut off surplus food programs in retaliation for voter registration attempts in 1962–63. Field secretary and director of the Holly Springs project in the summer of 1964, he has served more recently as advisor to Mayor Marion Barry in Washington, D.C.

Du Bois, W.E.B. (1868–1963): Black activist and intellectual who dedicated his research and writing to advancing the black race. Du Bois promoted a platform of racial unity. He disagreed with Booker T. Washington's accommodationist stance, instead advocating leadership by the black elite, which he termed the "talented tenth," and the participation of black people in all areas of American society. A cofounder of the NAACP in 1909, he edited its journal *The Crisis* from 1910 to 1934. Du Bois advocated fighting racial discrimination throughout the world, and was an early supporter of the Pan-African Congress. In 1961 he joined the Communist Party and immigrated to Ghana.

Dulles meeting: Former CIA director Allen Dulles flew to Mississippi as a special emissary of President Lyndon Johnson following the disappearance of James Chaney, Andrew Goodman, and Michael Schwerner in 1964. Dulles suggested that the civil rights demonstrations were creating too much friction, but Aaron Henry and SNCC members did not back down.

Durr, Clifford and Virginia: Montgomery, Alabama, activists, and friends to various civil rights leaders. Clifford Durr secured Rosa Parks's release from jail in 1955. *Outside the Magic Circle* (1985) is Virginia Durr's memoir.

Espy, Alphonso "Mike": The first African-American congressman from Mississippi since Reconstruction, elected in 1986. In 1993 President Clinton appointed him secretary of agriculture.

Evers, Medgar: Mississippi field secretary of the NAACP since 1954 and active in civil rights efforts. He was assassinated in the early morning of June 12, 1963. White Citizens Council member Byron de la Beckwith was accused of his murder, but juries deadlocked in two separate trials. In 1989 new information came to light and Beckwith was re-arrested. He was found guilty in 1994.

Expulsion meeting: A SNCC staff meeting held at black entertainer "Peg Leg" Bates's estate in New York in December 1966. The meeting was called to address concerns over Black Power and the void left by the large number of experienced SNCC workers who had quit the organization as a result of SNCC's new controversial focus. Separatists from SNCC's Atlanta Project had presented a position paper at a staff meeting in the spring of 1966 suggesting that only an all-black organization could achieve racial equality. They continued to press their agenda at the December meeting and after days of debate over white involvement, the separatists narrowly won.

Fanon, Frantz (1925–1961): An Algerian freedom fighter and psychiatrist expelled from Algeria in 1957. His writings about liberation struggles, in light of his own experience in the Algerian war with France, fostered concern among black Americans, particularly those who supported Black Power, for the colonial territories in Africa, and they drew links between his analysis of colonialism and their own experience. His *Wretched of the Earth* (1961) became an important book for many SNCC members.

Folsom, James "Big Jim": Governor of Alabama (1947–1951 and 1955-1959). A populist, he was a racial moderate relative to most of his southern colleagues.

Foster, Marie: A dental hygienist who began citizenship classes for her neighbors in Selma, Alabama.

Free Southern Theater: An integrated touring theater company, started by John O'Neal and Doris Derby of SNCC along with Gilbert Moses of the *Mis-*

sissippi Free Press, whose aim was to use drama to communicate the goals of the civil rights movement to African Americans throughout the South.

Free Speech Movement (FSM): In 1964, prohibited from distributing civil rights materials on campus, disenchanted students at the University of California at Berkeley protested their lack of political freedom and the inflexibility of the university bureaucracy. Led by Freedom Summer volunteer Mario Savio, the students held a sit-in. The university arrested 773 students. The next year the university changed its policy, allowing political freedom on campus. The FSM ushered in a period of turbulent student-administration relations and set a precedent for students around the country to increase their influence over the management of institutions of higher education. Many students politicized by the FSM went on to become involved in other social movements.

Freedom Rides: Organized by CORE, the Freedom Rides sought to test *Boynton v. Virginia* (1960), which had declared segregation in railway and bus terminals unconstitutional. James Farmer, national director of CORE, and twelve others left Washington, D.C., in May 1961 for Georgia, Alabama, and Mississippi. Although a bus was destroyed and the Riders were attacked by mobs, the Freedom Riders persisted, augmented by Nashville students and SNCC volunteers. By November 1961, when the Interstate Commerce Commission prohibited segregated accommodations, over one thousand people had participated in Freedom Rides.

Freedom Schools: Based on SNCC's experience with Burgland High School in 1961, Freedom Schools were planned in Mississippi in 1963 to help students and adults with basic skills. Students were taught black history and its importance to the civil rights movement. The focus was also on cooperative education and black culture. The schools enrolled about 3,500 students in fifty schools around the state of Mississippi. They were officially established during the summer months of 1964 as a base for the Mississippi Freedom Democratic Party, but many continued beyond Freedom Summer.

Freedom Singers: A singing group established in 1962 for fund-raising. Most of its members were SNCC members involved in the Albany, Georgia, protests. The songs united civil rights workers and demonstrators and sustained morale.

Freedom Summer: A project organized and coordinated in 1964 by SNCC and the Council of Federated Organizations with help from CORE and others. Its purpose was to register blacks to vote (through the Mississippi Freedom

Democratic Party) and to teach reading and other skills in Freedom Schools in rural Mississippi. Over one thousand volunteers participated. Most were white northern college students. The project embodied SNCC's commitment to interracialism and nonviolence, but volunteers often met violent white resistance. Many of the volunteers went on to become involved in other social movements; some remained in the South beyond the summer.

Freedom Vote: As a protest against voting discrimination and to prove that if given the chance to register, black people would vote, SNCC sponsored a mock election, the Freedom Vote campaign, in November 1963. Aaron Henry ran as the gubernatorial candidate. With the help of Allard Lowenstein and northern white college student volunteers, over 83,000 African Americans voted during the campaign. (Mississippi law stated that voters who claimed illegal exclusion from voting registration could cast ballots which would then be set aside while they were appealing their exclusion.)

Gaither, Tom: Field secretary for CORE. Gaither came from Claflin College in Orangeburg, South Carolina, where he had led sit-ins and demonstrations and taught the fine points of civil disobedience to other activists.

Garrison, William Lloyd (1805–1879): Prominent white abolitionist. He was a founder of the American Anti-Slavery Society and editor of *The Liberator.*

Garvey, Marcus (1887–1940): A Jamaican Pan-African nationalist and founder of the Universal Negro Improvement Association (UNIA) in 1914. The UNIA urged all people of African descent to unite for their collective improvement, and in August 1920 the group elected Garvey the provisional president of Africa. He had come to the United States in 1916; in 1925 he was convicted of mail fraud and after serving half of his five-year sentence, was deported. His vision inspired many civil rights leaders.

Goodman, Andrew: A northern white Freedom Summer volunteer. In 1964, along with James Chaney and Michael Schwerner, he was arrested in Philadelphia, Mississippi, as they were on their way to visit a Longdale, Mississippi, church that had been burned by the Ku Klux Klan. Upon their release they were killed by white supremacists. Their bodies were uncovered in a dam after a massive FBI search.

Greene, George: A Greenwood, Mississippi, native active in the youth movement there, he became a SNCC field secretary and helped organize the Freedom Vote campaign in Adams County.

Greenville meeting: A November 1963 planning meeting for Freedom Summer that lasted three days. A discussion of the role of whites surfaced with respect to the proposed involvement of a large number of northern white students. Many SNCC workers believed whites would want to assume leadership roles and would not be able to relate to blacks in the community. Others like Fannie Lou Hamer, Bob Moses, and Lawrence Guyot emphasized the need for white participants in Freedom Summer, both to ensure national attention to the problems of voting rights and to break down racial barriers within SNCC as the group was seeking to do in the broader community. The latter view prevailed.

Gregory, Dick: A comedian, popular lecturer, and civil rights activist. He became known for focusing national attention on efforts to register black voters during Freedom Summer. He was jailed several times in 1963 and during the Watts riot in 1965.

Grimké, Angelina (1805–1879): South Carolina–born abolitionist and women's rights activist along with her sister Sarah. Opposed to slavery, she moved north in 1829, where she joined the Philadelphia Female Anti-Slavery Society and began writing and speaking for the cause. Public speaking by women was frowned upon, but Grimké refused to stop and added women's rights to her list of causes. She married prominent abolitionist Theodore Weld.

Hamer, Fannie Lou (1917–1977): Born into a sharecropping family in Mississippi, from 1962 Hamer was a central figure in Mississippi voter registration projects. Fired from her plantation job, she became a SNCC field secretary in 1963. She was instrumental in starting the Delta Ministry and the Mississippi Freedom Democratic Party, for which she was a delegate to the 1964 Democratic National Convention. She continued her activism after the MFDP and founded the Freedom Farms Corporation, a nonprofit organization created to provide social service, scholarships, and help to destitute families.

Hansen, Bill: An activist from Cincinnati, Hansen joined the Freedom Rides and did time in notorious Parchman Penitentiary. One of the first whites to join SNCC, he worked (and was frequently jailed) in Maryland, southwest Georgia (where his jaw was broken), and Mississippi. He organized SNCC's project in Arkansas and was a member of the 1964 SNCC delegation to Africa.

Harris, Donald: A SNCC staffer in Sumter County, Georgia, and a graduate of Rutgers University. He was arrested in 1963 for insurrection along with Zev

Aelony, John Perdew, and others for protesting in Americus, Georgia, and was a member of SNCC's 1964 delegation to Africa.

Hayes, Curtis: A high school student in McComb, Mississippi, when he became involved in the movement, Hayes became a SNCC field secretary in Mississippi.

Henry, Aaron: A black pharmacist and civil rights and political leader. He organized a branch of the NAACP in Coahoma County, Mississippi. Throughout the 1960s he ran campaigns, economic boycotts, and voter registration projects. Gubernatorial candidate in the Freedom Vote, he also directed Freedom Summer as the president of the Council of Federated Organizations and served as the convention delegation chairman for the Mississippi Freedom Democratic Party.

Aaron Henry Campaign: A 1963–64 voting rights project in Mississippi (Freedom Vote) for which student volunteers, predominantly white, were recruited to work alongside local activists.

Highlander Folk School (Monteagle, Tennessee): Founded by Myles Horton and Don West in 1932 as a community folk school in the Danish tradition. Highlander then worked with trade unions. The school's focus shifted to civil rights in the 1950s, and it was one of the few places in the South where interracial meetings could be held. By the 1960s it had become a training school for civil rights leaders.

Highlander meeting (SNCC): A SNCC meeting was held at Highlander in 1961 to determine the future direction of SNCC and to train SNCC workers in voter registration strategies. Staffers argued over whether to focus on direct action or on voting rights, and ultimately agreed to do both.

Hollings, Ernest, Jr.: Governor of South Carolina (1959–1963) and later senator, who opposed the civil rights movement.

Holloway, Frank: An Atlanta student who participated in the Freedom Rides, Holloway was active in the Mississippi project.

Holloway, Lucius: One of the first black residents of Terrell County, Georgia, to register to vote, Holloway was fired from his job. He headed the subsequent voter registration drive, and housed SNCC workers in his home.

House Un-American Activities Committee (HUAC): Established in 1938 as a special committee by the United States House of Representatives, HUAC became a standing committee in 1945. Its original intent was to halt Axis propaganda in the United States; by the 1940s it considered its primary mission the investigation and uncovering of communists and subversives in government and society at large.

Howard, Ruth: Director of SNCC's voter registration project in Greenwood, Mississippi.

Hulett, John: Founder of the Lowndes County Christian Movement for Human Rights and chairman of the Lowndes County Freedom Organization, Hulett became the county's first black sheriff in 1970.

Jackson, Jimmie Lee: Attacked by state troopers during a voter registration march in Selma in February of 1965, he later died. The SCLC organized the Selma to Montgomery march the following month to protest his death.

Jemison, Reverend Theodore J.: Pastor of the Mt. Zion Baptist Church in Baton Rouge, Louisiana, and president of the local NAACP, he led a successful bus boycott there in the summer of 1953 and organized a car pool to transport protesters which the later Montgomery bus boycott used as a model. One of the founders of SCLC, he became president of the National Baptist Convention in 1982. His father, David V. Jemison, had served as Convention president from 1940 to 1953.

Jemmott, Janet: As SNCC field secretary in Natchez, Mississippi, Jemmott coordinated voter registration efforts there. She later married Bob Moses.

Jones, Charles (C.J.): Originally from Charlotte, North Carolina, and a sit-in veteran, Jones was director of SNCC's voter registration project in southwest Georgia. He also worked in Mississippi and North Carolina. When SNCC divided over voter registration and direct action, Jones became head of the voter registration wing.

Kennard, Clyde: A Forrest County, Mississippi, native whose attempts to enroll at the all-white Mississippi Southern College (now University of Southern Mississippi) were thwarted. Arrested twice on false charges and sentenced to seven years in jail, he developed cancer and died upon his release, having been denied medical care.

Kenyatta, Reverend Muhammad Isaiah (Bagley) (1944–1992): A Civil rights activist and educator from Chester, Pennsylvania, where he began his protest activities by opposing discrimination by local businesses. Kenyatta became director of the Black Economic Development Conference, project director for the National Council of Churches, and taught law at the University of Buffalo.

King, Lonnie: A student leader in Atlanta, he, along with Julian Bond, headed its first sit-ins.

Kinoy, Arthur: A white attorney for the National Lawyers Guild who provided legal assistance for both SNCC and the Council of Federated Organizations. He was one of the three lawyers (with William Kunstler and Benjamin Smith) hired by SNCC to challenge the seating of the Mississippi congressional delegation in 1965.

Kopkind, Andrew: A journalist with the *New Republic* (later with *The Nation)*, Kopkind was a Freedom Summer volunteer who later became active in the Free Speech Movement.

Ladner, Dorie: A native of Mississippi, she became a SNCC field secretary there. Dorie and her sister, Joyce, became involved in the movement during high school.

Lawson, James: A theology student at Vanderbilt University who had gone to India to study Gandhi's philosophy of nonviolence. Following his return to the United States, he became a Fellowship of Reconciliation field secretary in the South. As a theology student he met many future SNCC staffers, including Diane Nash and John Lewis, during his nonviolence workshops in Nashville. With them, he helped organize sit-ins in an effort to persuade Nashville business owners to desegregate their lunch counters. Lawson was also instrumental in helping to organize SNCC. Because of such activities Lawson was expelled from Vanderbilt three months before he was to graduate.

Lawyers' Committee for Civil Rights Under Law: A volunteer group formed after the Birmingham demonstrations to aid in civil rights cases.

Lee, Reverend George: A pastor in Humphreys County, Mississippi, who helped African Americans register to vote. He was gunned down on Mother's

Day in 1955 following a confrontation over his refusal to remove the names of black voters from the registry.

Lee, Herbert: A SNCC supporter shot to death in 1961 in Liberty, Mississippi, by a member of the state legislature.

Lewis, John: An avid supporter of nonviolence, Lewis was one of the early leaders in the Nashville student protests (1960) as a seminary student. He was instrumental in the establishment of SNCC, participated in the Freedom Rides, and served as SNCC chairman from 1963 to 1966. As SNCC's representative to the March on Washington, he wrote a fiery speech, highly critical of the administration. Although he was prevailed upon to temper his remarks, his speech nonetheless remained forceful and hard hitting. He has served as congressional representative from Georgia's Fifth District since 1987.

Lewis, Rufus: A funeral director who served as transportation chairman for the Montgomery bus boycott (1955-56) and a member of the executive board of the Montgomery Improvement Association (MIA). He nominated Martin Luther King, Jr., for the presidency of the MIA.

Liuzzo, Viola: A white demonstrator from Detroit shot to death on March 25, 1965 following the Selma to Montgomery march.

Love, John: SNCC's field secretary in Selma following Bernard Lafayette's departure.

Lowndes County Christian Movement for Human Rights: Founded by John Hulett following discussions with SCLC members. Hulett started working with SNCC when SCLC did not send a full-time organizer to the county.

Lowndes County Freedom Organization (LCFO): An independent political party established by SNCC organizers and local residents in 1965 on the basis of a provision in the Alabama law code that permitted the formation of independent political parties on the county level. The party, chaired by John Hulett, chose as its symbol a black panther and was nicknamed the Black Panther Party.

Madhubuti, Haki (Don Lee): Poet and essayist. Born in 1942, he was a leader in the Black Arts Movement of the 1960s and early 1970s. He promoted black cultural nationalism (political activism and cultural preservation to heighten racial awareness and black unity) through his writings, which include *Think Black* (1967), *Black Pride* (1968), and (written after attending the Sixth Pan-African Congress in Tanzania in 1974), *Enemies: Clash of Races* (1978).

March on Washington: Inspired by A. Philip Randolph's call for a March on Washington in 1941 (which did not take place) to protest racial discrimination, Bayard Rustin, Martin Luther King, Jr., Randolph, and other civil rights leaders organized the March on Washington for jobs and freedom on August 28, 1963. Over 250,000 marched from the Washington Monument to the Lincoln Memorial to press for civil rights and economic justice. Initially skeptical, President Kennedy endorsed the march. King delivered his famous "I Have a Dream" speech there, and John Lewis of SNCC, although prevailed upon to temper his planned remarks, nonetheless offered a forceful call for further action.

Marshall, Burke: Assistant attorney general of the United States (1961–1965), in charge of the Civil Rights Division of the Department of Justice. He directed the federal government's efforts to integrate the University of Mississippi (1962) and acted as a negotiator between Birmingham, Alabama, city officials and civil rights leaders during the 1963 desegregation campaign. He helped to draft the Civil Rights Act of 1964.

Matthews, Z. T. (Zeke): Sheriff of Terrell County, Georgia.

McComb (Mississippi) Freedom School: SNCC workers opened a makeshift school called Nonviolent High in 1961 after Burgland High School students were expelled for civil rights protests. When the impending trials for sit-in arrests forced it to close its doors, Campbell College in Jackson offered high school–level classes for the students.

Medical Committee for Human Rights: Formed by New York doctors and nurses who had come to Mississippi for Freedom Summer to provide medical assistance.

Meredith, James: In September 1962, amid much opposition by white students and state officials and with the aid of federal troops, Meredith became the first black student to enter the University of Mississippi. On June 6, 1966, following the publication of his autobiography *Three Years in Mississippi*, Meredith was shot and wounded at a civil rights march in Mississippi. He went from being a militant civil rights activist to a moderate one in the late 1960s, and by the 1980s had become a conservative Republican.

Minnis, Jack: SNCC's research director and staff member in the Atlanta office. Minnis also worked on the Voter Education Project and taught social studies at Louisiana University.

Mississippi Freedom Democratic Party (MFDP): Established in the spring of 1964, the MFDP was a response to the exclusion of black people by the state Democratic convention, which opposed the national party's commitment to civil rights. The MFDP's goal was to elect delegates (including delegation chairman Aaron Henry, Fannie Lou Hamer, Victoria Gray, and Annie Devine) to serve at the Democratic National Convention to replace the official all-white delegation. When the delegates went to Atlantic City they were offered a compromise by Hubert Humphrey and Walter Mondale, who promised two at-large seats for their pledge of loyalty to the Democratic Party. They rejected the offer and were ejected when they attempted to take Mississippi's seats on the convention floor. The party also filed a successful reapportionment suit. Lawrence Guyot served as chairman and Fannie Lou Hamer as vice chairman of the Mississippi Freedom Democratic Party.

Mississippi reapportionment suit: In 1965 the Mississippi Freedom Democratic Party filed a state reapportionment suit, *Connor v. Johnson*, which was ultimately successful. Using similar reasoning, the MFDP also called for all of Mississippi's congressional seats to be vacated in 1965 and for new elections to be held. That challenge failed.

Montgomery, Lucy: One of SNCC's most loyal financial supporters, Montgomery, originally from the South, lived in Chicago.

Montgomery bus boycott: The 381-day boycott began in December of 1955 with Rosa Parks's refusal to give up her seat on a Montgomery public bus. After a year of boycotting and protesting, the Supreme Court ruled that segregation on common carriers violated the due process and equal protection clauses of the Fourteenth Amendment. The decision was used by civil rights activists to argue against all existing forms of segregation. The boycott was coordinated by Martin Luther King, Jr., president of the Montgomery Improvement Association. The boycott was successful largely because of grass-roots organizing by citizens and ministers such as Jo Ann Robinson, Ralph Abernathy, and Fred Shuttlesworth. As a result of the boycott, King and other boycott leaders established the Southern Christian Leadership Conference (SCLC) in 1957.

Montgomery Improvement Association: On December 5, 1955, African Americans in Montgomery, Alabama, formed this organization to lead the new bus boycott. With Martin Luther King, Jr., as president, the association provided a free transportation system for the tens of thousands of black people who were affected by what became a year-long boycott.

Moore, Amzie: President of the NAACP's Cleveland, Mississippi, chapter. Moore helped organize Mississippi's voting rights campaign, and suggested that Bob Moses send students to Mississippi to focus on voter registration.

Morgan, Charles: The Kentucky-born Birmingham lawyer became the American Civil Liberties Union's southern regional director from 1964 to 1972. The cases he won included *Reynolds v. Sims* (1964), which reaffirmed the principle of one person–one vote.

Morrisroe, Father Richard: A Roman Catholic priest from Chicago who went south and was wounded in the same Klan ambush that killed Jonathan Daniels in Hayneville, Alabama.

Moses, Robert (Parris): A native New Yorker and a graduate student at Harvard University, he was teaching in New York when he heard about the sit-ins and traveled to Atlanta to work with SCLC on voter registration. Dissatisfied with his role in the SCLC, he accepted Jane Stembridge's invitation to join SNCC and recruit southern black leaders for SNCC's impending conference in the fall of 1960. Modest, Moses nevertheless became one of SNCC's most powerful and influential members. In 1965 Moses took a leave of absence from SNCC, and following his return in 1966 from a trip to Africa, he insisted that blacks needed to work alone for their own liberation. In 1968 Moses and his wife, Janet Jemmott, traveled to Tanzania, where they taught math and English, respectively, for nearly ten years. They returned to the United States in 1977, and Moses resumed graduate studies at Harvard University. Most recently Moses has established the Algebra Project to help poor youths master mathematics.

Move on Mississippi (MOM): A direct action project set up by SNCC in 1961 to challenge Mississippi's segregated institutions.

National Association for the Advancement of Colored People (NAACP):
Motivated by violence against African Americans and by opposition to Booker T.
Washington's accommodationist strategy, black and white activists founded the
NAACP in 1909. The purpose of the NAACP was to protest black inequality
and racial injustice and to address grievances through the legal system. Its Legal Bureau, and later its Legal Defense and Educational Fund, helped to abolish grandfather clauses, restrictive covenants by city ordinance, all-white juries,
and segregation in public facilities, including public education.

National Lawyers Guild: Founded in 1937 as a progressive and racially integrated alternative to the American Bar Association, its work has focused primarily on issues involving labor, civil rights, and progressive social change.

National Student Association (NSA): A national union of students established in 1947, it received covert funds from the CIA, which hoped the NSA
could help it monitor foreign student groups. The liberal NSA became deeply
involved in the civil rights movement, opening an Atlanta civil rights office in
1959 headed by Connie Curry. It also became active in the antiwar movement
in the 1960s. In 1967 the CIA funding became public knowledge, which almost
destroyed the NSA. The organization then remade itself along more radical
lines. In 1978 it merged with the United States Student Association and now
conducts lobbying efforts on issues of education and multiculturalism.

New Left: A loose political movement that arose during the 1960s among
young middle-class white critics of capitalism. Many came out of the civil rights
movement. Spearheaded by the Students for a Democratic Society, the New
Left maintained at its core opposition to the Vietnam War.

Niagara Conference/Movement: Organized by W.E.B. Du Bois in 1905, black
leaders met and drew up a declaration of aggressive action and demanded full
suffrage, equal economic and educational opportunities, an end to segregation,
and full civil rights. Although the movement was short-lived, it was a forerun-
ner to the NAACP and is considered the first significant, organized black protest movement of the twentieth century.

Nkrumah, Kwame: Prime minister of Ghana who led his country to independence in 1957. With the granting of independence to Ghana and the emergence of the Black Power movement in the late 1960s, many blacks began to
develop new pride in their African heritage.

Orangeburg (South Carolina) massacre: On February 8, 1968, thirty students were shot, three of whom died, at South Carolina State College when patrolmen opened fire upon a group of students they mistakenly thought had shot an officer. This massacre followed beatings that had occurred two nights earlier when the student NAACP chapter tried to integrate the local bowling alley. SNCC organizer Cleveland Sellers was arrested following the massacre and found guilty of inciting a riot. Nine of the patrolmen involved were tried; all were found not guilty.

Orangeburg Movement for Civic Improvement: In an effort originated by CORE and generally backed by the local NAACP, students in Orangeburg organized sit-ins and demonstrations in the summer of 1960 using techniques of nonviolent civil disobedience. Several participants went on to join SNCC.

Owen, Robert: Justice Department attorney.

Paine, Thomas (1737–1809): British-born sympathizer with the American Revolution, essayist. A believer in democracy, his writings include *Common Sense* (1776) and *Rights of Man* (1792).

Parchman Penitentiary: Notoriously brutal prison in Jackson, Mississippi. The Freedom Riders were imprisoned there, as were many later civil rights protesters.

Parks, Rosa: On December 1, 1955, Rosa Parks, a black seamstress and local leader trained at Highlander Folk School, refused to move to the rear of a Montgomery public bus. The black community rallied around her to organize a boycott. The 381-day Montgomery bus boycott was a success, and Parks became a symbol of nonviolent direct action.

Peacock, Willie: A native of the Mississippi Delta, Peacock became a SNCC field secretary working in Sunflower and Leflore counties. He ran for district attorney in the Freedom Vote.

Perdew, John: A white Harvard University student from Denver, Colorado, Perdew went to work for SNCC in Georgia in 1963. Although he had intended to stay for a summer, he remained, and endured frequent and sometimes long arrests.

Ponder, Reverend. L. P.: Pastor of St. John's Methodist Church in Palmer's

Crossing, Mississippi. He supported civil rights efforts and participated in the movement in Hattiesburg.

Potter, Paul: President of the National Student Association. He also worked on an SDS project in 1965 to organize white communities using SNCC organizing tools.

Poussaint, Alvin: African-American psychiatrist from Harvard Medical School active with SNCC and field director for the Medical Committee for Human Rights in Mississippi; he has written widely about African Americans, self-esteem, and mental health.

Powell, Adam Clayton, Jr.: A black politician from New York from the 1940s through the 1960s. He succeeded his father to become pastor of Harlem's Abyssinian Baptist Church, was elected to New York's city council and in 1945 to the U.S. House of Representatives, where he served eleven successive terms. He pushed for employers in Harlem to hire blacks and, while in Congress, fought for federal involvement against discrimination and segregation.

Pritchett, Laurie: As Albany, Georgia, police chief and implacable foe of civil rights, he arrested, beat, and imprisoned dozens of SNCC workers and demonstrators during the Albany protests in 1962.

Progressive Labor Party: A Maoist group within the Students for a Democratic Society (SDS). The group had little influence until the late 1960s, when it proposed a "worker-student alliance" in which students would foster a proletarian revolution. After the 1969 SDS convention, the Progressive Labor Party declared itself the real SDS, but soon after the organization withered.

Public Accommodations Act: Title II of the Civil Rights Act of 1964, it prohibited discrimination in the use of public accommodations such as hotels, motels, restaurants, gas stations, and places of amusement whose operations involved interstate commerce.

Rabinowitz, Victor: A New York City attorney who helped to supply bail money for picketers in Mississippi. He later became disenchanted: at a 1965 staff meeting, he asserted that SNCC had become a traditional bureaucracy by creating a secretariat to make policy decisions and proposing mainstream political demands.

Raines, "Mama Dolly": An elderly but strong and self-sufficient black woman in Lee County, Georgia, who hosted SNCC voter registration staff in her house.

Raskin, Barbara: Feminist, novelist. Her writings include *Hot Flashes* (1987) and *Current Affairs* (1990).

Reagon, Cordell: SNCC field secretary who opened the Albany office along with Charles Sherrod. He had been a Freedom Rider and active in the Nashville student movement. He died in 1996.

Reese, Reverend Frederick: President of the Dallas County Voters League.

Republic of New Africa (RNA): Founded in 1968 with Robert F. Williams (who was exiled in Cuba) as president, the RNA advocated black separatism in an independent country that was to include Louisiana, Mississippi, Alabama, Georgia, and South Carolina. Significant RNA activity ended in 1971 with a shootout in Jackson, Mississippi, between members and FBI agents and local police.

Revolutionary Action Movement (RAM): An all African-American organization formed in 1964 by supporters of Robert F. Williams. It advocated guerrilla warfare to attain nationalist goals. SNCC's Atlanta separatists were influenced by RAM in the late 1960s.

Richards, Dona: University of Chicago graduate, Richards worked for SNCC in Mississippi and took part in Freedom Summer. She was Bob Moses's first wife.

Richardson, Judy: Atlanta staff worker who also worked in Mississippi.

Ricks, Willie: Ricks joined SNCC as a Chattanooga high school student in the early 1960s. He was part of SNCC's advance group organized to mobilize black support in small communities. A self-described black nationalist known within SNCC as "The Reverend," he shortened the slogan "Black power for Black people" to the popular "Black Power." He was later expelled from SNCC for refusing to distance himself from the Black Panther Party.

Robinson, Jo Ann: An English professor at Alabama State College and president of the Women's Political Council. Established in 1946, this organization consisted of black professional women. Robinson was responsible for sending out the leaflets organizing the Montgomery bus boycott two years after a WPC meeting with black leaders to discuss the bus situation.

Robinson, Ruby Doris (Smith) (1942–1967): Robinson joined SNCC after participating in the early sit-ins in Atlanta as a Spelman College student and member of Atlanta Committee on Appeal for Human Rights. A Freedom Rider, Ruby Doris worked for SNCC in Atlanta, Charleston, Nashville and McComb, served as administrative secretary to James Forman, and became executive secretary in 1966 following Forman's departure.

Ruffin, Susan: A Mississippi civil rights worker, Ruffin published the Mississippi Freedom Democratic Party newsletter.

Sales, Ruby: Sales was a sixteen-year-old Tuskegee high school student when she became involved with SNCC in Lowndes County in 1965. She then joined the voter registration project in Fort Deposit, Mississippi.

Salinger, Pierre: White House press secretary from January 1961 to March 1964, under Presidents Kennedy and Johnson.

Savio, Mario: Leader in Berkeley's Free Speech Movement (FSM). Savio had been a Freedom Summer volunteer, and he drew direct connections between that experience and his work in the FSM.

Schrader, Emmie: White Radcliffe College graduate who joined SNCC during Freedom Summer and remained involved in the movement. She worked with Mary King and Casey Hayden in Mississippi.

Schwerner, Michael: A northern white college student who had been working for CORE in Mississippi. In 1964, along with James Chaney and Andrew Goodman, he was arrested in Philadelphia, Mississippi, as they were on their way to visit a Longdale, Mississippi, church that had been burned by the Ku Klux Klan. Upon their release they were killed by white supremacists. Their bodies were uncovered in a dam after a massive FBI search.

Selma to Montgomery march: During a march for voter registration in February of 1965, Jimmie Lee Jackson was attacked by state troopers and later died. The SCLC decided to organize a march from Selma to Montgomery to protest his death. On March 7 between five and six hundred attempted to march. They were stopped by Sheriff Jim Clark and state troopers on horseback who attacked them at the Edmund Pettus Bridge ("Bloody Sunday"). A federal judge ordered the SCLC not to march again, but protesters insisted. Martin Luther King compromised, leading marchers to the bridge on March 10 and then turning around. Many felt betrayed by this decision. Following this, whites attacked and killed a white marcher, the Reverend James Reeb. President Johnson sent the National Guard to secure the route for the marchers who left Selma March 21 and rallied in Montgomery on the 25th.

Shuttlesworth, Reverend Fred: He joined with Martin Luther King, Jr., and Ralph Abernathy to form the SCLC, in which he held the position of secretary from 1958 to 1970. As leader of the Birmingham, Alabama, civil rights movement, he survived two bombings, a mob beating, and numerous jailings.

Sitton, Claude: *New York Times* reporter, one of the first national reporters to cover the civil rights movement. His coverage helped the fledgling movement gain publicity and sympathy.

Smith, Charles: A leader in the Lowndes County Christian Movement for Human Rights and the Lowndes County Freedom Organization. He later became its first black county commissioner.

Smith, Frank: Morehouse College student who joined SNCC in 1965 as field secretary in Mississippi.

Smith, Scott B.: SNCC worker in Lowndes County.

Southern Christian Leadership Conference (SCLC): Established in 1957 after the Montgomery bus boycott to organize nonviolent, direct action protests in the South. It was led by Martin Luther King, Jr., and dominated by Baptist ministers. Through mass marches, sit-ins, and demonstrations, the SCLC mobilized blacks and helped fight discrimination and secure voting rights. After the passage of the Voting Rights Act of 1965, SCLC turned to the problems of discrimination and poverty in northern cities. After King was killed Ralph Abernathy became head of the SCLC.

Southern Conference Educational Fund (SCEF): Established in 1946 in Birmingham by the Southern Conference for Human Welfare (SCHW) to further its work in race relations. Dedicated to civil rights reform, it sought to create a democratic South and overcome white supremacy. During the 1950s and 1960s, SCEF took an active role in school desegregation, especially higher education, as well as in voter registration drives. It contributed to SNCC, gave it exposure in SCEF's journal *Southern Patriot,* and provided a $5,000 grant for a white field secretary to recruit on white college campuses. SCEF often came under investigation as a result of its allegedly communist ties.

Spike, Reverend Robert: Executive director of the National Council of Churches' Commission on Religion and Race, and strong financial and moral supporter of civil rights, SNCC and the Mississippi Freedom Democratic Party.

Stembridge, Jane: A southern-born white theology student studying in New York when Ella Baker asked her to serve as SNCC's first executive secretary in May of 1960. She is also a poet.

Student Voice: SNCC's newsletter, produced regularly beginning in June of 1960.

Students for a Democratic Society (SDS): Founded in 1962 when two dozen white students, including Tom Hayden, gathered to draft the Port Huron Statement. They wished to create a new left-wing political movement not bound to Marxist ideology or labor union politics, to help people play larger roles in their communities. SDS was committed to racial justice, the abolition of poverty, and the creation of a more participatory democracy. In 1968 SDS split into rival factions, some of which advocated armed struggle. Many members were lost, and the organization collapsed after the Progressive Labor Party faction took control.

Taconic Foundation: Founded by Stephen and Audrey Currier in 1958 in New York City to open doors of opportunity to all Americans. The foundation financed several civil rights programs, including SNCC's voter registration projects and the March on Washington. More recently, Taconic has been concerned with youth unemployment and urban housing.

Thoreau, Henry David (1817–1862): American Transcendentalist, essayist, and abolitionist. His writings include "Civil Disobedience" (1849), which laid out the arguments for nonviolent civil disobedience against immoral laws, and *Walden* (1854).

Till, Emmett: A fourteen-year-old black boy from Chicago killed in Leflore County, Mississippi, in 1955 for allegedly making sexual advances toward a white woman. Till's body was found in the Tallahatchie River. The widely reproduced picture of Till's bloated body spurred many to become involved in the emerging civil rights movement. The killers were acquitted.

Tillinghast, Muriel: Black volunteer from Howard University and SNCC project director in Greenville during and after Freedom Summer. She later became SNCC's state office manager.

Travis, Brenda: She was fifteen when she joined SNCC protests in McComb, Mississippi. She helped to organize a month-long voter registration drive and stage sit-ins. White resistance was immediate, and she was sentenced to a year in a state school for delinquents.

Travis, Jimmy: A former Tougaloo student from Jackson, Mississippi, who became a SNCC field secretary, Travis was shot and nearly killed on February 28, 1963, in Greenwood, Mississippi.

Trotter, William Monroe: (1872–1934): A black Bostonian who rose to prominence when he denounced Booker T. Washington's accommodationist stance. He formed the Niagara Movement with Du Bois, which challenged Washington's view through direct political and social protest. Trotter founded the National Equal Rights League in 1908 to advance the rights of black people. Later his ideas were denounced as too radical by the NAACP.

Truth, Sojourner (c. 1799–1883): Abolitionist and women's rights advocate. Born Isabella Bornefree, a slave in New York, she was freed through state law in 1827. She began preaching soon after and spoke often on abolition and women's rights. After the Civil War she worked on behalf of the new freedmen and -women.

Tubman, Harriet (1821–1913): Runaway slave known as "Moses" for leading more than two hundred slaves to Canada and freedom in over fifteen trips. During the Civil War she served as nurse, scout, and spy, and later helped freedmen and -women and the families of black soldiers.

Turnbow, Hartman: The first black voter applicant in Holmes County, Mississippi, in 1963, he became voter registration leader there. He was arrested after firing on whites who bombed his home.

Turner, Albert : Local leader from Marion, Alabama, and SCLC staff member.

Universal Association of Ethiopian Women: An organization opposing lynching and advocating welfare and prisoners' rights, founded by nationalist leader and political organizer Queen Mother (Audley) Moore, Mother Langley, and Dara Collins.

Varela, Maria (Mary): A member of Students for a Democratic Society, she established an adult literacy program in Selma, Alabama, in 1963.

Vietnam War, Mississippi Freedom Democratic Party position: In 1965 the Mississippi Freedom Democratic Party published an article in its newsletter stating five reasons why blacks should not fight in the Vietnam War. Mississippi Freedom Democratic Party's dissent from the war was a result of John Shaw's death. Prior to serving in Vietnam, Shaw had been active in direct action campaigns in Mississippi, and MFDP members argued that a man should not lose his life overseas when he had not gained freedom at home. Many blacks from Mississippi, however, disagreed with MFDP's antiwar position. Lawrence Guyot issued a statement declaring that the leaflet was not a representation of MFDP policy, and he assured readers in a *New York Times* article that if drafted he would serve. SNCC came out against the war in 1966; and Martin Luther King, Jr., did so in 1967.

Vivian, Reverend C. T.: A minister from Chattanooga, Tennessee, he was arrested in Jackson, Mississippi, for participating in the Freedom Rides and beaten by the police. He served as advisor to students involved in the Nashville sit-ins.

Voter Education Project (VEP): Founded in 1962 by the Southern Regional Council, a biracial organization to promote southern black voter registration, the VEP provided seed money for civil rights groups conducting voter registration efforts. In 1965 the VEP began its own voter registration and voter education projects, and in 1969 became an independent organization.

Voting Rights Act of 1965: The law prohibited discriminatory tactics that prevented blacks from voting. The act also made provision for federal registrars to enter any area practicing blatant discrimination. Before the act was passed scarcely one hundred African Americans held elective offices. Today there are thousands, most of whom serve in the South.

Wallace, George: Governor of Alabama (1963–1967, 1971–1977, 1983–1987) and militant segregationist. On June 11, 1963, he physically blocked the entrance of two black students to the University of Alabama. In September of that year, Wallace delayed the opening of elementary and secondary schools that the federal courts had ordered desegregated. In 1968 he ran for President as an independent and received 13.6 percent of the vote. By his 1982 campaign he had recanted his segregationist position.

Washington, Booker T. (1856–1915): Educator, president of the Tuskegee Normal School (Tuskegee Institute) in Alabama. Born a slave, considered a spokesman for his race, he advocated a separate but equal doctrine for blacks and whites and was willing to trade civil rights for economic gains. At the same time he fought segregation and discrimination by secretly financing court cases. His accommodationist views were opposed by more militant black leaders such as W.E.B. Du Bois.

Washington, Cynthia: Headed a SNCC project in Greene County, Alabama; head of the Community Center in Cleveland, Mississippi.

Waveland meeting (1964): A retreat for SNCC members following Freedom Summer in Waveland, Mississippi. The meeting's focus was to discuss the future and structure of the organization, and SNCC members were asked to bring position papers on issues they believed were important for the organization to consider. The position papers ranged from SNCC's past successes and failures to white involvement in the movement to the role of women in the organization.

Wells, Samuel B.: Wells led the Albany march (July 1962) despite a federal court injunction against demonstrating. He and over one hundred people were arrested by Chief Laurie Pritchett.

White Citizens Councils: Organizations of whites devoted to white supremacy but generally unwilling to resort to Klan-like violence. They sought to dominate state and local governments and fight integration through legal means.

Wilkins, Roy: Executive director of the NAACP from 1955 until his retirement in 1977. His tenure there coincided with significant achievements in black civil rights, including school desegregation, fair housing, and voting rights legislation.

Williams, Avery: SNCC staffer in Mississippi and Alabama from Alabama State College.

Williams, Hosea: SCLC staff member from 1963. He was elected to the Georgia State Assembly in 1974, to the Atlanta city council in 1985, and ran unsuccessfully for mayor of Atlanta in 1989.

Williams, Robert F.: Former president of the NAACP's Union County, North Carolina, chapter. He was expelled from the NAACP after urging the use of violence against violence. He published the *Crusader,* a monthly newsletter, and was chairman of the Revolutionary Action Movement.

Winona: On their way home from the SCLC citizenship school in the summer of 1963 a group of Mississippi civil rights workers attempted to desegregate a bus rest stop and lunch counter. Authorities arrested the activists, and Fannie Lou Hamer and June Johnson were among those who were severely beaten by Winona police authorities. The Justice Department brought charges against the sheriff, police chief, and others for their brutality, but they were found not guilty.

Wright (Edelman), Marian: Atlanta sit-in participant as a student at Spelman College, she became a lawyer. Wright worked on voter registration in 1963 and defended protesters in Mississippi. She heads the Children's Defense Fund, a child advocacy agency she founded in 1973 dedicated to promoting public policies that benefit children.

Young, Andrew: Young joined the staff of the SCLC in 1961, becoming its executive director and executive vice president. Congressional representative from Georgia's Fifth District (1973–1978), he has also served as United Nations ambassador, and was elected mayor of Atlanta in 1981.

Younge, Samuel, Jr.: A Navy veteran recruited by SNCC during the Montgomery demonstrations. He worked in SNCC projects in Mississippi and Alabama and was killed while attempting to use a "white" bathroom at a gas station on January 3, 1966.

Zellner, Dorothy (Dottie) (Miller): She worked with Julian Bond on SNCC's communications from 1961 to 1963 doing publicity and preparing SNCC's newsletter the *Student Voice.* Later she worked for the Center for Constitutional Rights in New York.

Zwerg, Jim: University of Wisconsin exchange student attending Fisk University. He was beaten in Alabama along with John Lewis and William Barbee during the 1961 Freedom Rides.

Biographies of Participants

Victoria Jackson Gray Adams was a local, independent businesswoman living in Hattiesburg, Mississippi, when she became involved in SNCC's voter registration campaign. Among her many activities, she opposed Senator John Stennis in the 1964 Mississippi primary and was national committeewoman of the Mississippi Freedom Democratic Party delegation to the 1964 National Democratic Convention. She continued her work in social and human justice issues, and, now a retired realtor, is a part-time campus minister at Virginia State University in Petersburg.

Ralph Allen was a Trinity College student when he went to work with the southwest Georgia voter registration project in the summer of 1962. He is now a secondary school teacher at Germantown Academy in Philadelphia.

Julian Bond left Morehouse College to enter the civil rights movement. After helping organize the Atlanta student movement, he became director of communications for SNCC, editing its newsletter, *The Student Voice,* and writing most of SNCC's press releases. Bond was elected to the Georgia legislature, where he served until 1987. At the 1968 Democratic convention in Chicago, Bond was the first African American nominated for the Vice Presidency. He was a University of Pennsylvania Pappas Fellow in 1989 and American University's Distinguished Visiting Professor in 1991. He teaches history and politics at the University of Virginia and is the author of *A Time to Speak, a Time to Act: The Movement in Politics* (1972).

Clayborne Carson was the second historian to write a book on SNCC. *In Struggle: SNCC and the Black Awakening of the 1960s* (1981) remains the most thorough scholarly study of the organization. Carson is professor of history at Stanford University and the director of the Martin Luther King Papers Project.

Jack Chatfield, a Trinity College student, worked with SNCC in southwest Georgia. He is now associate professor of history at Trinity College, Hartford, Connecticut.

Courtland Cox was involved in the Nonviolent Action Group (a SNCC affiliate) at Howard University from 1961 to 1964. He served as coordinator for the 1963 March on Washington; field secretary for Mississippi Freedom Summer, 1964; SNCC program director until 1965; field secretary in Lowndes County, Alabama in 1965–66; and representative to the Bertrand Russell War Crimes Tribunal in Stockholm in 1966. Most recently he was deputy mayor for economic development in Washington, D.C., under Mayor Marion Barry.

Theresa Del Pozzo worked with SNCC in Mississippi.

James Forman served as SNCC's executive secretary from 1961 to 1966 and as director of its International Affairs Department from 1966 to 1969. Prior to his involvement with SNCC he worked with the Emergency Relief Committee (a CORE affiliate), which aided evicted sharecroppers in Tennessee. Following SNCC, Forman was an officer in the Black Workers' Congress and served as neighborhood commissioner in Washington, D.C. He received a Ph.D. from the Union Institute. In 1990 he was the recipient of the Fannie Lou Hamer Freedom Award from the National Conference of Black Mayors. He is the author of several books, including *Self Determination: An Examination of the Question and Its Application to the African-American People* (1985); *The Making of Black Revolutionaries* (1972); *The Political Thought of James Forman* (1970); and *High Tide of Black Resistance and Other Political and Literary Writings* (1993). he currently heads the Unemployment and Poverty Action Council, a social action organization in Washington, D.C.

Joanne Grant was founder of New York Friends of SNCC, a major source of SNCC funding. She covered the movement for the *National Guardian* and served as an unpaid SNCC staff member for six years. She taught in a Freedom School in Jackson, Mississippi, in 1964. The author of *Black Protest: History, Documents, and Analyses, 1619 to the Present*, she is the writer/producer of the award-winning film *FUNDI: The Story of Ella Baker*. Her biography of Baker is forthcoming.

Lawrence Guyot, a native Mississippian and graduate of Touglaoo College, was SNCC field secretary in Mississippi (1961–1964), chairman of the Mississippi Democratic Freedom Party (1964–1968), and a candidate for Congress in Mississippi's Fifth Congressional District (1965). He currently works for the city of Washington, D.C.

Prathia Hall (later Prathia Hall Wynn) worked with SNCC from 1962 to 1966. She served as field secretary in Atlanta and as staff member on the southwest Georgia voter registration project, and was a member of SNCC's delegation to Africa. She is currently a pastor at Mt. Sharon Baptist Church in Philadelphia and dean of African American Ministries and lecturer in Christian social ethics at United Theological Seminary in Dayton, Ohio.

Casey Hayden, a student at the University of Texas, worked with SNCC from 1960 to 1966, serving on its staff from 1963 to 1966. She traveled the South for a campus YWCA human relations project directed by Ella Baker in 1961–62 and was an initial member of Students for a Democratic Society. Subsequently she worked for a variety of social change and public interest organizations, including for the city of Atlanta under Mayor Andrew Young. She currently lives in Tucson and is part of a collaborative book project by ten women about their experiences in the movement.

Tom Hayden was cofounder of Students for a Democratic Society and the primary author of SDS's founding "Port Huron Statement." He was a staff member of SNCC in 1963. He served in the California State Assembly between 1986 and 1992 and has been a member of the California State Senate since that time.

Faith Holsaert, a Barnard College student, left school to join the Albany Movement. Following the mandate to work in the white community, she lived and organized in West Virginia for twenty years. She is currently a teacher and writer in the Washington, D.C., area.

Gloria House was field secretary for SNCC in Lowndes County, Alabama (1965–1967). She is now associate professor in the Interdisciplinary Studies Program at Wayne State University in Detroit. She is the author of two collections of poetry, *Blood River* (1983) and *Rainrituals* (1989), and *Tower and Dungeon: A Study of Place and Power in American Culture* (1991).

John Jackson was a high school student when SNCC went to Lowndes County, Alabama. His father offered SNCC workers a vacant house to live in while working there. He became SNCC field secretary in Lowndes County from 1964 to 1966, and has been mayor of Whitehall, Alabama, since 1980.

June Johnson was born in Greenwood, Mississippi. She joined the movement at age fourteen as president of the local NAACP youth chapter. While still a teenager, she organized the Greenwood Voters' League and worked with the Mississippi Freedom Democratic Party and the Council of Federated Organizations. She now works for the Department of Human Services in Washington, D.C.

Mary King was on SNCC's communication staff in Danville, Atlanta, and Jackson, Mississippi, from 1963 to 1966. During the Carter administration she served as deputy director of ACTION, which oversaw national volunteer-service programs. In 1988 she won a Robert F. Kennedy Book Award for *Freedom Song: A Personal Story of the 1960s Civil Rights Movement* (1987). She currently heads the research organization Global Action, Inc., based in Washington, D.C. A political scientist specializing in the use of nonviolence, she is also the author of *The Power of Nonviolent Action: Gandhi, King, and the Continuing Quest* (1997).

Joyce Ladner was born in Mississippi and began her activism by attending NAACP meetings while in high school. She was a field secretary for SNCC from 1962 to 1964. Following SNCC she chaired the TransAfrica Forum, which opposed apartheid in South Africa. She is a sociologist and a professor of social work at Howard University and the author of *Tomorrow's Tomorrow: The Black Woman* (1971, 1995). She served as interim president of Howard University in 1994–95.

Bernard Lafayette, Jr., was a member of the Nashville Student Christian Movement from 1959 to 1961, and a participant in SNCC's Jackson, Mississippi, direct action project in 1961. He was a Freedom Rider, field director for SNCC's Selma project from 1962 to 1963, and one of the Nashville campaign's chief song leaders. He has been president of American Baptist College in Nashville since 1992 and is a scholar in the area of nonviolence education and training.

Paul Lauter worked for the American Friends Service Committee and traveled through Mississippi during Freedom Summer bringing films and leading discussions in Freedom Schools. He participated in the Selma to Montgomery march, and raised money for SNCC in the North. In 1965 he returned to the South to help integrate the Natchez schools, then worked on a community school project in Washington, D.C., and in opposition to the Vietnam War. He is currently Allan K. and Gwendolyn Miles Smith Professor of Literature at Trinity College, Hartford, Connecticut, general editor of the *Heath Anthology of American Literature*, and recent president of the American Studies Association.

Danny Lyon was SNCC's official staff photographer and publicist in 1963–64. His photos filled *The Movement* (1964), SNCC's official history. Lyon has published widely, including *Memories of the Southern Civil Rights Movement* (1992) and *Conversations with the Dead: Photographs of Prison Life* (1971). He has also made numerous films.

Robert Mants was field secretary of SNCC's southwest Georgia project in 1963–64 and field director of its Lowndes County, Alabama, project in 1965–1966. Still living in Alabama, he has purchased a farm in Lowndes County in an attempt to reverse black abandonment of southern agricultural lands. He served as county commissioner in Lowndes County (1985–1989).

Allen Matusow is professor of American history at Rice University in Texas, and most recently the author of *The Unraveling of America: A History of Liberalism in the 1960s* (1984).

Charles McDew, while in college at South Carolina State in Orangeburg, became a leader in the local sit-in movement of 1960. Serving as chairman of SNCC from 1960 to 1963, he was an active participant in the 1961 McComb, Mississippi, protests and raised funds for SNCC in the North. A native of Massillon, Ohio, he teaches at Metropolitan State University in St. Paul, Minnesota.

Diane Nash, as a student at Fisk University, organized the first Nashville sit-ins in 1960 that became the Nashville movement. She was a coordinator of Freedom Rides in 1961, director of SNCC's direct action wing in 1961, and part of the SCLC field staff from 1961 to 1965. She has since served in a number of social service agencies and lectures nationally on issues pertaining to women's rights and the civil rights movement.

Martha Prescod Norman was a field secretary for SNCC in Mississippi in 1963 and in Selma, Alabama, in 1965–66. She also headed Friends of SNCC in Ann Arbor and Detroit, Michigan. At the time of the conference, she was pursuing her doctorate and had taught African American history at the University of Toledo and Wayne State University.

Silas Norman, Jr., graduated from Paine College in Augusta, Georgia, where he had been a sit-in leader in 1960. He became field secretary for SNCC and served as SNCC's Alabama project director in Selma in 1964–65. He is currently the medical director for Wayne County Jails, Detroit, Michigan.

Penny Patch, a Swarthmore student, worked for SNCC from 1962 to 1965 in southwest Georgia and Mississippi. She is currently enrolled in the Frontier School of Nurse-Midwifery in Kentucky.

Bernice Johnson Reagon, native of Albany, Georgia, joined SNCC as a field secretary and member of the Freedom Singers in 1962. She was founder of the Harambee Singers in Atlanta, and currently performs with Sweet Honey in the Rock, the female African-American a cappella ensemble she founded in 1973. She is Distinguished Professor of History at American University and curator emeritus at the Smithsonian Institution. She is also the author of *We Who Believe in Freedom: Sweet Honey in the Rock—Still on the Journey* (1993) and the editor of *We'll Understand It Better By and By: Pioneering African American Gospel Composers* (1992).

James "Sparky" Rucker, a performer and commentator on African-American folk culture and history, has been involved with the civil rights movement and the Highlander Folk School since 1963. He has produced numerous recordings, videos, and articles, and he serves on the boards of several musical, cultural, and labor groups.

Mendy Samstein was a Ph.D. candidate at the University of Chicago and on the faculty at Morehouse College when he joined SNCC in Mississippi in 1963. He has since been teaching in the New York public schools.

Kathie Sarachild (then Kathie Amatniek) came to Mississippi as a Freedom Summer volunteer, and returned to work with SNCC again for the spring of 1965. Her experiences led her to organizing in the women's liberation movement, where she helped pioneer the technique of consciousness raising. She was an editor of Redstockings' anthology *Feminist Revolution* (1975, 1978) and continues to work with the Redstockings Women's Liberation Archives in New York.

Cleveland Sellers served as a SNCC field secretary in Mississippi (1964–65) and as its national program director (1965–1967). He received his Ed.D. from the University of North Carolina and currently teaches in the History Department and African-American Studies Program at the University of South Carolina. On the board of numerous political and educational organizations, he is the author of *The River of No Return: The Autobiography of a Black Militant and the Life and Death of SNCC* (1990).

Charles Sherrod left divinity school in Virginia to join SNCC. He was field director for SNCC's southwest Georgia voter registration project from 1961 to 1966, a member of the Freedom Ride Coordinating Committee in 1963, and a participant in the Mississippi Freedom Democratic Party. He subsequently served as city commissioner in Albany, Georgia (1977–1991). Since 1966 he has been executive director of the Southwest Georgia Project for Community Education, Inc., the successor to SNCC's southwest Georgia project, and is presently a chaplain in the Georgia state prison system.

Jean Wheeler Smith was a field organizer for SNCC in Mississippi and Georgia (1963–1965) and a campus traveler in Virginia and Tennessee. She is currently a child psychiatrist practicing in the Washington, D.C., area. She has been an assistant professor in the Department of Psychiatry at Howard University and at Georgetown University.

Michael Thelwell served as field secretary of SNCC (1963–64) and director of the SNCC/MFDP Washington office (1964–65). He is presently professor of Afro-American Studies at the University of Massachusetts, Amherst, and author of *The Harder They Come: A Novel* (1980); *Duties, Pleasures, and Conflicts: Essays In Struggle* (1987); and *Black Writers Redefine the Struggle: A Tribute to James Baldwin* (1989).

Kwame Toure, formerly Stokely Carmichael, graduated from Howard University where he was a participant in the Nonviolent Action Group, a SNCC affiliate, and the Freedom Rides. He became a full-time SNCC worker in 1964. He directed the Council of Federated Organizations office in Mississippi's Second Congressional District, became a field secretary with the Lowndes County voter registration project, and chaired SNCC from 1966 to 1967. He then served as honorary prime minister for the Black Panther Party. Toure is a Central Committee member of the All African Peoples Revolutionary Party and the Democratic Party of Guinee of the African Democratic Revolution, and lives in Guinea, Africa. He is the author of *Stokely Speaks: Black Power Back to Pan-*

Africanism (1973) and, with Charles Hamilton, *Black Power: The Politics of Liberation* (1967).

Hollis Watkins at eighteen, with Curtis Hayes, organized the first sit-in in the history of McComb, Mississippi. He joined SNCC in 1961 and served as a field secretary in Mississippi, where he worked on voter registration projects and became a member of the Mississippi Freedom Democratic Party. He continues to live and organize in Mississippi.

John Robert (Bob) Zellner was a SNCC field secretary in 1961–1963 and remained on the SNCC staff through 1967. An Alabama native, Zellner became part of SNCC through a grant by the Southern Conference Educational Fund to support white organizers in the civil rights movement. Since that time he has been a labor organizer in New Orleans and has lectured around the country. He currently teaches history at Tulane, where he is pursuing his doctorate, and lives in Southampton, New York.

Howard Zinn is a historian and professor emeritus at Boston University, where he taught for over twenty years. At the time of SNCC's founding he was teaching at Spelman College, and he served as a senior advisor to SNCC for much of its history. Author of the first serious study of SNCC, *SNCC: The New Abolitionists* (1964), he has also written many other books, including *A People's History of the United States* (1980); *Declarations of Independence: Cross-examining American Ideology* (1990); and *You Can't Be Neutral on a Moving Train: A Personal History of Our Times* (1994).

Index

Braden, Carl, 4, 107, 217, 224–225
Broder, David, 67
Brown, Benjamin, 93, 225
Brown, H. Rap, 5, 12, 159, 195, 225
Brown, Rev. Brother, 123
Brown Chapel, 98
Brown v. Board of Education, x, 2
Bruner, Deacon and Mrs., 59
Burgland High School (McComb, Miss.), 62, 63, 225, 231, 238. *See also* "Nonviolent High"
bus boycotts, 182; Baton Rouge (1953), 27, 29, 222–223, 235; Montgomery (1955–56), 2, 20, 29, 117–119, 126, 237, 239, 242, 245

capitalism, 165, 166, 169
Carmichael, Stokely (Kwame Toure), xv, 12, 97–106 passim, 139, 143, 148, 157, 163, 183, 191–198 passim, 207, 225, 259–260; and All African Peoples Revolutionary Party, 221; and Black Power, 152, **164–173**, **174**, 223; chairs SNCC, 5, 11; and COINTELPRO, 159, 162; on urban black communities, 154; visits Cuba, 195; and voter registration drive of 1965, 11; on women in SNCC, 10, 129–130, 136–137, 145
Carson, Clayborne, **196–199**, 254
Carter, Amy, 128
Carter, Jimmy, 36, 56
cattle prods, 95
Center for Constitutional Rights, 251
Central Intelligence Agency (CIA), 20, 78, 161–162; funds NSA, 241
Chaney, James, 9, 61, 64, 70, 103, 127–128, 131, 137, 156, 225, 229, 232, 245
"Charge to Keep I Have, A" (song), 125
Charles, Ray, 118
Chatfield, Jack, ix–xvi, 5, 12, 36, 52, 59, **191–192**, 254
Chester (Pa.), protests in, 29–30
Chestnut, J. L., 90, 225
Children's Defense Fund, 251

Christian, Joanne, 59
churches, and civil rights movement, xiv, 27, 62, 76, 77, 92, 98, 118, 119–120, 180, 206, 228, 235, 236, 247
Churchville, John, 54, 225
civil disobedience, 2–3, 4, 24, 33, 73
"Civil Disobedience" (Thoreau), 247
Civil Rights Act of 1957, 42, 225–226
Civil Rights Act of 1964, xiv, 11, 43, 55, 56, 79, 94, 127, 159, 181, 194, 216, 226, 238, 243; Public Accommodations Act, 94, 243
Civil Rights Commission, federal, 226
Clark, Jim, 10, 94, 226, 245
Cobb, Charles, 129, 226
COINTELPRO, 12, 43, 152, 158, 159, 161–162, 173, 226
Cold War, and climate for integration, 3
Collins, Dara, 249
Commission on Religion and Race, National Council of Churches, 247
Common Sense (Paine), 242
Communist Party, 189
Congressional Black Caucus, 174, 227, 229
Congress of Racial Equality (CORE), 4, 8, 142, 221, 226, 227, 232; and Ella Baker, 24; and Freedom Rides, 224, 231; Journey of Reconciliation (1947), 6; role of, in sit-ins, 180
Connor, Eugene "Bull," 227
Connor v. Johnson, 239
conscientious objection, 83. *See also* Vietnam War, opposition to
Conversations with the Dead (Lyon), 257
Council of Federated Organizations (COFO), 8, 9, 63, 77, 226, 227, 228, 231, 234, 236, 256, 259
County Consolidation Law (Miss.), 68
Cox, Courtland, 5, 80, 97, 99, 103, 106, **108–109**, 139, **162–164**, 168, 254
Cox, Elton, 92, 227
Crisis, The, 229
Crusader (Williams, ed.), 251

About the Editor

Cheryl Lynn Greenberg, associate professor of African-American and twentieth-century American history at Trinity College in Hartford, Connecticut, is the author of *"Or Does It Explode?" Black Harlem in the Great Depression* and the forthcoming "Troubling the Waters: Black-Jewish Relations in the American Century."

Printed in the United States
136212LV00008B/80/A